Square up to GCSE Maths exams with CGP!

Worried about GCSE Maths? Practise answering exam questions until you can do them in your sleep — it's the perfect way to ease your mind.

That's why we've packed this brilliant CGP book with hundreds of exam-style questions, all matched to the Higher Tier CCEA GCSE course! They are all marked up to show you which unit (M3, M4, M7 & M8) they prepare you for.

We've also included detailed answers, so if you drop any marks, it's easy to find out exactly where you went wrong. By the time the real exams come round you'll be ready to show them who's boss.

CGP — still the best! ☺

Our sole aim here at CGP is to produce the highest quality books — carefully written, immaculately presented and dangerously close to being funny.

Then we work our socks off to get them out to you — at the cheapest possible prices.

Contents

Use the tick boxes to check off the topics you've completed.

Published by CGP

Editors:
Paul Jordin, Rachael Rogers and George Wright

With thanks to Mona Allen, Luke Bennett and Glenn Rogers for the proofreading.

ISBN: 978 1 78908 564 8

Clipart from Corel®
Printed by Bell and Bain Ltd, Glasgow

Based on the classic CGP style created by Richard Parsons.

How to Use This Book

- Hold the book upright, approximately 50 cm from your face, ensuring that the text looks like this, not sıɥʇ. Alternatively, place the book on a horizontal surface (e.g. a table or desk) and sit adjacent to the book, at a distance which doesn't make the text too small to read.
- In case of emergency, press the two halves of the book together firmly in order to close.
- Before attempting to use this book, familiarise yourself with the following safety information:

Each topic has been given a stamp to show which unit exams it could appear in. Use this handy table to see which topics you need to practise:

Unit exam you're preparing for	M3	M4	M7	M8
Material you need to practise	M3 only	M3 and M4	M3 and M7	M3, M4, M7 and M8 (that's all of them — sorry)

The questions are arranged into topics, so you can get exam practice on exactly the bit of the course that you want.

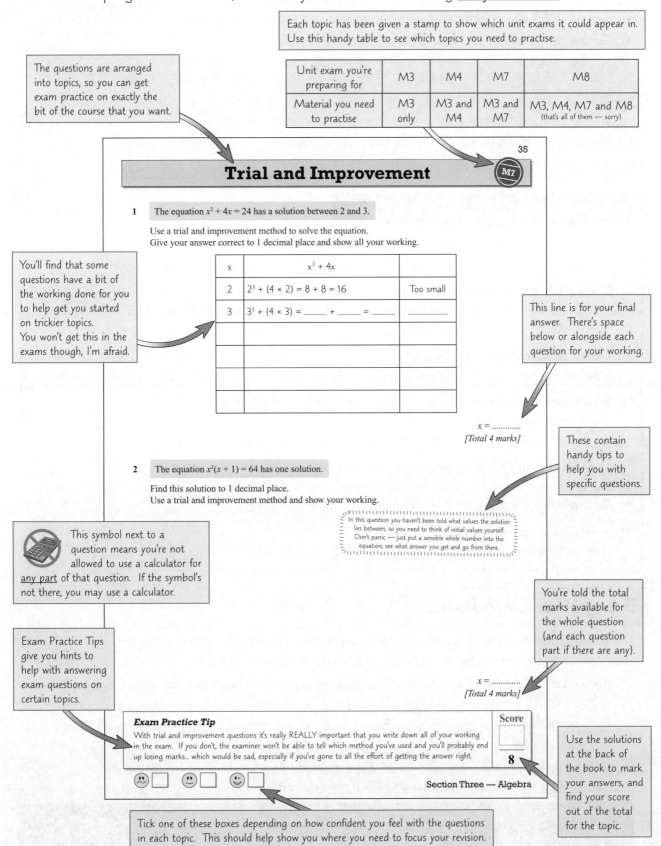

35

Trial and Improvement

M7

1 The equation $x^3 + 4x = 24$ has a solution between 2 and 3.

Use a trial and improvement method to solve the equation.
Give your answer correct to 1 decimal place and show all your working.

x	$x^3 + 4x$	
2	$2^3 + (4 \times 2) = 8 + 8 = 16$	Too small
3	$3^3 + (4 \times 3) =$ .... + ... = ...	....

$x =$ ....
[Total 4 marks]

You'll find that some questions have a bit of the working done for you to help get you started on trickier topics. You won't get this in the exams though, I'm afraid.

This line is for your final answer. There's space below or alongside each question for your working.

2 The equation $x^2(x + 1) = 64$ has one solution.

Find this solution to 1 decimal place.
Use a trial and improvement method and show your working.

In this question you haven't been told what values the solution lies between, so you need to think of initial values yourself. Don't panic — just put a sensible whole number into the equation, see what answer you get and go from there.

These contain handy tips to help you with specific questions.

This symbol next to a question means you're not allowed to use a calculator for any part of that question. If the symbol's not there, you may use a calculator.

You're told the total marks available for the whole question (and each question part if there are any).

$x =$ ....
[Total 4 marks]

Exam Practice Tips give you hints to help with answering exam questions on certain topics.

Exam Practice Tip
With trial and improvement questions it's really REALLY important that you write down all of your working in the exam. If you don't, the examiner won't be able to tell which method you've used and you'll probably end up losing marks... which would be sad, especially if you've gone to all the effort of getting the answer right.

Score
8

Section Three — Algebra

Use the solutions at the back of the book to mark your answers, and find your score out of the total for the topic.

Tick one of these boxes depending on how confident you feel with the questions in each topic. This should help show you where you need to focus your revision.

Exam Tips

Exam Stuff

1) You will sit three exam papers in total — one for unit M3 or M4 and then two for unit M7 or M8 (one of these will be a non-calculator paper).
2) The M3/M4 exam lasts 2 hours and there are 100 marks.
3) The M7/M8 papers both last 1 hour 15 minutes and each has 50 marks.
4) Timings in the exams are really important, so here's a quick guide...

The unit exams you take will depend on the grade you're hoping to get. M3 and M7 are targeted at grades B-E, while M4 and M8 are targeted at grades A*-C. You could even sit a combination of Foundation and Higher unit exams — your teacher should be able to tell you more about this.

- You should spend about a minute per mark working on each question (e.g. 2 marks = 2 mins).
- That'll leave about 20 minutes at the end of each exam to check back through your answers and make sure you haven't made any silly mistakes.
- If you're totally, hopelessly stuck on a question, just leave it and move on to the next one. You can always go back to it at the end if you've got enough time.

There are a Few Golden Rules

1) **Always, always, always make sure you read the question properly.** For example, if the question asks you to give your answer in metres, don't give it in centimetres.
2) **Show each step in your working.** You're less likely to make a mistake if you write things out in stages. And even if your final answer's wrong, you'll probably pick up some marks if the examiner can see that your method is right.
3) **Check that your answer is sensible.** Worked out an angle of 450° or 0.045° in a triangle? You've probably gone wrong somewhere...
4) **Make sure you give your answer to the right degree of accuracy.** The question might ask you to round to a certain number of significant figures or decimal places. So make sure you do just that, otherwise you'll almost certainly lose marks.
5) **Look at the number of marks a question is worth.** If a question's worth 2 or more marks, you probably won't get them all for just writing down the final answer — you're going to have to show your working.
6) **Write your answers as clearly as you can.** If the examiner can't read your answer you won't get any marks, even if it's right.

Obeying these Golden Rules will help you get as many marks as you can in the exam — but they're no use if you haven't learnt the stuff in the first place. So make sure you revise well and do as many practice questions as you can.

Using Your Calculator

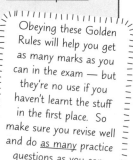

1) Your calculator can make questions a lot easier for you but only if you know how to use it. Make sure you know what the different buttons do and how to use them.
2) Remember to check your calculator is in degrees mode. This is important for trigonometry questions.
3) If you're working out a big calculation on your calculator, it's best to do it in stages and use the memory to store the answers to the different parts. If you try and do it all in one go, it's too easy to mess it up.
4) If you're going to be a renegade and do a question all in one go on your calculator, use brackets so the calculator knows which bits to do first.

REMEMBER: Golden Rule number 2 still applies, even if you're using a calculator — you should still write down all the steps you are doing so the examiner can see the method you're using.

Types of Number and BODMAS (1)

M3

1 Use your calculator to work out $\frac{197.8}{\sqrt{0.01 + 0.23}}$.

Give your answer to 2 decimal places.

....

[Total 2 marks]

2 Use your calculator to work out $\sqrt{\frac{12.71 + 137.936}{\cos 50° \times 13.2^2}}$.

Give your answer to 2 decimal places.

....

[Total 2 marks]

3 x and y are integers and $0 < x < y$.

Write down two sets of values for x and y such that $6 = \sqrt{3x + 2y}$.

x = ... , y = ...

or x = ... , y = ...

[Total 2 marks]

4 Find the reciprocal of $(4 + 28 \div 7)^2 \div (2 \times 4^2)$.

Write your answer as a fraction.

....

[Total 4 marks]

Score: ☐ / **10**

M8 Types of Number and BODMAS (2)

1 Circle the irrational numbers from the list below.

5.5 π 2.5^2 $\sqrt{3}$ 0.6π $\sqrt{16}$ $\frac{7}{9}$

[Total 2 marks]

2 State whether each of the following expressions is rational or irrational. Show your working.

a) $\sqrt{5^2 - 5 \times 3}$

The expression is ....

[2]

b) $\dfrac{\sqrt{6}}{4\sqrt{10 - 2 \times 2}}$

The expression is ....

[2]

[Total 4 marks]

3 For each of the following shapes, explain whether the perimeter is a rational or irrational number. Show your working.

a)

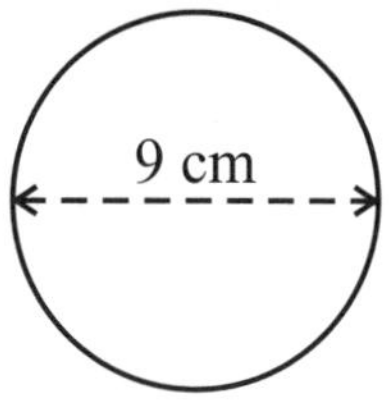

....

....

[1]

b)

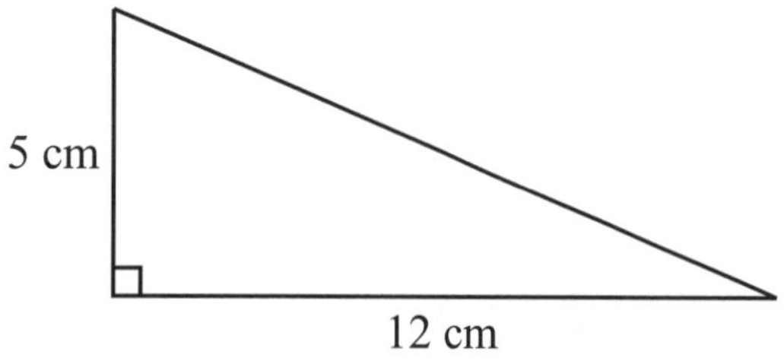

....

....

....

....

Diagrams not drawn accurately

[3]

[Total 4 marks]

Score: / **10**

Multiples, Factors and Prime Factors

M3

1 Express:

a) 210 as a product of its prime factors.

....

[2]

b) 105^2 as a product of its prime factors.

....

[2]

[Total 4 marks]

2 Declan says "even square numbers always have more factors than odd square numbers".

Find examples to show that Declan is wrong.

....

[Total 2 marks]

3 A number, x, is a common multiple of 6 and 7, and a common factor of 252 and 420.

Given that $50 < x < 150$, find the value of x.

$x =$ ....

[Total 4 marks]

Exam Practice Tip

Multiples, factors and prime factors can be a bit confusing at first. Remember, multiples of a number are the numbers that are in its times table, and factors are the numbers that divide into the original number. A prime factor is — yep, you guessed it — a factor that is also a prime number.

Score

10

M3 LCM and HCF

1 Find:

a) the HCF of 54 and 72.

....

[1]

b) the LCM of 54 and 72.

....

[1]

[Total 2 marks]

2 $P = 3^7 \times 11^2$ and $Q = 3^4 \times 7^3 \times 11$.

Write as the product of prime factors:

a) the LCM of P and Q,

....

[1]

b) the HCF of P and Q.

....

[1]

[Total 2 marks]

3 $X = 2^8$, $Y = 2^5 \times 5^3$ and $Z = 2^6 \times 5^2 \times 7$.

Write as the product of prime factors:

a) the LCM of X, Y and Z,

....

[2]

b) the HCF of X, Y and Z.

....

[2]

[Total 4 marks]

Score: ☐ / **8**

Fractions

M3

1 Write the following in order of size, starting with the smallest.

65% $\quad \frac{2}{3}$ $\quad 0.065$ $\quad \frac{33}{50}$

.... , ... , ... , ...

[Total 2 marks]

2 Work out:

Make sure each fraction has the same denominator.

a) $3\frac{1}{2} + 2\frac{3}{5}$

....

[3]

b) $3\frac{3}{4} - 2\frac{1}{3}$

....

[3]

[Total 6 marks]

3 Francis owns all the shares of his company.
He sells $\frac{2}{15}$ of the shares to Sharon and $\frac{5}{12}$ of the shares to Jamal.

What fraction of the shares does Francis still own? Give your answer in its simplest form.

....

[Total 3 marks]

4 Work out the following, giving your answers as mixed numbers.

a) $1\frac{2}{3} \times \frac{9}{10}$

....

[3]

b) $3\frac{1}{2} \div 1\frac{2}{5}$

....

[3]

[Total 6 marks]

5 A factory buys 25 tonnes of flour. $17\frac{1}{2}$ tonnes of the flour is used to make scones. $\frac{1}{5}$ of the scones are cheese scones.

a) What fraction of the total amount of flour is used to make cheese scones?

....

[2]

b) What percentage of the total amount of flour is used to make cheese scones?

.... %

[1]

[Total 3 marks]

6 Write each of the following fractions as a decimal.

a) $\frac{7}{40}$

....

[2]

b) $\frac{10}{11}$

....

[3]

c) $\frac{7}{33}$

....

[3]

[Total 8 marks]

Score: ☐ / **28**

Recurring Decimals into Fractions

M8

1 Write each of the following in the form $\frac{a}{b}$. Simplify your answers as far as possible.

a) $0.\dot{7}$

Let $r = 0.\dot{7}$

so, $10r =$ ....

$10r - r =$ .... $- 0.\dot{7}$

$9r =$ ....

$r =$ ....

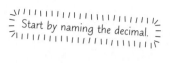

Start by naming the decimal.

....

[2]

b) $0.\dot{2}\dot{6}$

....

[2]

c) $1.\dot{3}\dot{6}$

....

[3]

[Total 7 marks]

2 Show that $0.5\dot{9}\dot{0} = \frac{13}{22}$.

Hint: start by trying to get only the non-repeating part before the decimal point.

[Total 3 marks]

Score: /10

M3 Rounding Numbers

1 Josie runs a race in 58.445 seconds.

Write Josie's time correct to the following levels of accuracy:

a) 1 decimal place.

.... seconds
[1]

b) 1 significant figure.

.... seconds
[1]

[Total 2 marks]

2 Round 10.9961 to two decimal places.

....
[Total 1 mark]

3 Use your calculator to find $\frac{4.32^2 - \sqrt{13.4}}{16.3 + 2.19}$.

Give your answer to 3 significant figures.

....
[Total 2 marks]

4 Answer the following questions.

A mountain is measured to be 1800 m tall, to 2 significant figures.

a) What is the smallest height that the mountain could be?

.... m
[1]

The average September temperature at a village on the mountain is recorded as 16.3 °C, to 3 s.f.

b) The average temperature was measured to 4 s.f. What is its highest possible value?

.... °C
[1]

[Total 2 marks]

Score: ___ / **7**

Estimating

M7

1 Look at the following calculation: $\frac{215.7 \times 44.8}{460}$

a) By rounding each number to 1 significant figure, give an estimate for $\frac{215.7 \times 44.8}{460}$.

....

[3]

b) Will your answer to part a) be larger or smaller than the exact answer? Explain why.

....

....

[1]

[Total 4 marks]

2 Work out an estimate for $\sqrt{\frac{2321}{19.673 \times 3.81}}$.

Show all of your working.

....

[Total 3 marks]

3 A cone has a radius (r) of 10 cm and a vertical height (h) of 24 cm.

Find an estimate for the volume of the cone.

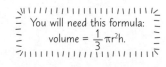

You will need this formula: volume = $\frac{1}{3}\pi r^2 h$.

.... cm^3

[Total 2 marks]

4 Estimate the square root of 108 to one decimal place.

....

[Total 2 marks]

Score: ____ / **11**

M3 Bounds (1)

1 The width of a rectangular piece of paper is 23.6 centimetres, correct to 1 decimal place. The length of the paper is 54.1 centimetres, correct to 1 decimal place.

a) Write down the lower bound for the length of the paper.

.... cm

[1]

b) Calculate the lower bound for the perimeter of the piece of paper.

.... cm

[2]

[Total 3 marks]

2 Here is a rectangle.
$x = 55$ mm to the nearest 5 mm.
$y = 30$ mm to the nearest 5 mm.

Calculate the upper bound for the area of this rectangle.
Give your answer to 3 significant figures.

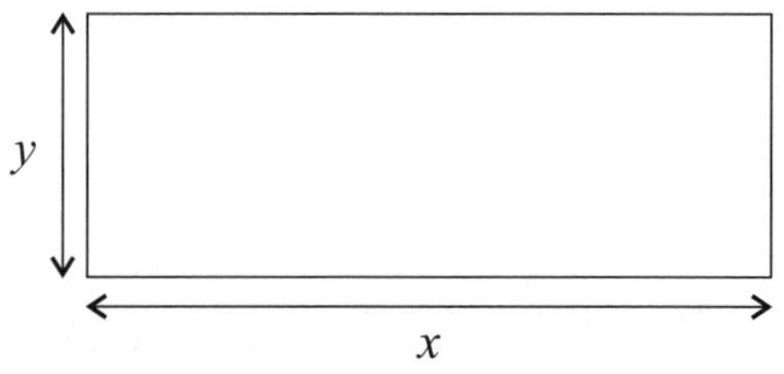

Diagram not drawn accurately

.... mm^2

[Total 3 marks]

3 Given that $x = 2.2$ correct to 1 decimal place, find the interval that contains the value of $4x + 3$. Give your answer as an inequality.

....

[Total 4 marks]

4 A cuboid measures 0.94 m by 0.61 m by 0.21 m, each measured to the nearest cm.

Find the volume of the cuboid in m^3 to a suitable degree of accuracy.

.... m^3

[Total 4 marks]

Score: ____ / **14**

Bounds (2)

M4

1 Samantha is comparing the volume of two buckets. She measures the volume of each bucket to the nearest 0.1 litres and finds that bucket A has a volume of 8.3 litres and bucket B has a volume of 13.7 litres.

Calculate the lower bound of the difference, in litres, between the volumes of bucket A and bucket B.

.... litres

[Total 2 marks]

2 Rounded to 1 decimal place, a triangle has a height of 3.2 cm and an area of 5.2 cm^2.

Calculate the upper bound for the base length of the triangle, giving your answer to 2 d.p.

.... cm

[Total 3 marks]

3 Ridhi runs 100 m, measured to the nearest metre. Her time is 12.5 s to the nearest tenth of a second.

Find Ridhi's speed to a suitable number of significant figures.
Give a reason for your final answer.

speed = ... ÷ ....

lower bound for distance = ... m   upper bound for distance = ... m

upper bound for time = ... s   lower bound for time = ... s

lower bound for speed = ... m / .... s = ... m/s   upper bound for speed = ... m / .... s = ... m/s

to 2 s.f. = ... m/s   to 1 s.f. = ... m/s   to 2 s.f. = ... m/s   to 1 s.f. = ... m/s

TIP: compare your upper and lower bounds.

....

....

[Total 5 marks]

Exam Practice Tip

If you're stuck in the exam wondering which bounds to use in a calculation, think about what would happen if you used the upper or lower bound for each of the numbers in your calculation. And remember that dividing something by a bigger number gives you a smaller number — and vice versa.

Score

10

M7 Standard Form

1 Express the following numbers in standard form:

a) 648 200 000

.... *[1]*

b) 0.0000245

.... *[1]*

[Total 2 marks]

2 $A = 4.834 \times 10^9$, $B = 2.7 \times 10^5$, $C = 5.8 \times 10^3$

a) Express A as an ordinary number.

.... *[1]*

b) Work out $B \times C$. Give your answer in standard form.

.... *[2]*

c) Put A, B and C in order from smallest to largest.

.... , ... , ... *[1]*

[Total 4 marks]

3 Light travels at approximately 1.86×10^5 miles per second.
The distance from the Earth to the Sun is approximately 9.3×10^7 miles.

How long will it take light to travel this distance?
Give your answer in standard form.

.... seconds
[Total 2 marks]

4 $A = (5 \times 10^5) + (5 \times 10^3) + (5 \times 10^2) + (5 \times 10^{-2})$

Find the value of A. Give your answer as an ordinary number.

....
[Total 2 marks]

5 The distance from Neptune to the Sun is approximately 4.5 billion km.
The distance from the Earth to the Sun is approximately 150 million km.

Calculate the ratio of the Earth-Sun distance to the Neptune-Sun distance.
Give your answer in the form $1 : n$.

....
[Total 4 marks]

6 A patient has been prescribed a dose of 4×10^{-4} grams of a certain drug to be given daily.

a) The tablets that the hospital stocks each contain 8×10^{-5} grams of the drug.
How many tablets should the patient be given each day?

.... tablets
[3]

b) The doctor increases the patient's daily dose of the drug by 6×10^{-5} grams.
What is the patient's new daily dose of the drug?

TIP: you need matching powers to be able to add two numbers together in standard form.

.... grams per day
[3]

[Total 6 marks]

7 A cruise ship weighs approximately 7.59×10^7 kg.
Its passengers weigh a total of 2.1×10^5 kg.

Express the weight of the passengers as a percentage of the total combined weight of the ship and passengers. Give your answer to 2 decimal places.

.... %
[Total 3 marks]

Score: ___ / 23

M7 Different Number Systems

1 Convert the binary number 1011011 into a decimal number.

Use a table to show the place values:

64	....	....	....	....	....	1
1	0	1	1	0	1	1

So 1011011 as a decimal number = 64 + ... + ... + ... + 0 + ... + ...
= ....

....

[Total 1 mark]

2 Convert the decimal number 20 into a binary number.

Using the subtracting method:

32	....	....	4	....	1
....	....	....	....	....	....
20 – 32 = –12	....	....	....	....	0 – 1 = –1

So 20 in binary = ...

....

[Total 1 mark]

3 Perform the following conversions:

a) The decimal number 25 into a binary number.

....

[1]

b) The binary number 10110 into a decimal number.

....

[1]

[Total 2 marks]

Score: ___ / 4

Ratios

M7

1 Aoife is making a bird house. To make the walls, she takes a piece of wood and cuts it into four pieces in the ratio 5 : 6 : 6 : 7. The longest wall is 9 cm longer than the shortest wall.

How long was the original piece of wood?

.... cm

[Total 3 marks]

2 Hannah is making some green paint to paint her kitchen wall. She makes it by mixing together $3\frac{3}{4}$ tins of yellow paint and $1\frac{1}{2}$ tins of blue paint. The tins are all the same size.

a) Express the ratio of yellow to blue paint in its simplest form.

....

[2]

b) How much of each paint will Hannah need to make 2800 ml of green paint?

yellow paint .... ml

blue paint .... ml

[2]

[Total 4 marks]

3 Simone, Ariana, Nasir and Catrin shared £660. Nasir got four times as much money as Catrin, Simone got twice as much money as Nasir, and Ariana got a quarter as much money as Simone.

How much money did Simone get?

£ ....

[Total 3 marks]

4 Chocolate milkshake is made by mixing milk and ice cream in the ratio 2 : 9.

a) Give the amount of milk used as a fraction of the ice cream used.

....

[1]

b) How much milkshake is made if 801 ml of ice cream are used?

.... ml

[2]

c) On the axes below, draw a graph that can be used to work out the amount of ice cream needed, given the amount of milk used.

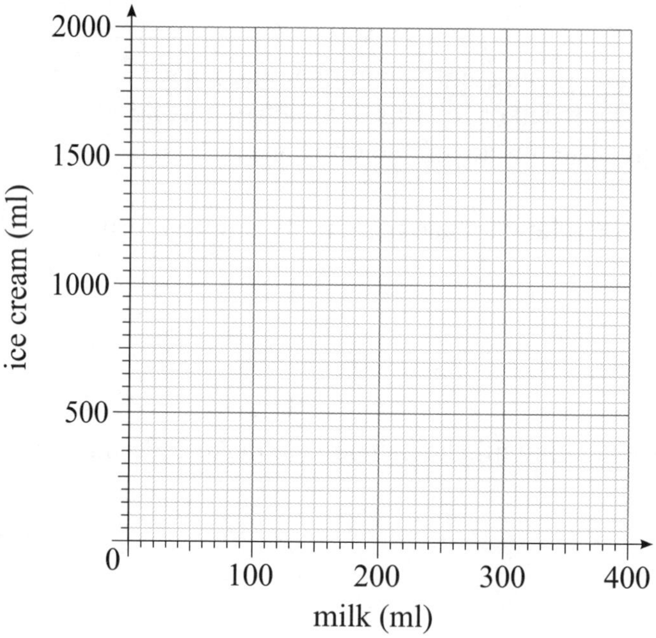

[2]

[Total 5 marks]

5 Mr Appleseed's Supercompost is made by mixing soil, compost and grit in the ratio 4 : 3 : 1. Soil costs £8 per 40 kg, compost costs £15 per 25 kg and grit costs £12 per 15 kg.

How much profit will be made if 16 kg of Mr Appleseed's Supercompost is sold for £10?

£ ....

[Total 5 marks]

6 In the morning a baker makes x muffins and y pastries.
After selling 5 muffins and 3 pastries, the ratio of muffins to pastries is 5 : 8.
He then makes 10 more of each item and the ratio becomes 5 : 7.

Find the values of x and y.

x − .... : y − .... = 5:8 and x + ... : y + ... = 5:7

$\frac{\ldots - \ldots}{\ldots - \ldots} = \frac{5}{8}$ and $\frac{\ldots + \ldots}{\ldots + \ldots} = \frac{5}{7}$

8(....... − ....) = 5(....... − ....) and 7(....... + ...) = 5(....... + ...)

Expand and simplify to give ......x − ......y = 25 [1] and ......x − ......y = 0 [2]

[1] − [2]: x = ...

Substitute x = ... into [1]: (........ × ....) − ....y = 25

........y = ... , so y = ...

x = ...

y = ...

[Total 5 marks]

7 Fabio has a large jar containing only black and green olives.
The probability of randomly choosing a black olive from the jar is $\frac{5}{16}$.
After eating 1 green and 3 black olives the probability of choosing a black olive is $\frac{3}{10}$.

How many black and green olives were originally in the jar?

Start by finding the ratios of black to green olives before and after he eats some — careful though, the original ratio of black:green isn't 5:16.

Black olives: ....

Green olives: ....

[Total 6 marks]

Exam Practice Tip

Ratio questions that include a changing ratio can be tough — you'll often need to set up a pair of equations and solve them simultaneously. Luckily you can always use the same method to do this. Write the ratios as equations, turn the ratios into fractions, multiply out the fractions and solve the equations simultaneously.

Score

31

M7 Direct and Inverse Proportion (1)

1 Ishmael is making some t-shirts. It takes 3 m^2 of cotton to make 5 t-shirts. 2 m^2 of cotton costs £5.50.

Ishmael is able to buy cotton by the square metre.
How much will it cost him to buy enough cotton to make 85 t-shirts?

£ ....

[Total 4 marks]

2 Elijah runs a go-kart track. It takes 12 litres of petrol to race 8 go-karts for 20 minutes. Petrol costs £1.37 per litre.

a) 6 go-karts used 18 litres of petrol. How many minutes did they race for?

.... minutes

[4]

b) How much does the petrol cost to run 8 go-karts for 45 minutes?

£ ....

[3]

[Total 7 marks]

3 Round a bend on a railway track, the height difference (h mm) between the outer and inner rails must vary in direct proportion to the square of the maximum permitted speed (S km/h).

When $S = 50$, $h = 35$. Calculate h when $S = 40$.

h = ...

[Total 3 marks]

Score: ___ / **14**

Direct and Inverse Proportion (2)

M8

1 **Sketch the following proportions on the axes below them.**

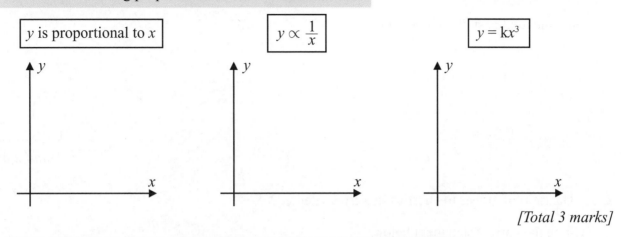

y is proportional to x

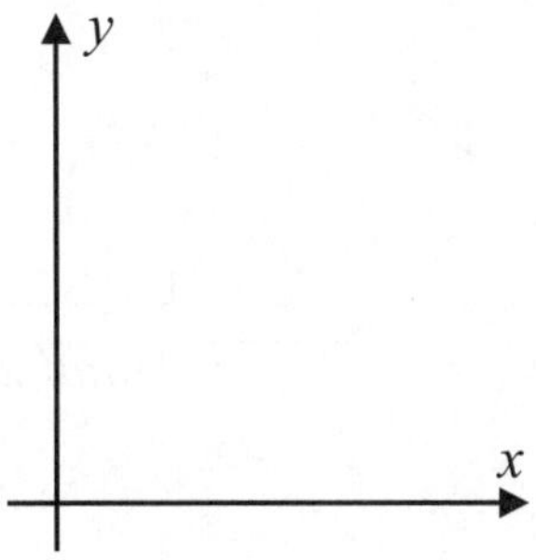

$y \propto \frac{1}{x}$

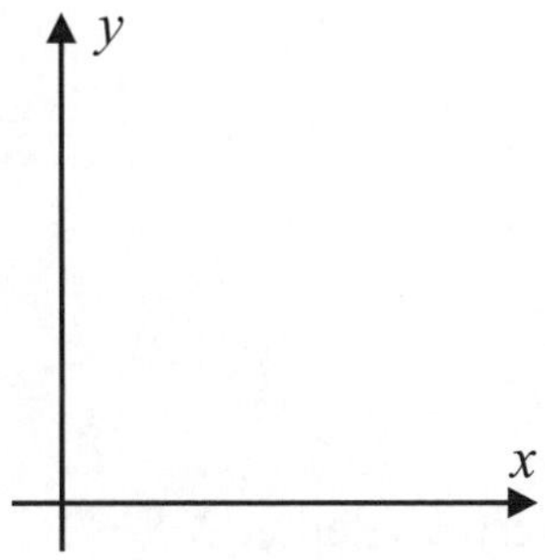

$y = kx^3$

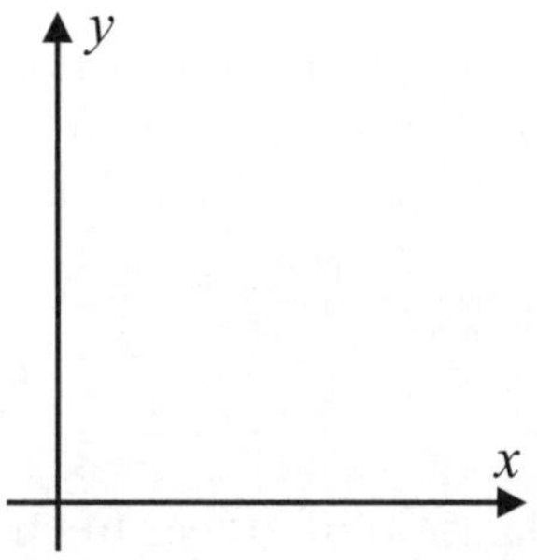

[Total 3 marks]

2 **The gravitational force, f, between two objects is indirectly proportional to the square of the distance, d, between them. When $d = 100$, $f = 20$.**

Write an equation connecting f and d and use it to find the value of f when $d = 800$.

$f =$ ....

[Total 3 marks]

3 **It takes two farmers one hour to shear a flock of 30 sheep. The time taken for shearing is directly proportional to the number of sheep and indirectly proportional to the number of farmers.**

a) How many sheep could be sheared by three farmers working for 80 minutes?

....

[4]

b) Write an equation for the time in minutes (t) it would take for s sheep to be sheared by f farmers.

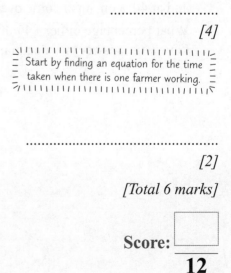

Start by finding an equation for the time taken when there is one farmer working.

....

[2]

[Total 6 marks]

Score: $\frac{\quad}{12}$

M3 Percentages

1 A computer costs £927 plus VAT, where VAT is charged at 20%.

Find the total cost of the computer.

£ ....

[Total 2 marks]

2 The ratio of grapes to cherries in a fruit salad is 2 : 5.

Circle the correct statement below.

The number of cherries is 50% more than the number of grapes.

There are 20% as many grapes as cherries.

The number of cherries is 80% more than the number of grapes.

There are 40% as many grapes as cherries.

[Total 1 mark]

3 After an 8% pay rise Mr Brown's salary was £15 714.

What was his salary before the increase?

£ ....

[Total 3 marks]

4 Jane has an annual salary of £45 000 before income tax.

She pays no income tax on the first £10 000 of her income — this is her tax-free allowance.
She pays income tax at 20% on any income between £10 000 and £41 865,
and at 40% on any income over £41 865.

What percentage of her £45 000 annual salary does Jane pay in income tax?
Give your answer to 1 decimal place.

.... %

[Total 4 marks]

5 A warehouse contains a stock of 17 500 folding chairs. The warehouse manager predicts that the stock will decrease by 12% (to 2 significant figures) each month over a three month period.

Calculate how many chairs, to the nearest hundred, will be in stock at the end of this period if the manager is correct.

....

[Total 3 marks]

6 Fergus makes and sells lobster pots. He sells them for £32 per pot, which is a 60% profit on the cost of the materials. He wants to increase his profit to 88%.

How much should Fergus start charging per lobster pot?

£ ....

[Total 3 marks]

7 Sophie and two friends are booking festival tickets online using their credit cards. Tickets cost £180 each, plus an additional charge of £5.40 per credit card transaction.

a) What is the percentage increase in the cost of buying one ticket if it's bought using a credit card, compared to the cost of buying it without a credit card?

.... %

[2]

b) What is the percentage saving if Sophie and her friends buy three tickets in one transaction rather than three separate transactions? Give your answer to 2 d.p.

.... %

[3]

c) Rebecca buys a single ticket separately using her credit card. The cost of borrowing on her credit card is 18% APR. Calculate the amount Rebecca would pay back for the ticket if she does not settle the credit card bill for one year.

£ ....

[3]

[Total 8 marks]

8 A hairdresser recorded some details about her customers one day.
The ratio of children : adults was 3 : 7.
60% of the children had blond hair and 20% of the adults had blond hair.

What percentage of all the customers had blond hair?

.... %

[Total 4 marks]

9 In the triangular prism below, the base and vertical height of the triangular face are x cm and the length of the prism is y cm.

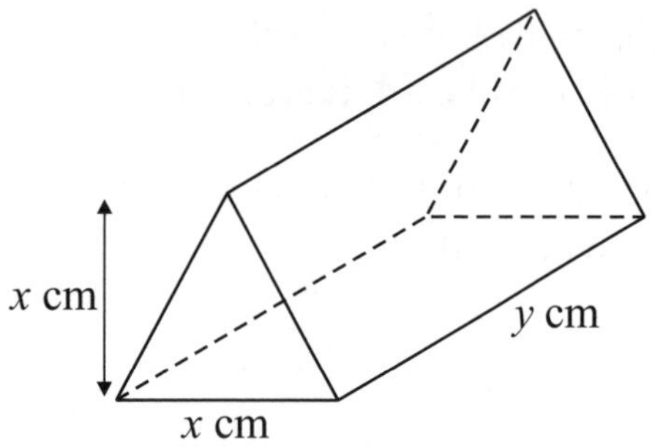

Diagram not drawn accurately

a) Work out the percentage increase in the area of the triangular face when x is increased by 15%.

.... %

[4]

b) Calculate the percentage decrease in y that is required to keep the volume of the prism unchanged when x is increased by 15%. Give your answer to 1 d.p.

.... %

[5]

[Total 9 marks]

Exam Practice Tip

One of the trickiest things about percentage questions can be figuring out which type of question you're dealing with. Think carefully about what the question is asking you to find and then use the correct method. Careful when you're giving your answer too — if the question asks for a percentage, don't give an amount.

Score

37

Compound Growth and Decay

M8

1 Mrs Burdock borrows £750 to buy a sofa.
She is charged 6% compound interest per annum.

Per annum just means per year.

If Mrs Burdock doesn't pay back any of the money for 3 years, how much will she owe?
Give your answer to the nearest penny.

Multiplier = 1 + ... = ...

In 3 years she will owe: £750 × (..............)..... = £ ....

£ ....
[Total 2 marks]

2 The population of fish in a lake is estimated to decrease by 8% every year.
The initial population is 2000.

a) How many fish will be left after 15 years?

....
[2]

b) How many years will it take for the population of fish to fall below 1500?

.... years
[3]
[Total 5 marks]

3 A conservation company plants pine trees in a forest to increase their number by 16% each year. At the end of each year, a logging company is permitted to cut down up to 75% of the number of new trees planted that year.

At the start of 2013 there were 5000 pine trees in the forest.
What was the minimum number of pine trees in the forest at the end of 2014?
Assume that no trees die from other causes.

....
[Total 4 marks]

4 Rich inherits £10 000, and wants to invest it. His bank is offering him two accounts.

Compound Collector Account	Simple Saver Account
5.5% compound interest per year, paid annually into your account. Rate is guaranteed for 5 years.	*6.2% simple interest paid annually into the account. Rate guaranteed for 5 years, no further deposits permitted after opening.*

a) After 5 years, which account will give him the largest balance? Explain your answer.

....

....

....

....

....

[4]

b) Why might Rich not want to invest in the Simple Saver Account?

....

....

[1]

[Total 5 marks]

5 Mrs Khan puts £2500 into a high interest savings account. Compound interest is added to the account at the end of each year. After two years Mrs Khan's account contains £2704.

Mrs Khan did not deposit or remove any money from the account over the two years.
What is the interest rate on the account?

.... %

[Total 3 marks]

6 The value of a football player decreases at a rate of 25% each year after the age of 30. On his 35th birthday, a player was valued at £2 000 000.

What was the player's value on his 31st birthday? Give your answer to the nearest £100 000.

£ ....

[Total 3 marks]

Score: ☐ / **22**

Algebra Basics

M3

1 Leah is tiling a section of her bathroom wall.
The tiles are *a* cm wide and *b* cm tall and she needs 20 tiles in total.

Find an expression for the area of the wall she is tiling in terms of *a* and *b*.

.... cm^2

[Total 1 mark]

2 On the diagram below, shade the area represented by $pq + 3pr$.

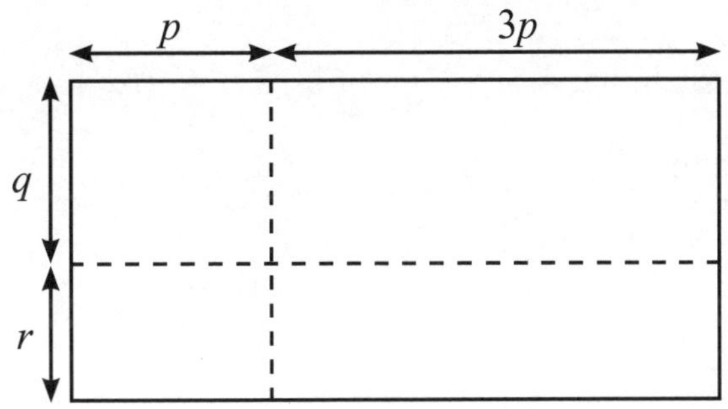

[Total 1 mark]

3 Peter is making a sculpture using different pieces of metal tubing.
He makes a tower by stacking 7 pieces that are $(f + g)$ cm tall, 9 pieces that are $(h - g)$ cm tall and 5 pieces that are $2h$ cm tall on top of each other.

Find a simplified expression for the height of the tower in terms of *f*, *g* and *h*.

.... cm

[Total 2 marks]

4 The diagram below shows a rectangle with sides that are $4x + 3$ cm and $5x - 9$ cm long.

Find an expression in terms of *x* for the side length of a regular hexagon with the same perimeter as the rectangle.

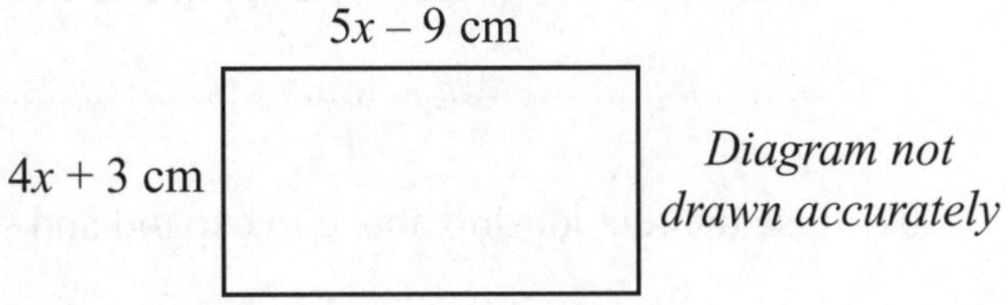

.... cm

[Total 3 marks]

Score: /7

M3

Multiplying Out Brackets

1 Expand the brackets in the following expressions.
Simplify your answers as much as possible.

a) $5p(6 - 2p)$

....

[2]

b) $(2t - 5)(3t + 4)$

....

[2]

[Total 4 marks]

2 a, b and c are integers such that $4(5x - 7) + 6(4 - 2x) = a(bx + c)$, and $a > 0$.

Find the values of a, b and c.

a = ..., b = ..., c = ...

[Total 3 marks]

3 Write an expression for the area of the triangle below.
Simplify your expression as much as possible.

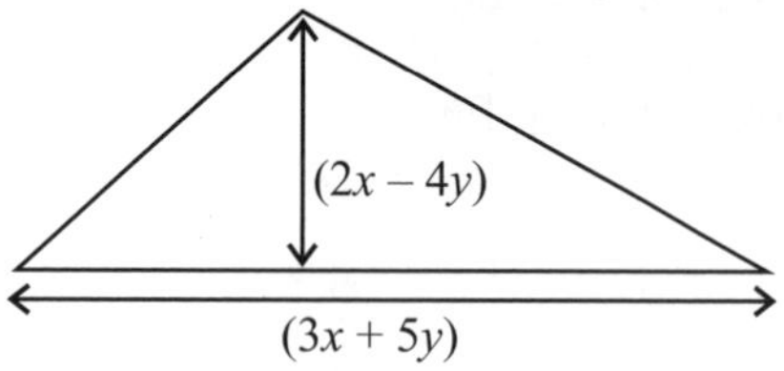

Diagram not drawn accurately

....

[Total 3 marks]

4 When expanding squared brackets, it can be stated that $(a - b)^2 \equiv a^2 - 2ab + b^2$.

a) What is meant by the $\equiv$ symbol in this context?

....

[1]

b) Use the relationship above to expand and simplify $2(3 - x)(6 - 2x)$

....

[3]

[Total 4 marks]

Exam Practice Tip

If you're struggling with double brackets in the exam, don't forget you can always use the FOIL method — multiply the First term in each bracket together, then multiply the Outside terms together, then the Inside terms, and finally multiply together the Last term in each bracket... easy.

Score

14

Factorising

M3

1 Factorise the following expressions fully.

a) $7y - 21y^2$

....

[2]

b) $2v^3w + 8v^2w^2$

....

[2]

[Total 4 marks]

2 Factorise the following expressions fully.

a) $x^2 - 16$

....

[1]

b) $x^2 - 121y^2$

....

[1]

c) $9n^2 - 4m^2$

....

[2]

[Total 4 marks]

3 Fully factorise $x^3 - 25x$.

....

[Total 3 marks]

Score: ☐ / **11**

☐ ☐ ☐

M7 Powers

1 Circle the correct value of 5^{-2}.

-25 $\quad$ 2.5 $\quad$ $\frac{2}{5}$ $\quad$ $\frac{1}{25}$ $\quad$ $\sqrt{5}$

[Total 1 mark]

2 Simplify the following.

a) $a^5 \times a^{-3}$

....

[1]

b) $\frac{(d^9)^2}{d^4}$

....

[2]

[Total 3 marks]

3 Evaluate the following.

a) 3^0

....

[1]

b) $\left(\frac{5}{4}\right)^{-2}$

....

[2]

[Total 3 marks]

4 Simplify the following expressions fully.

a) $3a^3 \times 2ab^2$

....

[2]

b) $\frac{4a^5b^3}{2ab^2}$

....

[2]

c) $\left(\frac{3a^2b^2 \times (b^{-1})^2}{2a^3}\right)^{-2}$

....

[3]

[Total 7 marks]

Score: ___ / **14**

Powers and Roots

M8

1 For values of $y \geq 2$, write the following expressions in order from smallest to largest.

y^{-3} y^{3} y^{1} y^{0} $y^{\frac{1}{3}}$

....

[Total 2 marks]

2 Show that $8^{\frac{4}{3}} = 16$.

$8^{\frac{4}{3}} = (8^{\frac{1}{3}})^4 = (\ldots\ldots\ldots)^4 = \ldots\ldots\ldots$

[Total 2 marks]

3 Simplify the following expressions:

a) $(64x^2)^{\frac{1}{3}}$

....

[2]

b) $\left(\frac{4}{y}\right)^{-\frac{1}{2}}$

....

[2]

[Total 4 marks]

4 Completely simplify the expression below.

$(9a^4)^{\frac{1}{2}} \times \frac{2ab^2}{6a^3b}$

....

[Total 3 marks]

5 Evaluate $64^{\frac{1}{3}} \times 4^{-2}$.

....

[Total 3 marks]

Score: $\frac{}{14}$

M8 Manipulating Surds

1 Write $(2+\sqrt{3})(5-\sqrt{3})$ in the form $a+b\sqrt{3}$, where a and b are integers.

....

[Total 2 marks]

2 Write the following expressions in the form $a\sqrt{b}$, where a and b are integers.

a) $\dfrac{\sqrt{54}}{\sqrt{3}}$

....

[1]

b) $2\sqrt{50}-(\sqrt{2})^3$

....

[2]

[Total 3 marks]

3 Express $\sqrt{396}+\dfrac{22}{\sqrt{11}}-\dfrac{220}{\sqrt{44}}$ in the form $a\sqrt{11}$, where a is an integer.

....

[Total 4 marks]

4 Rationalise the denominators of the following expressions.
Give your answers in their simplest form.

a) $\dfrac{33}{\sqrt{11}}$

....

[1]

b) $\dfrac{1+\sqrt{7}}{3-\sqrt{7}}$

Multiply by $3+\sqrt{7}$ to rationalise the denominator.

....

[4]

[Total 5 marks]

Score: $\dfrac{\quad}{14}$

Solving Equations

M3

1 Poppy, Felix and Alexi play a card game where they each score points. Poppy scores twice as many points as Felix, and Alexi scores 25 more points than Poppy. Their combined score is 700 points.

How many points did each of them score?

Poppy ....

Felix ....

Alexi ....

[Total 4 marks]

2 The diagram below shows an equilateral triangle.

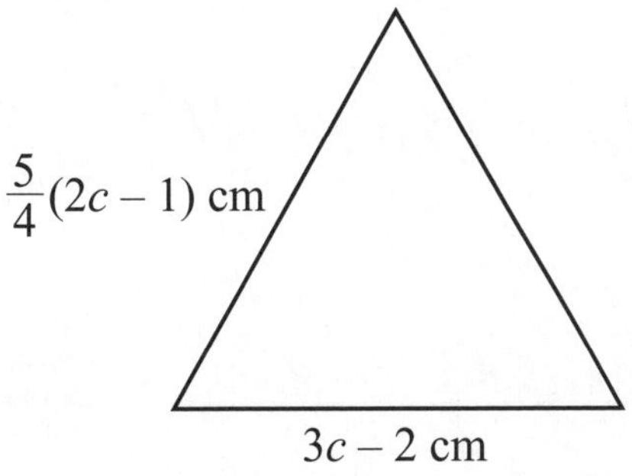

Find the length of one side of the equilateral triangle. Give your answer as a decimal.

.... cm

[Total 4 marks]

3 Liam and Neil want to buy a new games console, which costs £360. They both get weekend jobs, where they each get paid £4.50 per hour. When they can afford the games console, Liam has worked 30 more hours than Neil.

How many hours did each boy work?

Liam: .... hours, Neil: .... hours

[Total 3 marks]

4 Solve the following equations.

a) $\dfrac{28 - z}{4} = 5$

$z =$ ....

[2]

b) $5x^2 = 180$

$x =$ ....

[2]

c) $\dfrac{8 - 2x}{3} + \dfrac{2x + 4}{9} = 12$

$x =$ ....

[4]

d) $\dfrac{3 - 5x}{2} - \dfrac{4x - 7}{5} = -\dfrac{21}{3}$

$x =$ ....

[4]

[Total 12 marks]

5 Hassan thinks of two different positive integers.
Their product is 147, and one number is three times the other number.

What are the two numbers Hassan is thinking of?

....

[Total 3 marks]

Exam Practice Tip

It's a good idea to check your solutions by substituting them back into the equation and checking that everything works out properly. If the unknown appears on both sides of the equation, make sure you work out the value on each side. It certainly beats sitting and twiddling your thumbs or counting sheep to kill time.

Score

26

Trial and Improvement

M7

1 The equation $x^3 + 4x = 24$ has a solution between 2 and 3.

Use a trial and improvement method to solve the equation.
Give your answer correct to 1 decimal place and show all your working.

x	$x^3 + 4x$	
2	$2^3 + (4 \times 2) = 8 + 8 = 16$	Too small
3	$3^3 + (4 \times 3) =$ .... + ... = ...	....

$x =$ ....

[Total 4 marks]

2 The equation $x^2(x + 1) = 64$ has one solution.

Find this solution to 1 decimal place.
Use a trial and improvement method and show your working.

In this question you haven't been told what values the solution lies between, so you need to think of initial values yourself. Don't panic — just put a sensible whole number into the equation, see what answer you get and go from there.

$x =$ ....

[Total 4 marks]

Exam Practice Tip

With trial and improvement questions it's really REALLY important that you write down all of your working in the exam. If you don't, the examiner won't be able to tell which method you've used and you'll probably end up losing marks... which would be sad, especially if you've gone to all the effort of getting the answer right.

Score 8

Rearranging Formulas

1 The relationship between x and y is given by the formula $y = \frac{x-2}{3}$.

a) Rearrange this formula to make x the subject.

....

[2]

b) Find the value of x when $y = 5$.

$x =$ ....

[2]

[Total 4 marks]

2 The formula for finding the volume of a pyramid is $V = \frac{1}{3}Ah$, where A is the base area of the pyramid, and h is the height of the pyramid.

a) Rearrange the formula to make h the subject.

....

[2]

b) Find the height of a pyramid which has volume 18 cm^3 and base area 12 cm^2.

.... cm

[2]

[Total 4 marks]

3 Neela is on holiday in New York. The local weather forecast says that the temperature tomorrow will be 41 °F. Neela wants to know what this temperature is in °C.

The formula for converting temperatures in °C to °F is: $F = \frac{9}{5}C + 32$.

a) Rearrange the formula to make C the subject.

....

[2]

b) What will the temperature be in New York tomorrow in °C?

.... °C

[2]

[Total 4 marks]

4 Rearrange the formula $s = \frac{1}{2}gt^2$ to make t the subject.

....

[Total 3 marks]

5 The relationship between a, b and y is given by the formula $a + y = \frac{b - y}{a}$.

Rearrange this formula to make y the subject.

....

[Total 4 marks]

6 Rearrange the formula below to make n the subject.

$$x = \sqrt{\frac{(1+n)}{(1-n)}}$$

....

[Total 5 marks]

7 Pearse and Marek are both travelling to Belfast.

Pearse took the train. The train fare for Pearse's journey would normally cost £T, but Pearse got a discount of a third because he had a railcard.
Marek took a taxi. The taxi fare costs £4.50 plus an extra 50p per mile.
Marek's journey was d miles long and Marek paid twice as much as Pearse.

a) Show that $4.5 + 0.5d = \frac{4T}{3}$

[2]

Without the railcard discount, Pearse's journey would have cost £22.50.

b) Use algebra to determine how far Marek's taxi journey was.

.... miles

[3]

[Total 5 marks]

Score: ☐ / **29**

☐ ☐ ☐

M3 Factorising Quadratics (1)

1 Fully factorise the expression $x^2 + 9x + 18$.

....

[Total 2 marks]

2 Fully factorise the expression $y^2 - 4y - 5$.

....

[Total 2 marks]

3 The equation $x^2 - 9x + 20 = 0$ is an example of a quadratic equation.

a) Fully factorise the expression $x^2 - 9x + 20$.

....

[2]

b) Use your answer to part a) to solve the equation $x^2 - 9x + 20 = 0$.

$x =$ .... or $x =$ ....

[1]

[Total 3 marks]

4 Solve the equation $x^2 + 4x - 12 = 0$.

$x =$ .... or $x =$ ....

[Total 3 marks]

5 The product of two consecutive positive even numbers is 288.
By forming and solving an equation, find the larger of the two numbers.

Start by calling the smaller of the consecutive even numbers $2n$.

....

[Total 4 marks]

Score: /14

Factorising Quadratics (2)

M4

1 Fully factorise the following expressions:

a) $2x^2 + x - 28$.

....

[2]

b) $5x^2 - 19x + 18$.

....

[2]

[Total 4 marks]

2 Solve the following quadratic equations:

a) $3x^2 + 16x - 12 = 0$

....

[3]

b) $2x^2 - 7x + 3 = -3$

....

[3]

[Total 6 marks]

3 The shape on the right is made from a square and a triangle.

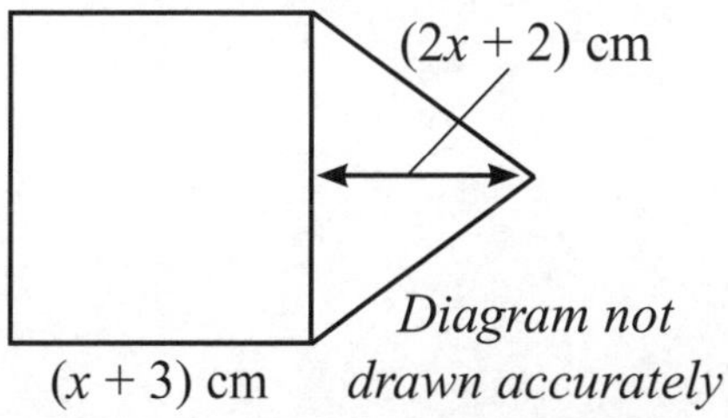

The sides of the square are $(x + 3)$ cm long and the height of the triangle is $(2x + 2)$ cm. The area of the whole shape is 60 cm^2.

a) Show that $2x^2 + 10x - 48 = 0$.

[4]

b) Solve the equation $2x^2 + 10x - 48 = 0$ to find a value for x.

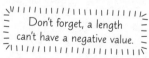

Don't forget, a length can't have a negative value.

$x =$ ....

[3]

[Total 7 marks]

Score: $\frac{\quad}{17}$

M4 The Quadratic Formula

1 Solve the quadratic equation $x^2 + 5x + 3 = 0$, giving your answers to 2 decimal places.

a = ..., b = ... and c = ...

$$x = \frac{-b \pm \sqrt{b^2 - 4ac}}{2a} = \frac{-\text{..............} \pm \sqrt{\text{..............}^2 - 4 \times \text{..............} \times \text{..............}}}{2 \times \text{..............}} = \frac{-\text{..............} \pm \sqrt{\text{..................}}}{\text{..................}}$$

$x =$ .... or $x =$ ....

[Total 3 marks]

2 Solve the equation $2x^2 - 7x + 2 = 0$. Give your answers correct to 2 decimal places.

$x =$ .... or $x =$ ....

[Total 3 marks]

3 Solve the equation $3x^2 - 2x - 4 = 0$. Give your answers to 3 significant figures.

$x =$ .... or $x =$ ....

[Total 3 marks]

4 The area of the rectangle on the right is 30 cm^2.
Find the length of the longer side of the rectangle to 1 decimal place.

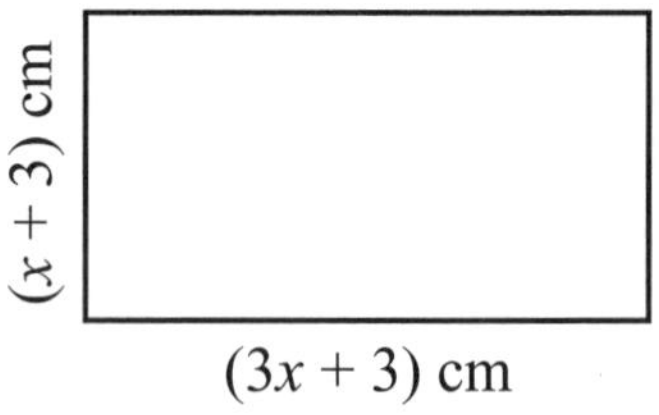

.... cm

[Total 5 marks]

Exam Practice Tip

One thing you really need to watch out for when it comes to using the quadratic formula are those pesky minus signs — especially if a, b or c are negative. Just take your time when you're putting them into the formula — you don't want to throw away easy marks simply because you've messed up your minuses.

Score

14

Algebraic Fractions (1)

M3

1 Write the following as a single fraction, giving your answers in their simplest form:

a) $\frac{6-2x}{4} - \frac{5-6x}{6}$

....
[3]

b) $\frac{2}{p} + \frac{4q}{r}$

....
[2]

c) $\frac{2x+6}{3} + \frac{4-2x}{5} - \frac{x-5}{4}$

....
[2]

[Total 7 marks]

2 Simplify the following algebraic fractions as much as possible.

a) $\frac{3x-12}{x^2-16}$

....
[3]

b) $\frac{x^2-4}{x^2+8x+12}$

....
[3]

[Total 6 marks]

3 Simplify the following:

a) $\frac{x^2}{3x} \times \frac{6}{x+1}$

....
[2]

b) $\frac{10x}{3+x} \div \frac{4}{5(3+x)}$

....
[3]

[Total 5 marks]

Score: $\frac{\square}{18}$

M4 Algebraic Fractions (2)

1 Simplify the fraction $\frac{4x^2 + 10x - 6}{16x^2 - 4}$ as much as possible.

....

[Total 3 marks]

2 Write $\frac{2}{3} + \frac{m - 2n}{m + 3n}$ as a single fraction.

$$\frac{2}{3} + \frac{m - 2n}{m + 3n} = \frac{2 \times \text{.......}}{3 \times \text{.......}} + \frac{\text{.......} \times (m - 2n)}{\text{.......} \times (m + 3n)} = \frac{2\text{.......} + \text{.......}(m - 2n)}{\text{.......}(m + 3n)}$$

$$= \frac{\text{..................}}{\text{..................}} = \frac{\text{..........}}{\text{..........}}$$

....

[Total 3 marks]

3 Write $\frac{3}{x} + \frac{2x}{x+4}$ as a single fraction.

....

[Total 3 marks]

4 Solve the equation $\frac{3}{x-5} + \frac{2}{x-1} = 1$.

....

[Total 6 marks]

5 Write $\frac{1}{x+2} + \frac{x+3}{x-2} - \frac{4}{x}$ as a single fraction.

....

[Total 4 marks]

Score: ____ / **19**

Simultaneous Equations (1)

M7

1 Solve this pair of simultaneous equations.

$x + 3y = 11$
$3x + y = 9$

$x =$ .... $y =$ ....
[Total 3 marks]

2 Solve this pair of simultaneous equations.

$2x + 3y = 12$
$5x + 4y = 9$

$x =$ .... $y =$ ....
[Total 4 marks]

3 A sweet shop sells bags of pick 'n' mix. A bag that contains 4 chocolate frogs and 3 sugar mice costs £3.69. A bag that contains 6 chocolate frogs and 2 sugar mice costs £3.96.

How much would a bag that contains 2 chocolate frogs and 5 sugar mice cost?
Show your working.

£ ....
[Total 5 marks]

Score: ___ / **12**

M8 Simultaneous Equations (2)

1 Solve the following pair of simultaneous equations.

$x^2 + y = 4$
$y = 4x - 1$

$x =$ .... , $y =$ ....

and $x =$ .... , $y =$ ....

[Total 5 marks]

2 Solve the following pair of simultaneous equations.

$2x^2 + y^2 = 51$
$y = x + 6$

$x =$ .... , $y =$ ....

and $x =$ .... , $y =$ ....

[Total 5 marks]

3 The lines $y = x^2 + 3x - 1$ and $y = 2x + 5$ intersect at two points.
The line joining the two points has length $k\sqrt{5}$. Find the value of k.

Use Pythagoras' theorem to find the distance between the two points.

$k =$ ....

[Total 6 marks]

Exam Practice Tip

When you're solving simultaneous equations in the exam, it's always a good idea to check your answers at the end. Just substitute your values for x and y back into the original equations and see if they add up as they should. If they don't then you must have gone wrong somewhere, so go back and check your working.

Score: / 16

Inequalities

M7

1 Circle the inequality that is shown on the number line below.

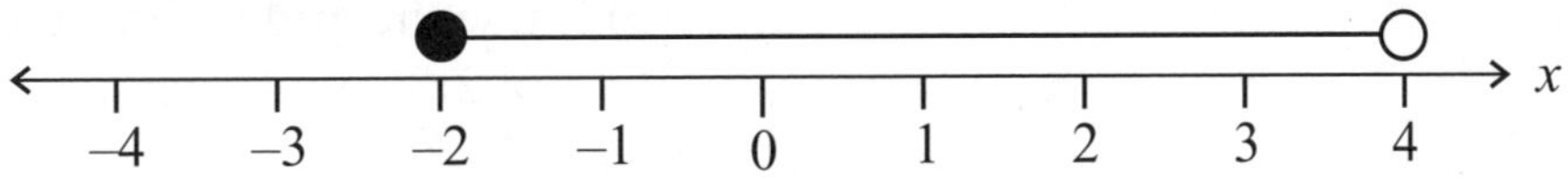

$-6 < 3x < 9$ $-4 \leq 2x < 8$ $-8 \leq 4x \leq 16$ $-10 \leq 5x < 15$

[Total 1 mark]

2 Solve the inequality $4x + 1 > x - 5$.

....

[Total 2 marks]

3 Find the integer values that satisfy both of the following inequalities:

$5n - 3 \leq 17$ and $2n + 6 > 8$

....

[Total 3 marks]

4 Possible values of x are given by the inequality $5 - 3x > 7 - x$.

a) Solve the inequality $5 - 3x > 7 - x$.

....

[2]

b) Represent your solution on the number line below.

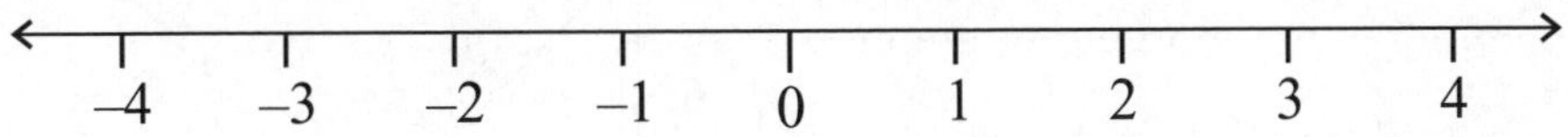

[1]

[Total 3 marks]

5 Find the largest three consecutive even numbers that sum to less than 1000.

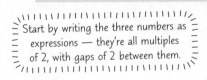

Start by writing the three numbers as expressions — they're all multiples of 2, with gaps of 2 between them.

....

[Total 3 marks]

Score: ☐ / **12**

M7 Graphical Inequalities

1 Look at the grid below.

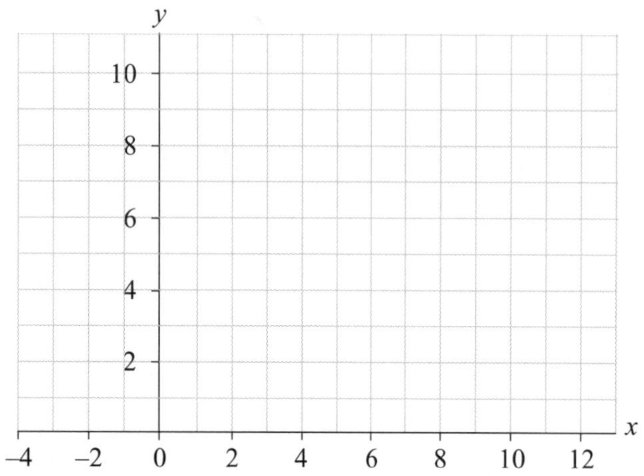

a) Use the grid to draw the graphs of $2x + y = 10$ and $y = x + 2$.

[2]

b) Shade and label, using the letter S, the area represented by the inequalities $x \geq 1,\ 2x + y \leq 10,\ y \geq x + 2$.

[2]

[Total 4 marks]

2 Look at the grid on the right.

On the grid, shade the region that represents these inequalities:

$x < 5$

$y \geq -2$

$y - x \leq 1$

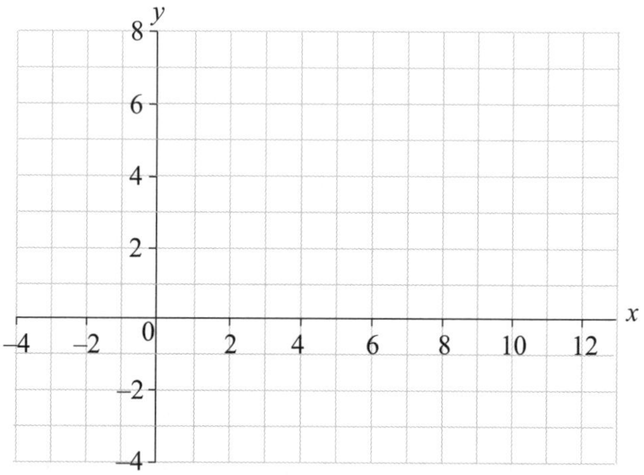

[Total 4 marks]

3 Look at the grid on the right.

a) The shaded region R is bounded by the lines $y = 2$, $y = x$ and $x + y = 8$.
Write down three inequalities which define R.

....

....

[3]

b) What is the lowest value of $y - x$ that satisfies this set of inequalities?

....

[2]

[Total 5 marks]

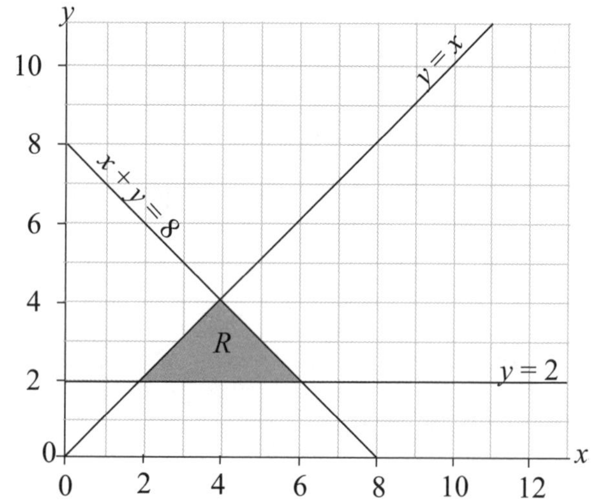

Exam Practice Tip

You need to pay close attention to whether the symbol is just < or > or whether it's ≤ or ≥. If it's < or >, draw a dashed line on the graph. If it's ≤ or ≥, you need to use a solid line. If you're not sure which side of the line you want, pick a point with coordinates that satisfy the inequality and see which side of the line it lies.

Score

13

Sequences

1 The nth term of a sequence is given by $3n + 2$.

What are the first 3 terms of this sequence?

....

[Total 2 marks]

2 The first four terms in a sequence are 3, 8, 13, 18, …

a) Write down the next two terms in the sequence.

....

[1]

b) Find the nth term of the sequence.

....

[2]

c) What is the 30th term of the sequence?

....

[1]

[Total 4 marks]

3 This question is about the sequence 3, 7, 11, 15, 19…

a) Find the nth term of the sequence.

....

[2]

b) Explain why 502 cannot be a term in this sequence.

....

....

....

[2]

[Total 4 marks]

4 Aine works as a music teacher. In her first week, she taught 9 piano lessons and 6 drumming lessons, then taught 5 piano lessons and 2 drumming lessons each week in the following weeks.

a) Show that the total number of lessons Aine has taught to date follows the rule $7n + 8$, where n is the number of weeks she has worked.

[3]

b) After six weeks of lessons, Aine wants to know what proportion of the lessons she taught were drumming lessons.
Use the rule for the total number of lessons to work this out.
Give your answer as a fraction.

....

[2]

[Total 5 marks]

5 Find an expression in terms of n that describes this sequence: $\frac{1}{3}, \frac{5}{12}, \frac{9}{21}, \frac{13}{30}, \frac{17}{39}$

....

[Total 4 marks]

6 The first four terms in a sequence are $\sqrt{2}$, 2, $2\sqrt{2}$, 4...

a) Find the next two terms in the sequence.

....

[2]

b) Circle the expression for the nth term of the sequence.

$\sqrt{2n}$ $\qquad n\sqrt{2}$ $\qquad (\sqrt{2})^n$ $\qquad n(\sqrt{2})^2$

[1]

[Total 3 marks]

7 A sequence begins 5, 12, 31, 68, ...

a) Find an expression for the nth term of the sequence.

....

[2]

b) Write down the next term in the sequence.

....

[1]

[Total 3 marks]

8 The patterns below are made up of grey and white squares.

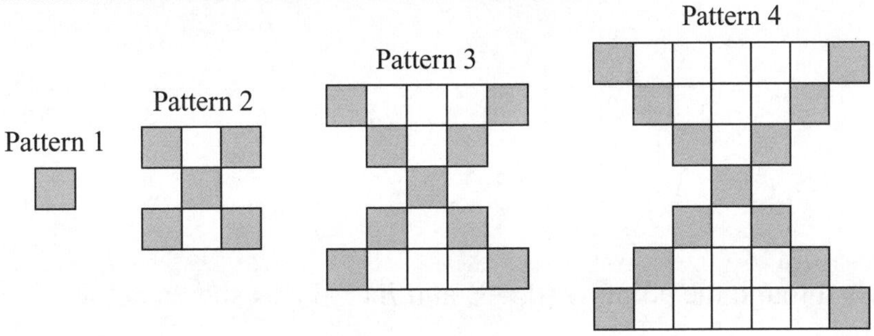

a) Find an expression for the number of **grey** squares in the nth pattern.

....

[2]

b) Giles makes two consecutive patterns in the sequence.
He uses 414 grey squares in total. Which 2 patterns has he made?

....

[3]

c) Find an expression for the **total** number of squares in the nth pattern.

....

[3]

[Total 8 marks]

Exam Practice Tip

Sequence questions are all about spotting the pattern — don't be put off if it's one you haven't come across before (examiners like to try and catch you off guard by throwing in things like coordinates and fractions). You might even come across a sequence where a numerator and denominator each follow a different rule.

Score

33

M3 Straight Line Graphs (1)

1 Draw the graph $2y + x = 7$ on the axes below, for values of x in the range $-2 \leq x \leq 10$.

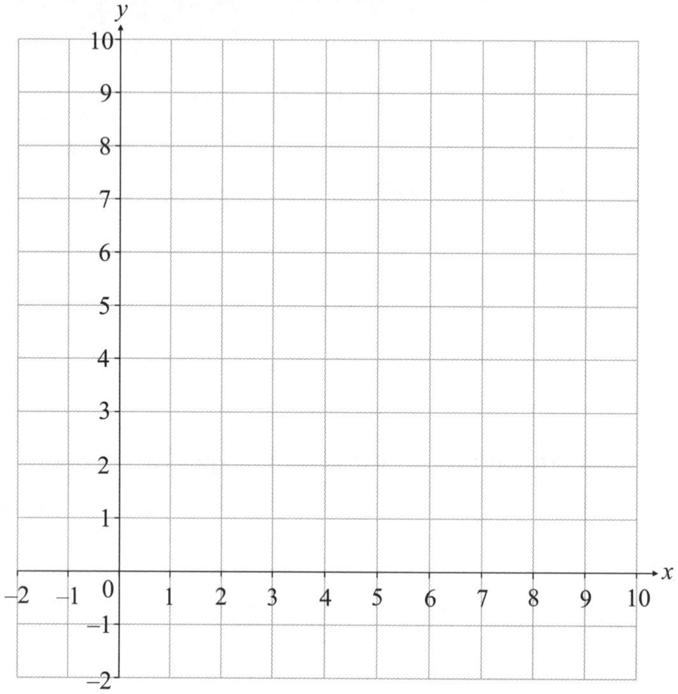

[Total 3 marks]

2 Line **L** passes through the points A (0, –3) and B (5, 7), as shown below.

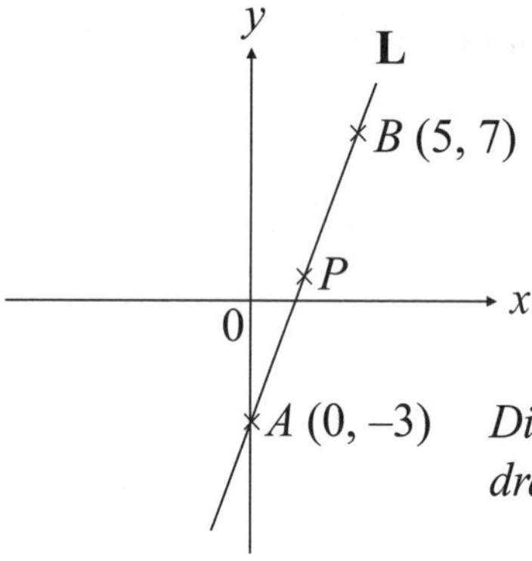

Diagram not drawn accurately

a) Find the equation of line **L**.

....

[3]

b) Write down the equation of the line which is parallel to line **L** and passes through the point (2, 10).

....

[2]

c) Point P is the midpoint of the line segment AB. What are the coordinates of P?

....

[2]

[Total 7 marks]

Score: $\frac{}{10}$

Straight Line Graphs (2)

M4

1 A straight line, **S**, passes through the points (a, b) and (c, d).

It is given that $2a + 4 = 2c$ and $b - 6 = d$.

a) What is the gradient of **S**?

Gradient = ...

[3]

b) Line **R** is perpendicular to Line **S** and passes through (6, 3). Find the equation of Line **R**.

....

[2]

[Total 5 marks]

2 Sakura plots the points A (5, 7), B (1, –1), C (13, 4) and D (3, –2). She claims she can draw a line perpendicular to AB that passes through the midpoint of both AB and CD.

Is she correct? Explain your answer.

Start by finding the midpoint of the lines AB and CD.

[Total 5 marks]

Exam Practice Tip

Sometimes questions include a real jumble of letters and coordinates and look pretty daunting. If you've got loads of information like this, try drawing a quick sketch — just seeing all the points plotted in roughly the right places on a set of axes often really helps with understanding what's going on in the question.

Score

10

M7 Quadratic Graphs

1 The graph below shows $y = x^2 - 3x + a$.

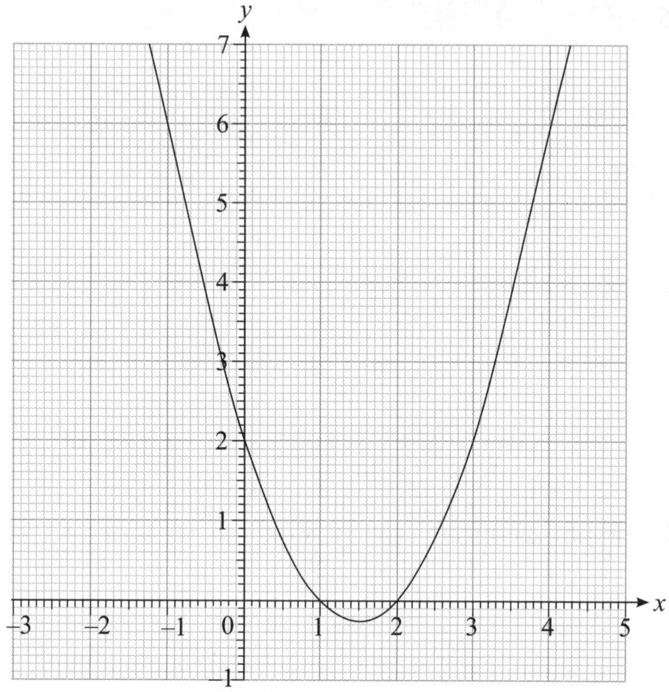

a) Estimate the coordinates of the turning point of $y = x^2 - 3x + a$.

(............. , ...)
[1]

b) Write down the value of a.

a = ...
[1]
[Total 2 marks]

2 The temperature (T) of a piece of metal changes over time (t) as it is rapidly heated and then cooled again. It is modelled by the equation $T = -5t^2 + 40t - 35$.

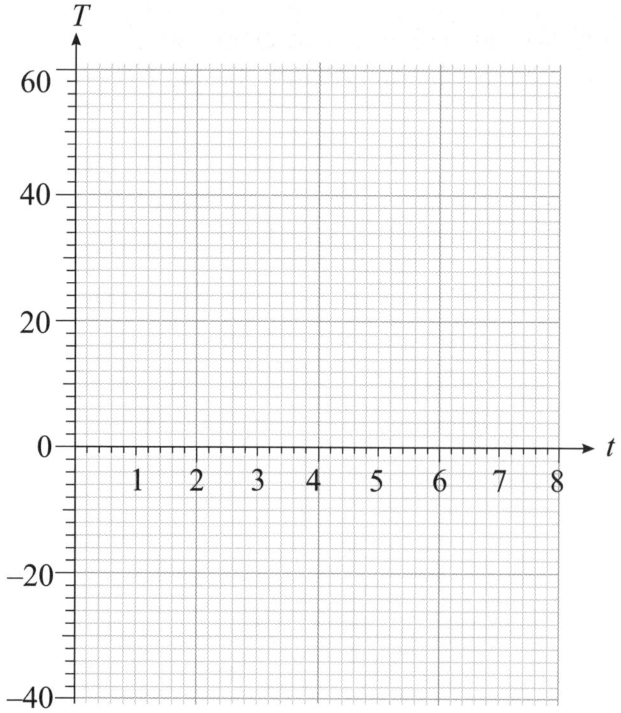

a) Plot the graph of $T = -5t^2 + 40t - 35$ on the grid. Show your working.

[4]

b) At what time did the metal reach its highest temperature?

t = ...
[1]

c) Using your graph, solve the equation $-5t^2 + 40t - 35 = 20$.

t = ... and t = ...
[2]
[Total 7 marks]

3 Find the turning point of $y = x^2 - 4x + 3$.

(............. , ...)

[Total 4 marks]

4 Sketch the graph of $y = 2x^2 + 10x - 12$. Label the turning point and any points where the curve intersects the axes with their coordinates.

[Total 6 marks]

Exam Practice Tip

If your curves don't look nice and smooth when you plot your quadratic graphs, you can be pretty sure you've gone wrong somewhere. Also remember that your graph should be symmetrical, with the turning point halfway between the points where the graph crosses the x-axis.

Score

/ 19

M7 Harder Graphs (1)

1 The sketch below shows two points from the graph $y = \frac{4}{x}$.

a) Complete the sketch below of the graph $y = \frac{4}{x}$, for $x > 0$.

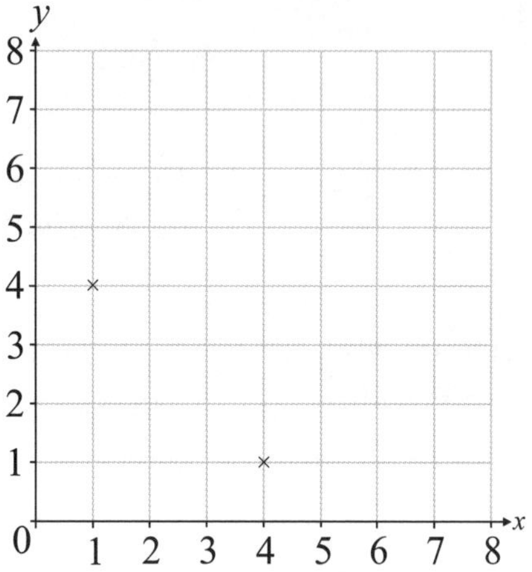

[2]

b) Find the coordinates of the point where $y = \frac{4}{x}$ crosses the line $y = x$ for $x > 0$.

(............... , ...)

[1]

[Total 3 marks]

2 On the grid below, draw the graph of $y = x^3 + x^2 - 6x - 6$ between $x = -3$ and $x = 3$. Show your working.

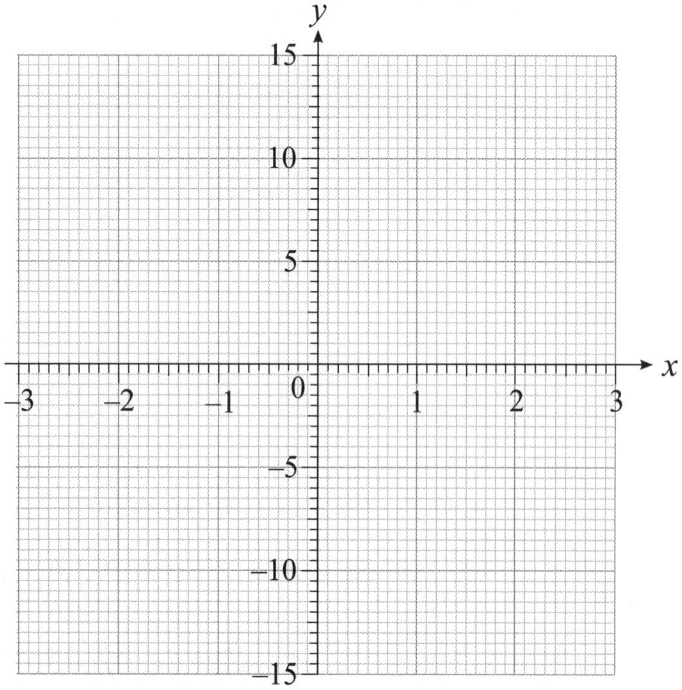

[Total 4 marks]

Score: /7

Harder Graphs (2)

M8

1 Sketches of different graphs are shown below.

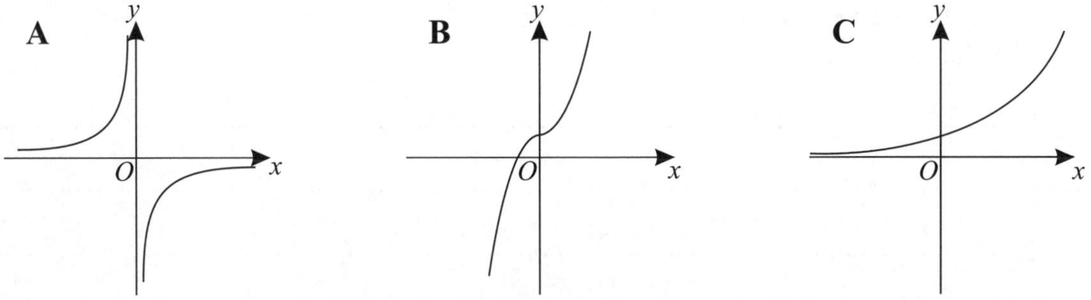

Match each equation below to one of the graphs above.

a) $y = x^3 + 1$ .... b) $y = \left(\frac{3}{2}\right)^x$ .... c) $y = -\frac{1}{x}$ ....

[Total 3 marks]

2 Ciarán bought a rare book which was worth £800 on 1st January 2018.

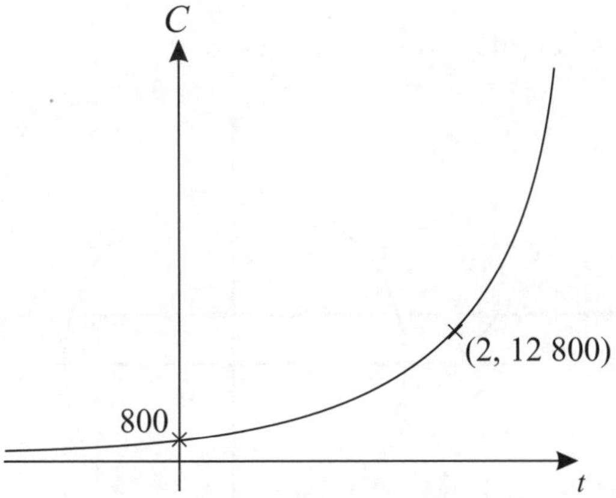

The book was worth £12 800 on 1st January 2020.

The value of the book over time is shown on the graph, represented by the equation

$$C = xy^t$$

where C is the value of the book in pounds, x and y are positive integers and t is the number of years since Ciarán bought the book ($-2 \leq t \leq 3$). $t = 0$ on 1st January 2018.

a) Find the values of x and y, using the information given above.

x = ... and y = ...

[3]

b) What was the value of the book on 1st January 2016?

£ ....

[2]

[Total 5 marks]

Score: /8

M8 Circle Graphs

1 A curve has the equation $x^2 + y^2 = 16$.

a) Does this curve pass through the origin?
Explain your answer.

....

....

....

[1]

b) Find the values of x for which the curve intersects the x-axis.

....

[1]

[Total 2 marks]

2 Find the equation of the tangent to the circle $x^2 + y^2 = 25$ at the point (–4, –3).

Start by finding the gradient of the radius that goes from (0, 0) to (–4, –3).

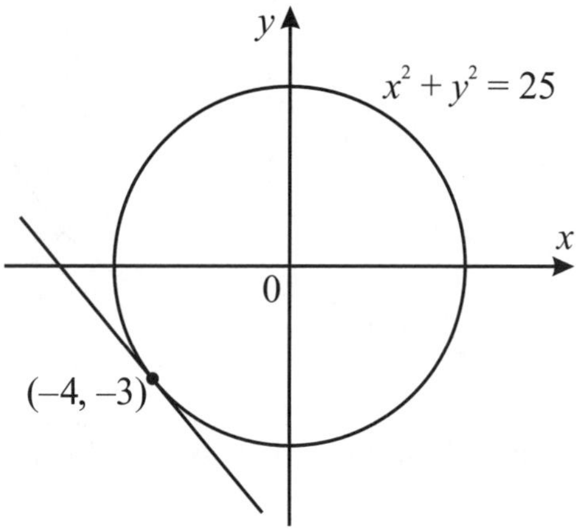

....

[Total 3 marks]

3 The point (–8, 15) lies on a circle centred at the origin.

Find the length of the radius and the equation of the circle.

Length of radius .... , Equation ....

[Total 4 marks]

Score: /9

Solving Equations Using Graphs (1)

M7

1 This is a question about the function $y = x^2 + 2x - 5$.

a) Draw the graph of $y = x^2 + 2x - 5$ on the grid below, for values of x in the range $-4 \leq x \leq 2$. Show your working.

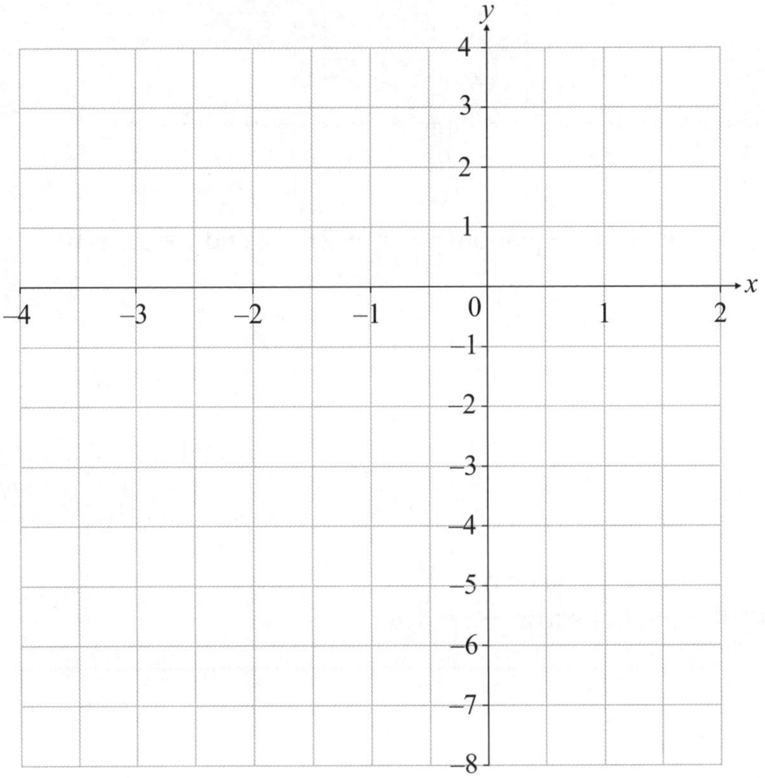

[4]

b) Using the graph you drew in part a), give estimates for the solutions of $x^2 + 2x - 5 = -1$.

x = ... and x = ...

[2]

c) Using the graph you drew in part a), find the coordinates where the line $x + y + 5 = 0$ intersects $y = x^2 + 2x - 5$.

....

[4]

[Total 10 marks]

Score: ___ / **10**

M8 Solving Equations Using Graphs (2)

1 The diagram below shows part of the graph of $y = x^2 + 2x - 2$.

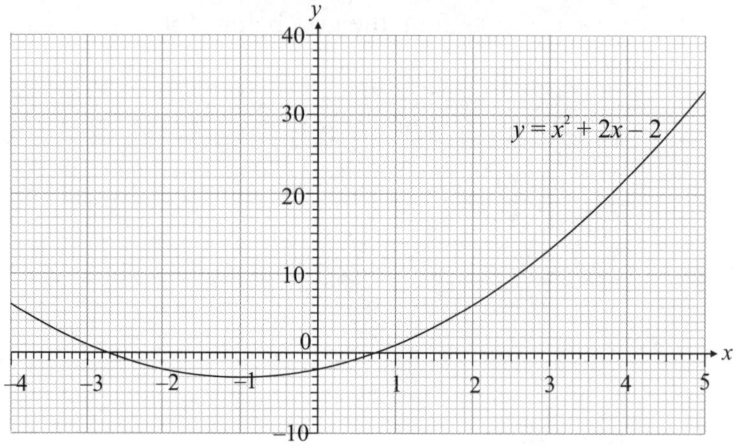

Use the graph to solve the simultaneous equations $y = x^2 + 2x - 2$ and $y = 3x + 10$.

$x =$ .... , $y =$ ....

and $x =$ .... , $y =$ ....

[Total 4 marks]

2 The graph of the curve $y = x^2 - x - 4$ is shown.
Use the graph to estimate the solutions to $x^2 + x = 1$.

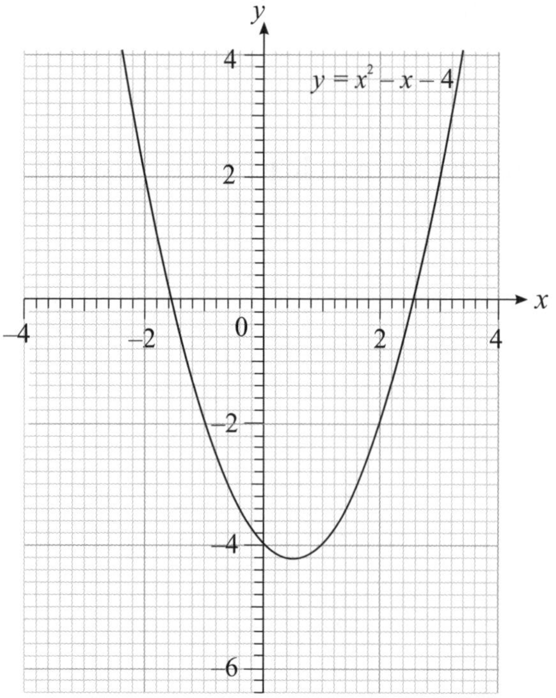

$x =$ ....

$x =$ ....

[Total 5 marks]

Exam Practice Tip

Questions like number 2, above, are much easier when you understand the trick — just find a way of getting two equations that you can draw graphs for on each side of the equals sign. And if you're having to balance or rearrange equations, check each step of your working to be sure you're doing the same thing to both sides.

Score

9

Real-Life Graphs (1)

M3

1 An electricity company offers its customers two different price plans.

Plan **A:** Monthly fee of £[redacted] plus [redacted] for each unit used.

Plan **B:** No monthly fee, just pay [redacted] for each unit used.

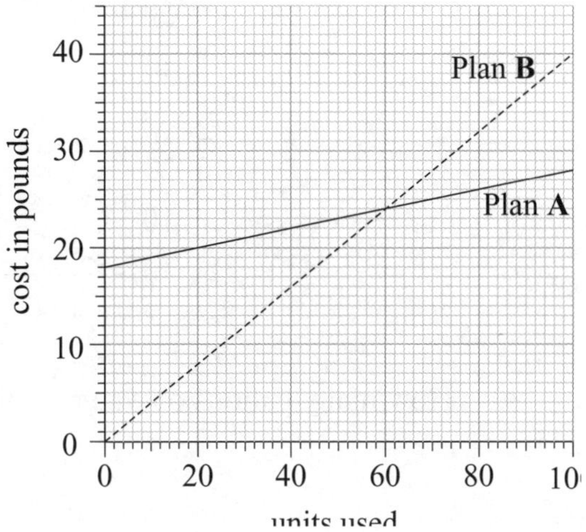

Some of the information is missing.

a) Use the graph to find:

i) The monthly fee for Plan **A**.

£ ....

[1]

ii) The cost per unit for Plan **B**.
Show your working.

.... p

[2]

b) Mr Barker uses about 85 units of electricity each month.
Which price plan would you advise him to choose? Explain your answer.

....

....

[2]

[Total 5 marks]

2 The table to the right shows how much petrol a car used on 3 journeys.

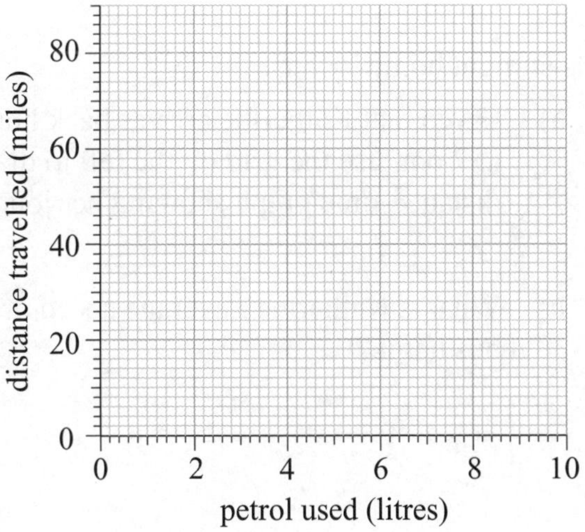

Distance (miles)	16	40	72
Petrol used (litres)	2	5	9

a) Plot a graph on the grid opposite to represent this information.

[2]

b) Use the gradient of the graph to work out how much petrol the car would use on a 190 mile journey. You must show your working.

....

[2]

[Total 4 marks]

Score: /9

Real-Life Graphs (2)

M7

1 Use the graph to help you answer the questions below.

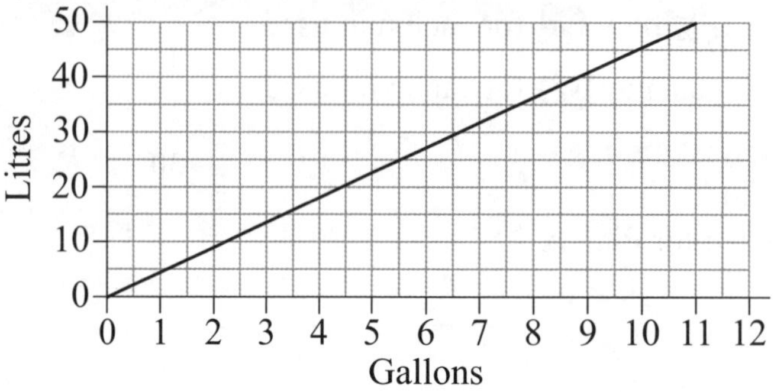

a) How many gallons of water would fit into a 25 litre container?

.... gallons
[1]

b) A paddling pool holds 80 litres of water. What is this in gallons?

.... gallons
[3]

[Total 4 marks]

2 Katherine is going to the cinema.

She leaves her house at 1 pm and walks at a constant speed of 3.5 mph.
Katherine arrives at the cinema 2 hours later.
She stays for 3 hours and 45 minutes, and then travels straight home by bus.

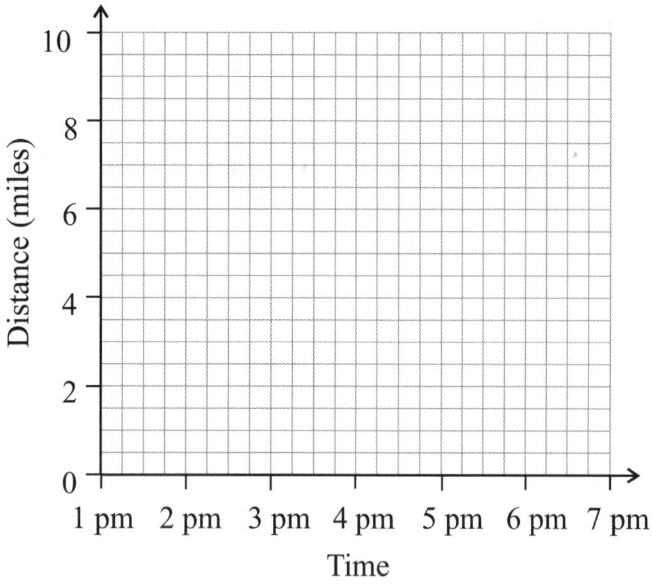

a) Given that Katherine arrives back home at 7 pm, use the grid on the left to draw a distance-time graph showing her journey.
[3]

b) What is Katherine's average speed on the bus home?

.... mph
[2]

[Total 5 marks]

Score: /9

Gradients of Real-Life Graphs

M8

1 Zuri rolls a ball along a sloped surface.

Zuri plots the distance, x m, of the ball from its starting position against time, t seconds, on the graph on the right.

Estimate the speed of the ball 1 second after it begins moving.

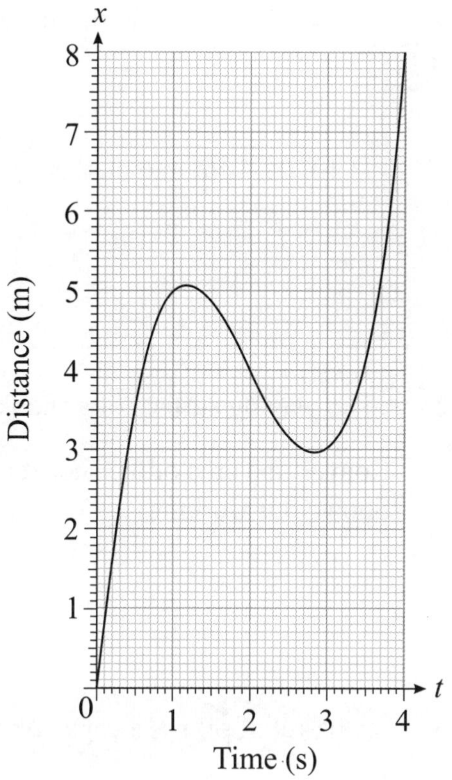

.... m/s

[Total 2 marks]

2 The graph below shows how the velocity of a moving vehicle changes over time.

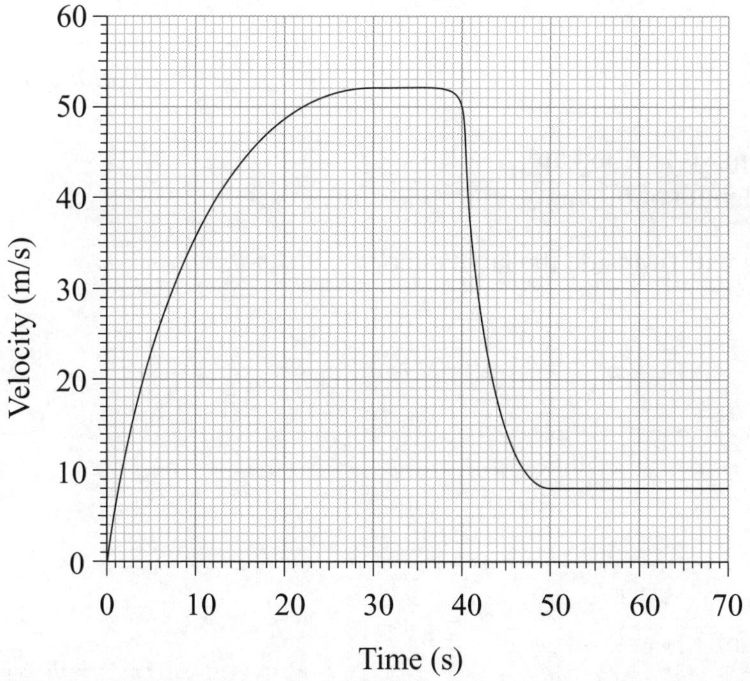

Estimate the acceleration of the vehicle at 45 seconds.

TIP: acceleration = velocity ÷ time.

.... m/s^2

[Total 2 marks]

Score: /4

Metric Units

M3

1 Convert the following:

a) 7.5 litres into millilitres.

.... ml
[1]

b) 8.7 cm into metres.

.... m
[1]

[Total 2 marks]

2 The playing surface of a snooker table has an area of 39 200 cm^2.

Convert the area of the snooker table into m^2.
Show your working.

.... m^2
[Total 2 marks]

3 A barrel of oil has a capacity of 150 litres.

How many cubic metres of oil does the barrel hold?

.... m^3
[Total 3 marks]

4 A large cube has side lengths of 3 m. It is filled up with small cubes each with a side length of 60 mm.

How many of the smaller cubes will fit inside the large cube?

....
[Total 3 marks]

Score: ___ / **10**

Imperial Units

M7

1 Cormac has just competed in a long jump competition.

His best jump measured 9½ feet. What is this distance in cm?
1 foot ≈ 30 cm.

.... cm
[Total 1 mark]

2 1 gallon = 8 pints. 9 litres ≈ 2 gallons.
Approximately how many litres are there in 64 pints?

.... litres
[Total 3 marks]

3 Farrah wants to post some books to a friend in another country.
Each book weighs 1.5 lb and each package can hold a maximum weight of 2500 g.

How many books can she send in one package?

....
[Total 4 marks]

4 Alex has a choice of two cars to hire for a holiday.
He wants to hire the most efficient car.

Car A will do 51.4 miles per gallon of petrol. Car B uses 6.2 litres of petrol per 100 km.
4.5 litres ≈ 1 gallon. Which car should Alex hire? Show your working.

....

[Total 3 marks]

Score: ___ / **11**

M3 Speed

1 John and Alan hired a van. Their receipt gave them information about how much time they spent travelling in the van, and how fast they went.

Travelling time: 1 hour 15 minutes
Average speed: 56 km/h

Calculate the distance that John and Alan travelled in the van.

.... km

[Total 2 marks]

2 Jhanvi has been caught speeding by a pair of average speed cameras. The speed limit was 50 mph.

The cameras are 2500 m apart. The time taken for her car to pass between them was 102 seconds.

a) What was Jhanvi's average speed between the cameras? Give your answer to the nearest mph. Take 1 mile as 1.6 km.

.... mph

[3]

b) If Jhanvi had been travelling within the speed limit, what is the minimum time it should have taken her to pass between the cameras? Give your answer to the nearest second.

.... s

[2]

[Total 5 marks]

3 In 2019 Mo ran a long-distance race (distance d) and finished with time t. In 2020 he finished the same race (distance d) but his time was 10% quicker.

By what percentage did his average speed for the race increase? Give your answer to 2 decimal places.

TIP: Start by expressing Mo's 2020 time in terms of t.

.... %

[Total 4 marks]

Score: /11

Density

M3

1 The mass of a metal statue is 360 kg.
The density of the metal alloy from which it is made is 1800 kg/m^3.

a) Calculate the volume of the statue.

.... m^3
[2]

b) It is decided that the metal statue is too heavy so a different metal alloy is used to make a new statue. The new statue has the same volume as the old one but has a mass of 220 kg. Calculate the density of the new statue.

.... kg/m^3
[2]

[Total 4 marks]

2 An iron cube has side length 4 cm and iron has a density of 7.9 grams per cm^3.

a) Work out the mass of the iron cube.

.... g
[3]

b) A larger iron cube has a mass of 63.2 kg.
What is the ratio of the side lengths of the smaller and larger cubes?

....
[4]

[Total 7 marks]

3 Brass is a metallic alloy. One type of brass consists of 70% copper and 30% zinc by volume. Copper has a density of 8.9 g/cm^3 and zinc has a density of 7.1 g/cm^3.

What is the density of this type of brass?

.... g/cm^3
[Total 4 marks]

Score: ___ / **15**

M3

Pressure

1 The cuboid opposite has three different faces (A, B and C). The cuboid has a weight of 40 N.

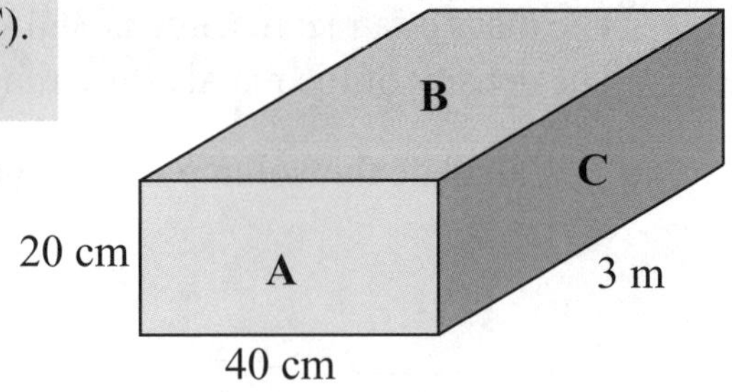

a) Calculate the pressure, in N/m^2, that the cuboid exerts on horizontal ground when it is resting on face A.

.... N/m^2

[3]

b) Three of these cuboids are stacked directly on top of each other and the bottom cuboid is resting on face B. What pressure are they exerting on horizontal ground?

.... N/m^2

[3]

[Total 6 marks]

2 The cone below has a base diameter of 20 cm. When the base of the cone rests on horizontal ground it exerts a pressure of 650 N/m^2.

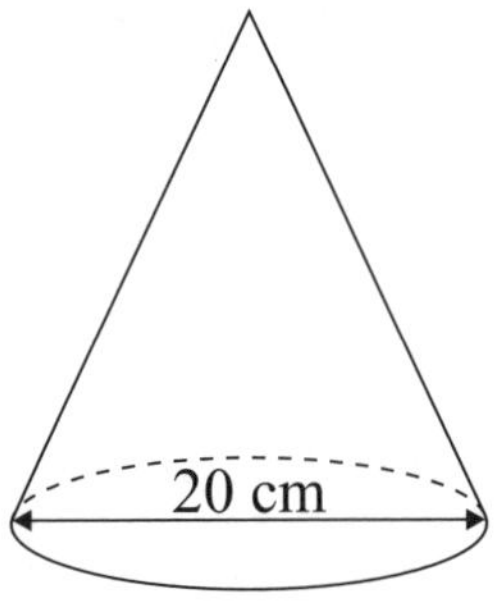

a) Calculate the weight of the cone.

.... N

[4]

b) The diameter of the cone is halved but the weight is kept the same. What effect will this have on the pressure exerted on the ground? Show working to explain your answer.

[2]

[Total 6 marks]

Exam Practice Tip

You might think remembering the formulas for speed, density and pressure is tough, but questions involving compound units often involve doing some conversions. Make sure you're happy converting between different units (particularly speeds, areas and volumes) so you don't make any silly mistakes when exam time comes.

Score

12

Angle Rules and Parallel Lines

M3

1 The diagram shows a pair of parallel lines with a straight line intersecting them.

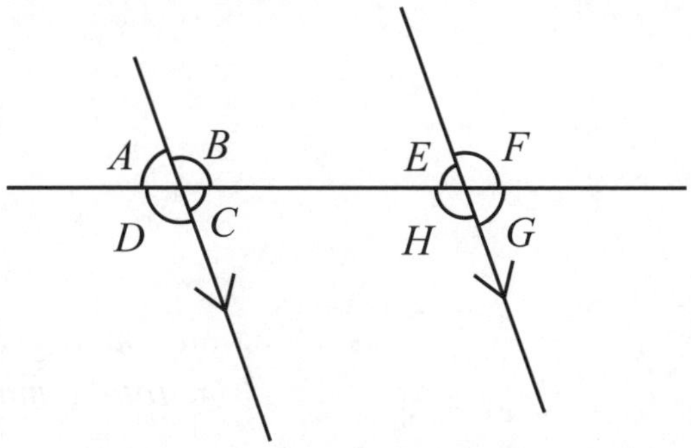

Diagram not drawn accurately

a) Identify one pair of alternate angles in the diagram.

Angle .... and angle ....

[1]

b) Identify one angle that is adjacent to angle F.

Angle ....

[1]

c) Angle A is 60°. What size is angle E?
Give a reason for your answer.

....

....

[1]

[Total 3 marks]

2 *DEF* and *BEC* are straight lines that cross at *E*.
AFB and *AC* are perpendicular lines.

a) Find angle *x*.
Give a reason for each stage of your working.

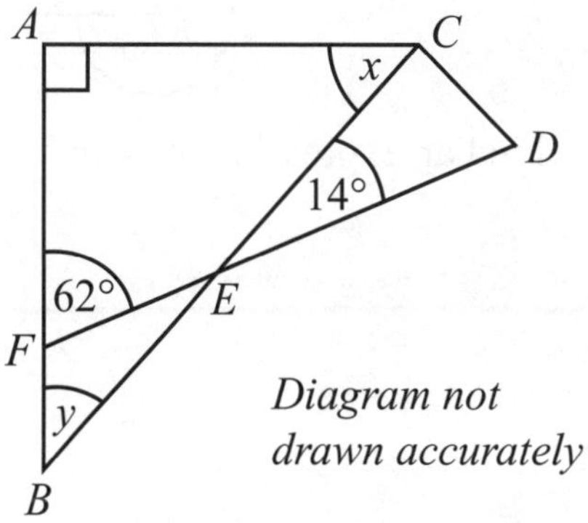

Diagram not drawn accurately

$x =$ .... °

[2]

b) Hence show that $y = 48°$.

[2]

[Total 4 marks]

3 A triangle is shown in the diagram on the right.

Show that $x = y + z$.

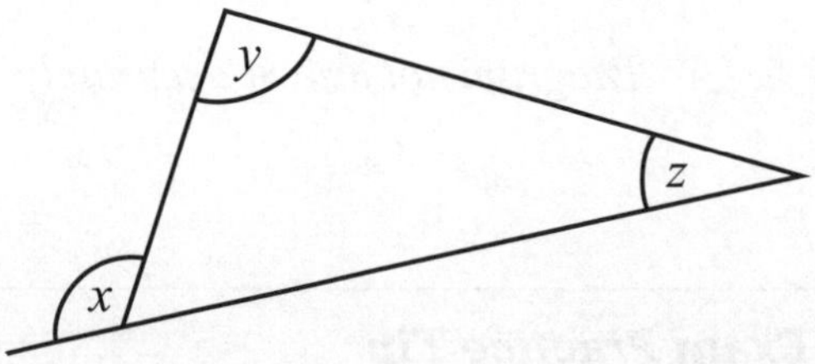

[Total 3 marks]

4 AB and CD are parallel lines. EF and GH are straight lines.

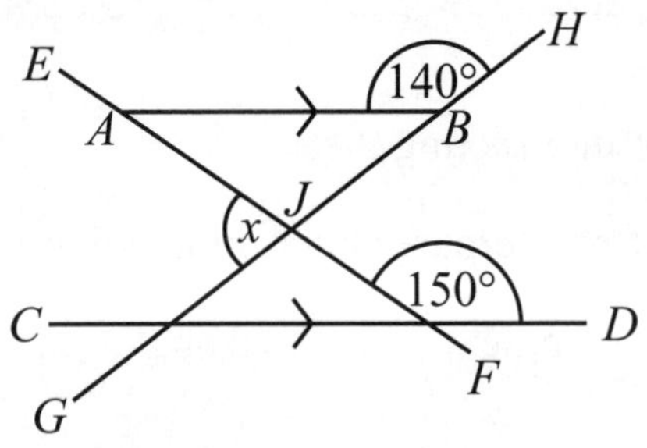

Diagram not drawn accurately

Work out the size of angle x.
Give reasons for each stage of your working.

....°

[Total 4 marks]

5 Lines AB and DE are parallel and ABC is a straight line. Lines AE, BC and BD are of equal length. ABDE is an isosceles trapezium, which has a vertical line of symmetry.

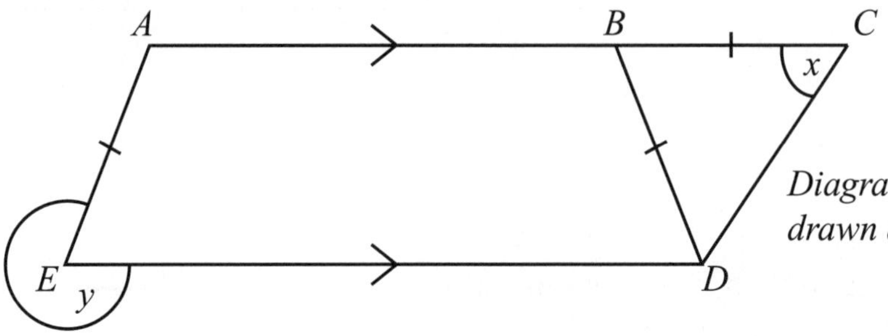

Diagram not drawn accurately

Find an expression for y in terms of x.

....

[Total 5 marks]

6 ABCD is a trapezium. Lines AB and DC are parallel to each other.

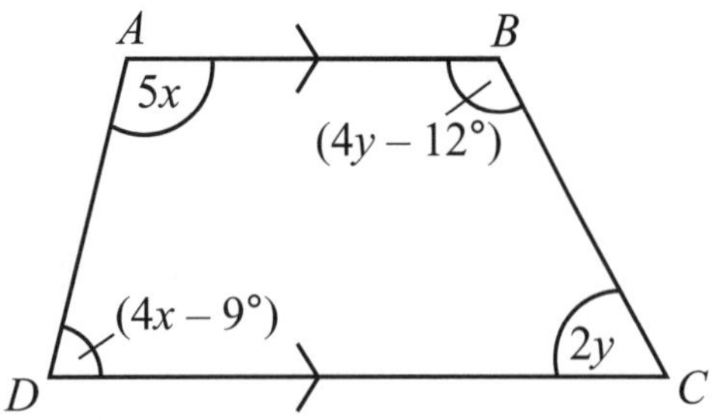

Diagram not drawn accurately

Find the values of x and y.

x = ...° y = ...°

[Total 4 marks]

Exam Practice Tip

If you find yourself staring at a geometry problem in the exam not knowing where to start, just try finding any angles you can — don't worry tooooo much at first about the particular angle you've been asked to find. Go through the rules of geometry one at a time, and apply them wherever you can.

Score

23

Angles in Shapes

1 Part of a regular polygon is shown below. The exterior angles of the polygon are 24°.

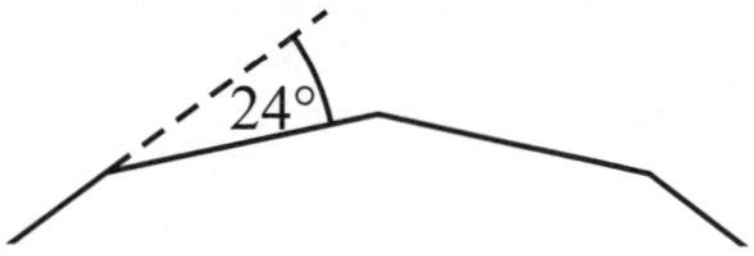

Diagram not drawn accurately

Work out the number of sides of the regular polygon.

....

[Total 2 marks]

2 Part of a regular polygon is shown below. Each interior angle is 150°.

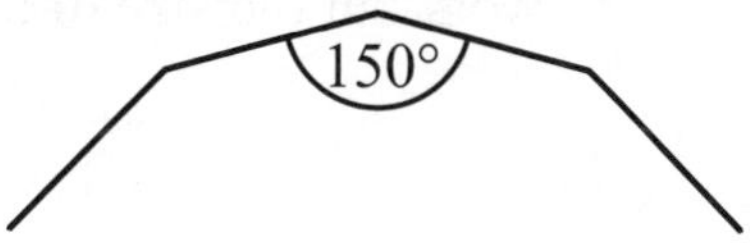

Diagram not drawn accurately

Calculate the number of sides of the polygon.

....

[Total 3 marks]

3 The shape on the right has six sides.

Work out the size of angle a in the shape.

Diagram not drawn accurately

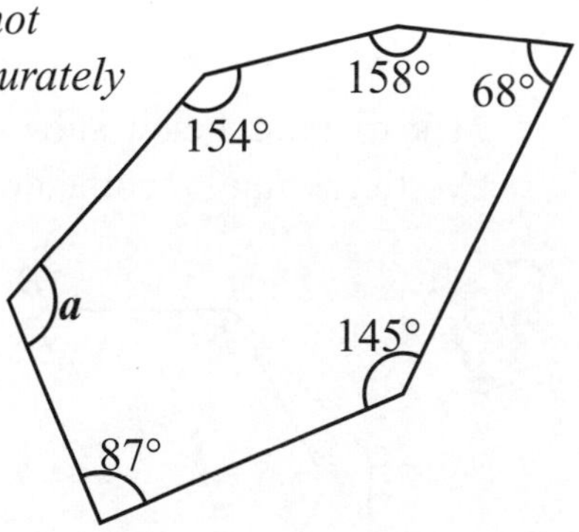

a = ...°

[Total 4 marks]

4 The diagram shows a regular pentagon and an equilateral triangle.

Work out the size of the angle p.

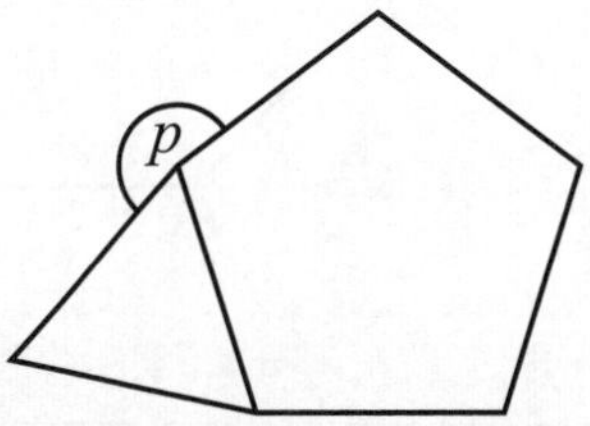

Diagram not drawn accurately

........................°

[Total 5 marks]

5 The diagram below shows a polygon.

Find the angle sum of the polygon by dividing it into triangles.
Show all your working.

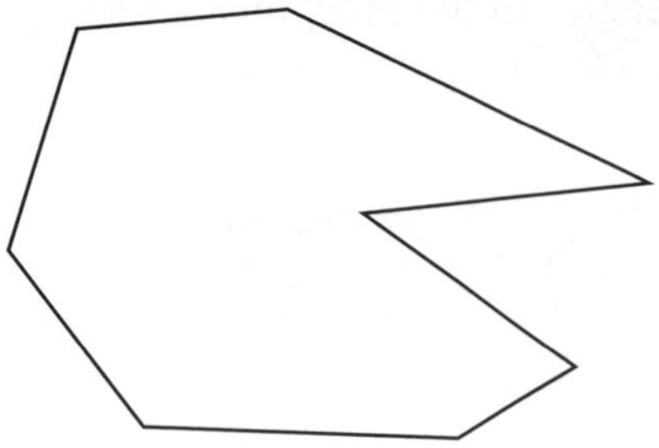

..........................°

[Total 3 marks]

6 The diagram shows a regular octagon. *AB* is a side of the octagon and *O* is its centre.

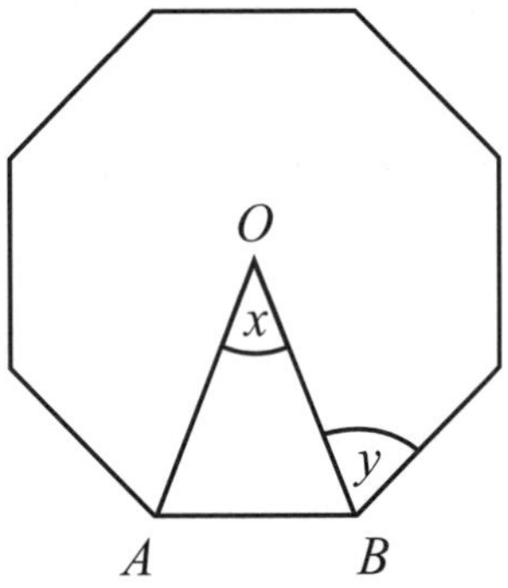

Diagram not drawn accurately

a) Work out the size of the angle marked x.

x = ...°

[2]

b) Work out the size of the angle marked y.

y = ...°

[2]

[Total 4 marks]

7 The diagram below shows a regular hexagon inside a regular octagon.
Vertices *A* and *B* coincide with vertices *I* and *J* respectively.

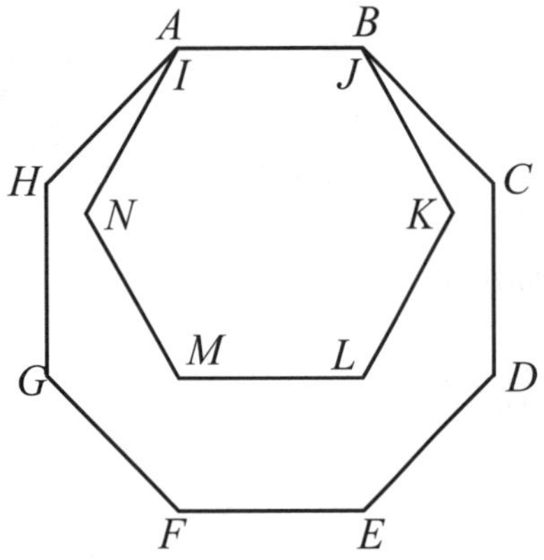

Find the size of angle *CBK*.

................°

[Total 3 marks]

Exam Practice Tip

You need to know the number of sides of a regular polygon to work out its interior and exterior angles — so make sure you've swotted up on the different types of polygon. Altogether now: equilateral triangle (3), square (4), pentagon (5), hexagon (6), heptagon (7), octagon (8), nonagon (9), decagon (10).

Score

24

Bearings

1 Two ships leave a port at the same time.
Ship *A* travels due west for 40 km. Ship *B* travels 60 km on a bearing of 110°.

a) Using a scale of 1 cm = 10 km, draw the journeys of the two ships in the space below and clearly mark their final positions.

[4]

b) Measure the final bearing of Ship *B* from Ship *A*.

.... °

[1]

c) Use your answer from part b) to find the final bearing of Ship *A* from Ship *B*.

.... °

[2]

[Total 7 marks]

2 The diagram shows the position of two villages, *A* and *B*.

a) A walker hikes from village *A* on a bearing of 035°.
After an hour's walk he stops when village *B* is directly east of his position.
Mark the walker's position on the diagram with a cross (×) and label it *W*.

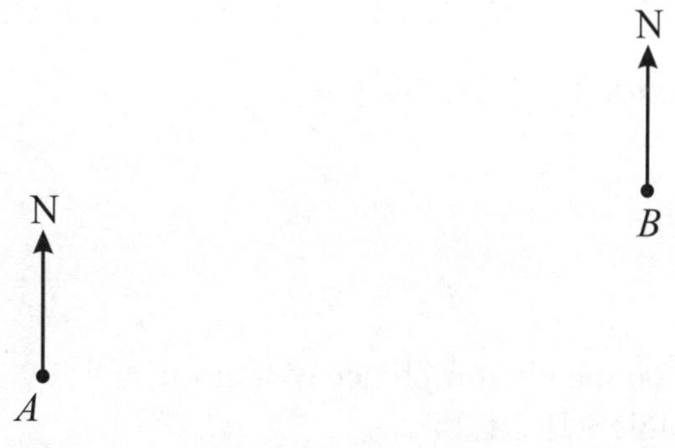

[2]

b) Another village, *C*, is on a bearing of 115° from village *A*, and on a bearing of 235° from village *B*. Mark the location of village *C* with a cross (×) and label it *C*.

[3]

c) Use a protractor to measure the bearing that the walker must hike on from his position at *W*, in order to reach village *C*.

.... °

[1]

[Total 6 marks]

Score: ____ / **13**

M4 Circle Geometry

1 The diagram shows a circle, centre *O*. *A*, *B*, *C* and *D* are points on the circumference.

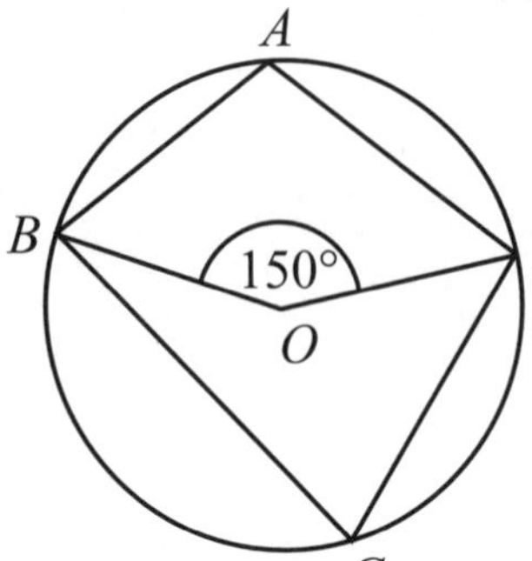

Diagram not drawn accurately

a) Work out the size of angle *BCD*. Give a reason for your answer.

....

....

[2]

b) Explain why angle *BAD* = 105°.

....

....

[1]

[Total 3 marks]

2 The diagram below shows a circle with centre *O*. *A*, *B*, *C* and *D* are points on the circumference of the circle and *AOC* is a straight line.

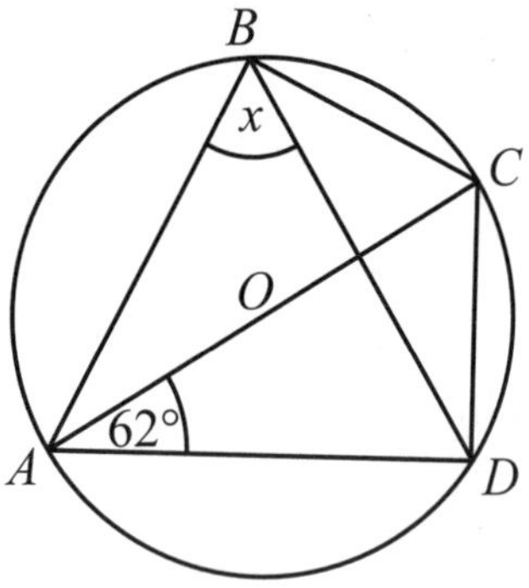

Diagram not drawn accurately

Work out the size of the angle marked *x*.
Give reasons for each step of your answer.

Angle *DBC* = ...° because ....

....

Angle *ABC* = ...° because ....

....

Angle x = ...° − ....° = ...°

x = ...°

[Total 3 marks]

3 *A*, *B*, *C* and *D* are points on the circumference of a circle.
Angle *BCD* is 28° and angle *ADC* is 24°.

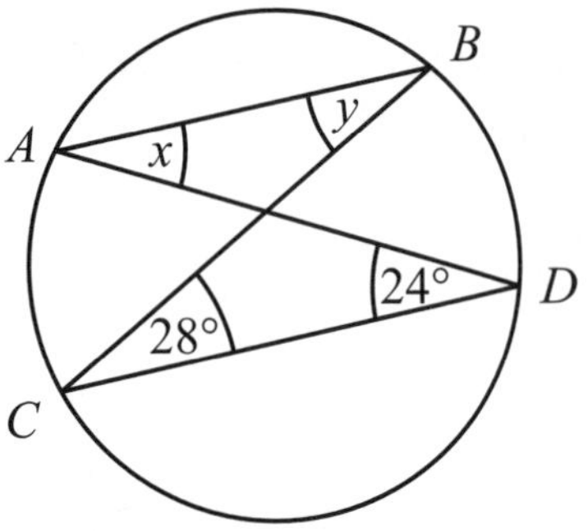

Diagram not drawn accurately

a) Find the sizes of angles *x* and *y*.

x = ...° *y* = ...°

[2]

b) Give a reason for your answers.

....

....

[1]

[Total 3 marks]

4 In the diagram, O is the centre of the circle. A, B, C and D are points on the circumference of the circle and DE and BE are tangents. Angle DEB is 80°.

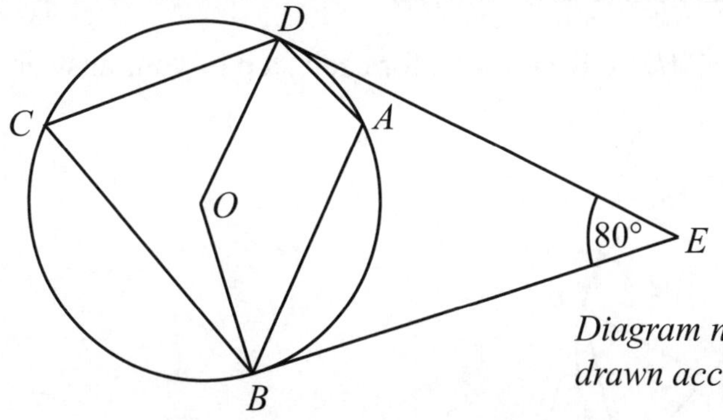

Diagram not drawn accurately

Work out the size of angle DAB, giving reasons for each step in your working.

Angles ODE and OBE are both ....° because a tangent always meets a radius at ....°.

Angle DOB = ...° because angles in a quadrilateral add up to ....°.

Angle DCB = ...° because an angle at the centre is twice the angle at the circumference.

Angle DAB = ...° because opposite angles of a cyclic quadrilateral add up to ....°.

...............................°

[Total 4 marks]

5 The diagram shows a circle with centre O. A, B and C are points on the circumference. AD and CD are tangents to the circle and ABE is a straight line. Angle CDO is 24°.

Diagram not drawn accurately

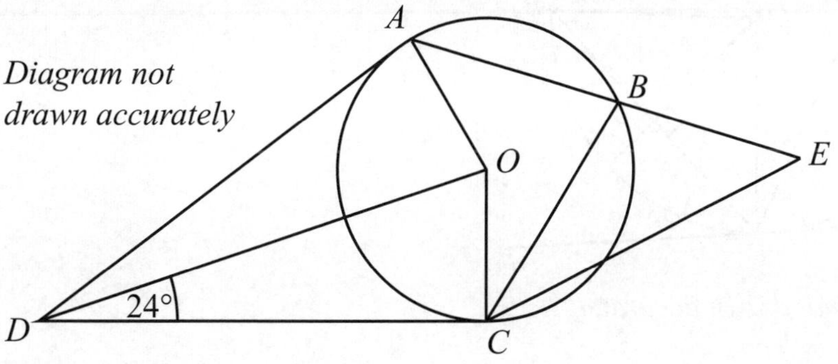

Find the size of angle CBE.
Give reasons for each step of your working.

...............................°

[Total 5 marks]

6 In the diagram below, A, B, C and D are points on the circumference of the circle. EDB is a straight line and FG is the tangent to the circle at point B. Angle FBD is 102° and angle EDC is 147°.

Find the size of angle CAD. Give reasons for each step of your answer.

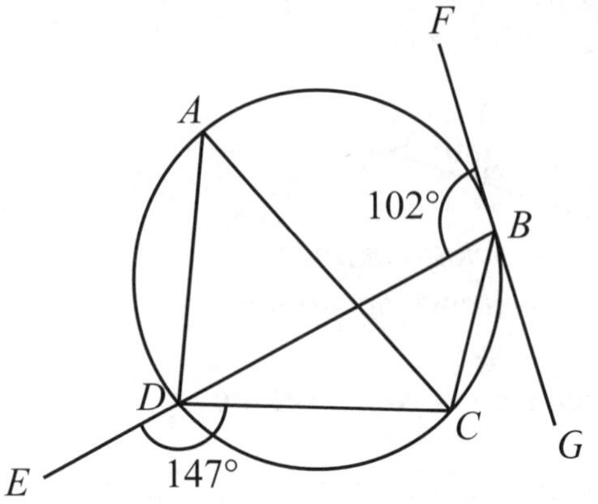

Diagram not drawn accurately

.............................°

[Total 4 marks]

7 A, B, C and D are points on the circumference of the circle with centre O. FE is the tangent to the circle at D and angle BDE = 53°.

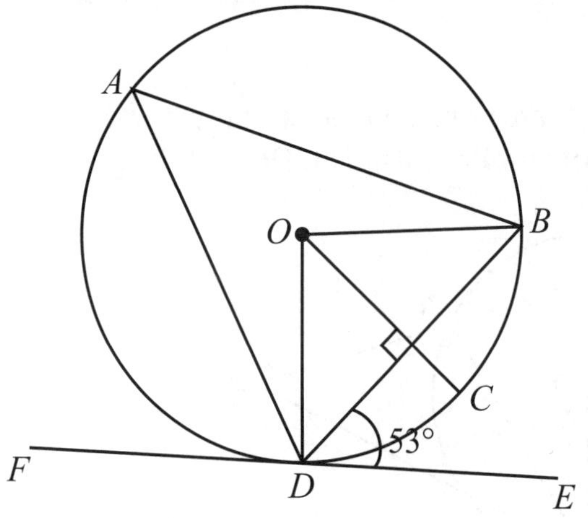

Diagram not drawn accurately

a) Find the size of angle DOB, giving reasons for each step of your answer.

.............................°

[2]

b) Explain why angle COB is half the size of angle DOB

....

....

....

[2]

[Total 4 marks]

Exam Practice Tip

Make sure you know the rules about circles really, really well. Draw them out and stick them all over your bedroom walls, your fridge, even your dog. Then in the exam, go through the rules one-by-one and use them to fill in as many angles in the diagram as you can. Keep an eye out for sneaky isosceles triangles too.

Score

26

Pythagoras' Theorem

M3

1 The diagram shows a right-angled triangle *ABC*. *AC* is 4 cm long. *BC* is 8 cm long.

Calculate the length of *AB*.

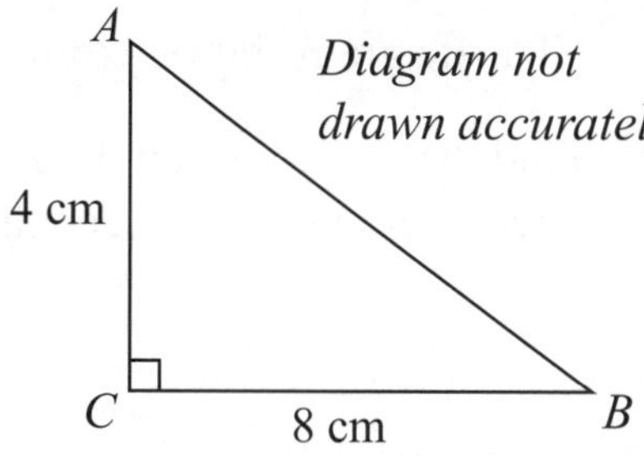

Diagram not drawn accurately

.... cm
[Total 3 marks]

2 Point *A* has coordinates (2, –1). Point *B* has coordinates (8, 7).

Calculate the length of the line segment *AB*.

....
[Total 3 marks]

3 A triangle has a base of 10 cm. Its other two sides are both 13 cm long.

Calculate the area of the triangle.

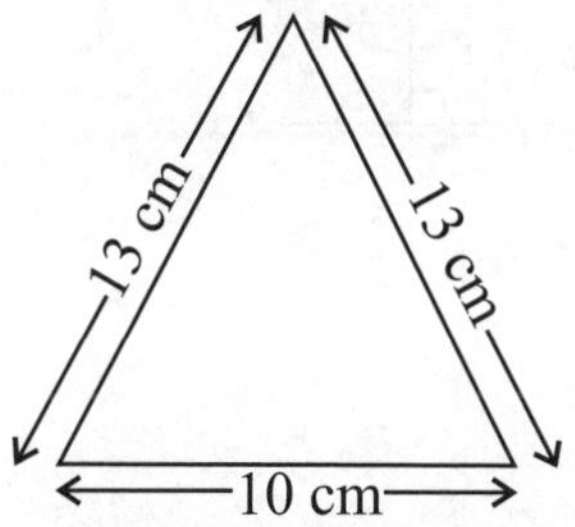

Diagram not drawn accurately

.... cm^2
[Total 4 marks]

4 The diagram shows a kite *ABCD*. *AB* is 28.3 cm long. *BC* is 54.3 cm long. *BE* is 20 cm in length.

Work out the perimeter of triangle *ABC*.
Give your answer to 1 decimal place.

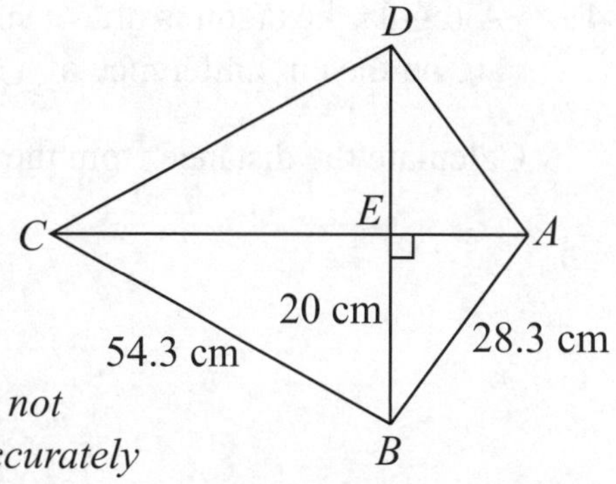

Diagram not drawn accurately

.... cm
[Total 5 marks]

Score: ___ / **15**

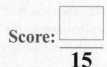

M3 Trigonometry

1 The diagram shows a right-angled triangle.

Find the size of the angle marked x.
Give your answer to 1 decimal place.

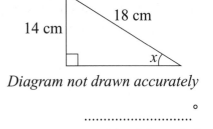

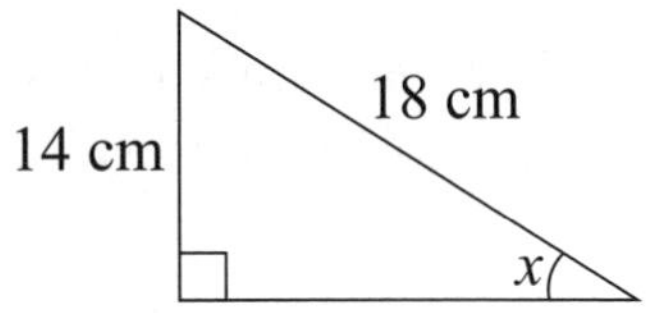

Diagram not drawn accurately

.... °

[Total 3 marks]

2 The diagram shows a right-angled triangle.

Find the length of the side marked y.
Give your answer to 2 decimal places.

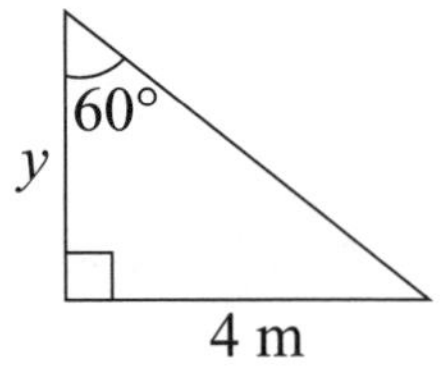

Diagram not drawn accurately

.... m

[Total 3 marks]

3 A shopkeeper needs a new access ramp for his shop. The top of the ramp must be level with the top of the step, which is 12 cm high. So that the ramp is not too steep, the angle of elevation from the bottom of the ramp to the top of the step should be 3.6°.

Diagram not drawn accurately

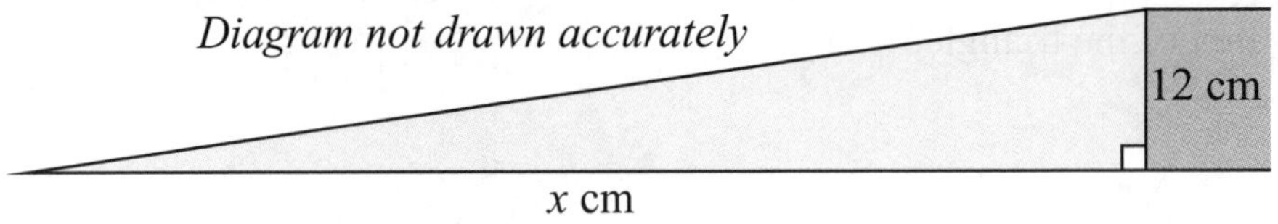

How far away from the bottom of the step should the ramp start?
Give your answer to 3 significant figures.

.... cm

[Total 3 marks]

4 A regular hexagon is drawn such that all of its vertices are on the circumference of a circle of radius 8.5 cm.

Calculate the distance from the centre of the circle to the centre of one edge of the hexagon.

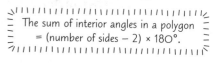

The sum of interior angles in a polygon = (number of sides − 2) × 180°.

.... cm

[Total 6 marks]

Exam Practice Tip

It'll help if you start trigonometry questions off by labelling the sides of the right-angled triangle for the angle you're using — the hypotenuse (H) is the longest side, and, of the two shorter sides, the opposite (O) doesn't touch the angle and the adjacent (A) is next to the angle. Make sure any angles you work out are sensible, too.

Score

15

The Sine and Cosine Rules

M8

1 In the triangle below, $AB = 10$ cm, $BC = 7$ cm and angle $ABC = 85°$.

a) Calculate the length of AC.
Give your answer to 3 significant figures.

$AC^2 = \dots\dots^2 + \dots\dots^2 - (2 \times \dots\dots \times \dots\dots \times \cos \dots\dots°)$

$AC = \sqrt{\dots\dots - \dots\dots \times \cos \dots\dots°}$

$AC = \dots\dots\dots\dots$

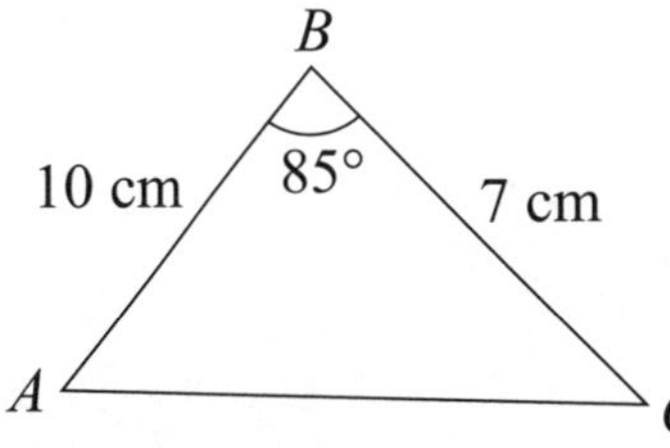

Diagram not drawn accurately

.... cm

[2]

b) Calculate the area of triangle ABC.
Give your answer to 3 significant figures.

.... cm^2

[2]

[Total 4 marks]

2 The diagram below is a sketch of a metal framework.
Some of the information needed to manufacture the framework has been lost.

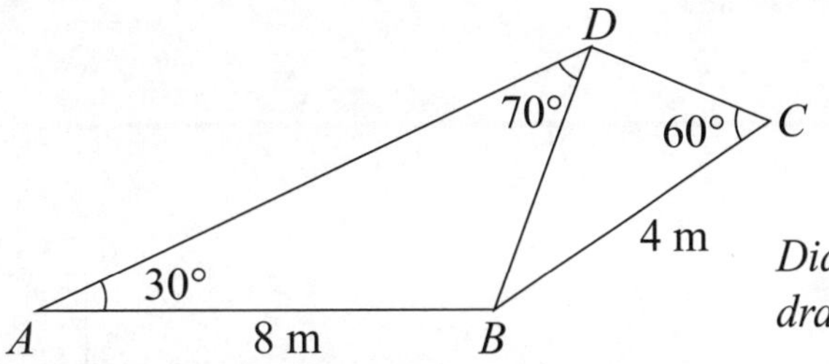

Diagram not drawn accurately

Complete the specification for the framework by calculating:

a) the length of BD.
Give your answer to 3 significant figures.

$\frac{BD}{\sin \dots\dots} = \frac{\dots\dots}{\sin \dots\dots}$

$BD = \frac{\dots\dots}{\sin \dots\dots} \times \sin \dots\dots$

$BD = \dots\dots\dots\dots$ m

.... m

[3]

b) the size of angle BDC.
Give your answer to 3 significant figures.

..........................°

[3]

[Total 6 marks]

3 In the triangle opposite, $AB = 12$ cm, $BC = 19$ cm and $AC = 14$ cm.

Calculate the area of the triangle.

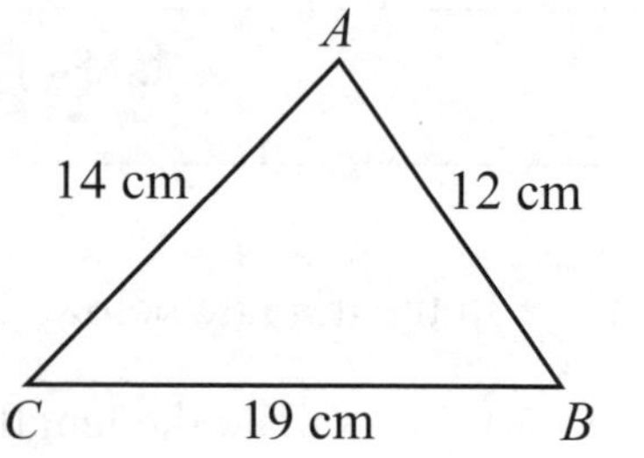

Diagram not drawn accurately

.... cm^2

[Total 4 marks]

4 A castle drawbridge is supported by two chains, *AB* and *AC*. Using the information on the diagram, calculate the total length of the drawbridge, *BD*, correct to 3 s.f.

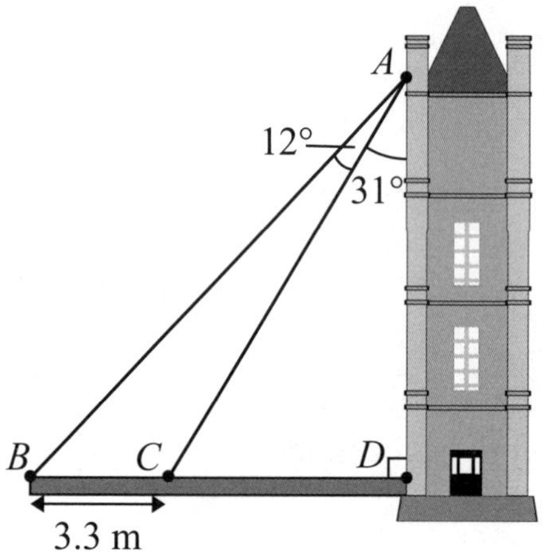

.... m

[Total 5 marks]

5 *ABCD* is a trapezium.

BC is parallel to *AD*.
$BC = x$ cm, $AD = 3x$ cm and angle $BAC = 30°$.

The perimeter of triangle *ACD* is $(a + \sqrt{b})x$ cm.
Find the values of *a* and *b*.

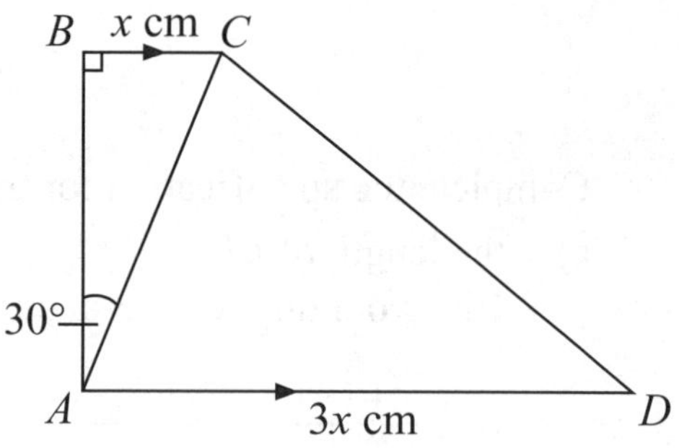

Diagram not drawn accurately

$a =$ .... , $b =$ ....

[Total 5 marks]

Score: $\frac{\quad}{24}$

3D Pythagoras and Trigonometry

M8

1 The diagram on the right is a cuboid *ABCDEFGH.*

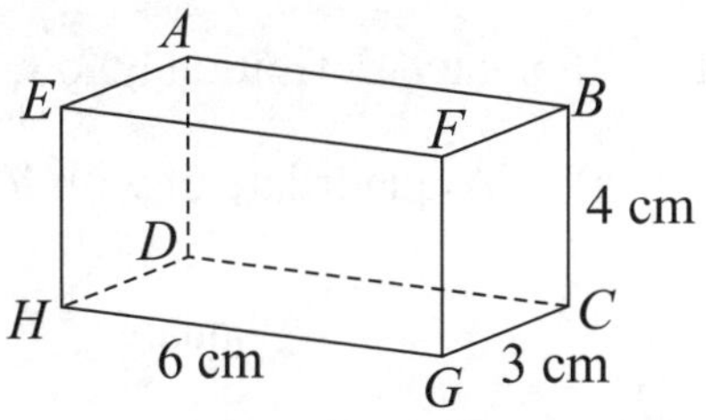

Diagram not drawn accurately

The cuboid has sides of length 6 cm, 4 cm and 3 cm.
Calculate the length of the diagonal *BH*.
Give your answer to 3 significant figures.

BH^2 = ...^{2} + ...^{2} + ...^{2}

$BH = \sqrt{\ldots\ldots\ldots\ldots}$

BH = ...

.... cm
[Total 3 marks]

2 The diagram below is a cuboid *ABCDEFGH.* It represents an empty box with a volume of 80 cm³ and 2 edges measuring 2 cm and 8 cm.

Find the size of the angle between the diagonal *DF* and the plane *CDHG*.
Give your answer to 2 significant figures.

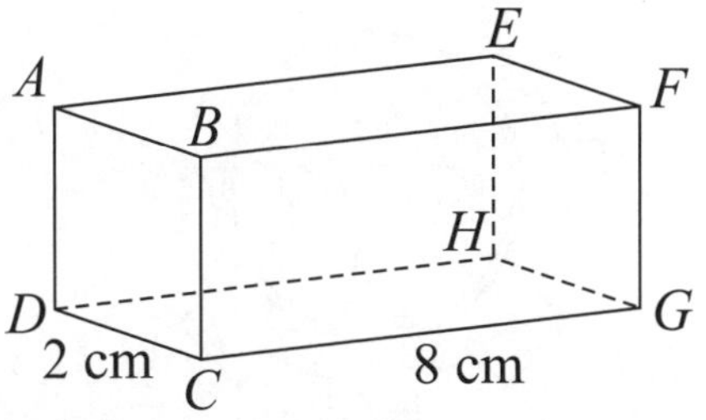

Diagram not drawn accurately

...........................°
[Total 5 marks]

3 The diagram shows a pyramid with a rectangular base. The vertex, *V*, of the pyramid is directly above the centre of the base *ABCD*.

VC = 8.9 cm, *VX* = 7.2 cm and *BC* = 4.2 cm.
Work out the length *AB*. Give your answer to 3 significant figures.

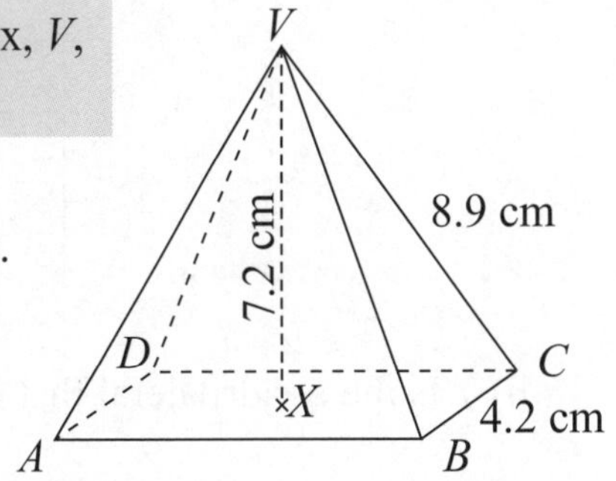

Diagram not drawn accurately

.... cm
[Total 4 marks]

Score: ☐ / **12**

M3 Properties of 2D Shapes

1 For each definition below, circle the shape from the list that it is describing.

a) 'A quadrilateral with four equal sides and rotational symmetry of order two.'

square rhombus trapezium rectangle

[1]

b) 'A triangle with one line of symmetry.'

equilateral triangle scalene triangle prism isosceles triangle

[1]

[Total 2 marks]

2 Below is an image of a cog.

a) Draw all the lines of symmetry for the cog.

[2]

b) What order of rotational symmetry does the cog have?

....

[1]

[Total 3 marks]

3 Meera's teacher asks her to draw a quadrilateral with the following properties:

- no lines of symmetry
- two pairs of equal angles
- two pairs of equal sides.

Meera says, "There is no quadrilateral which has all these properties."

a) Draw a shape on the grid to show that Meera is wrong.

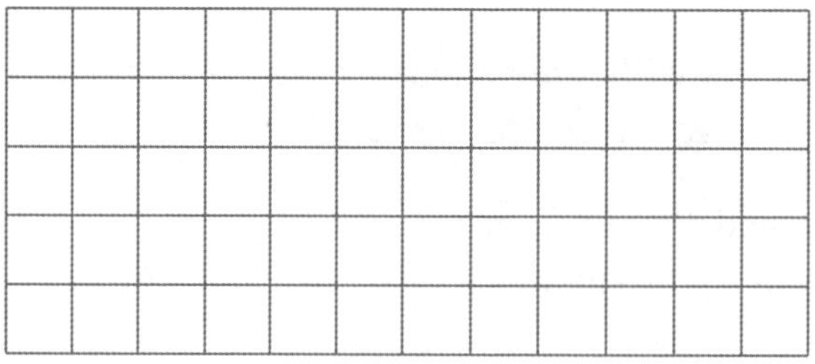

[2]

b) Is the quadrilateral that Meera was asked to draw a regular polygon? Explain your answer.

....

....

[1]

[Total 3 marks]

Score: ___ / 8

Similar Shapes

M7

1 The shapes *ABCD* and *EFGH* are mathematically similar.

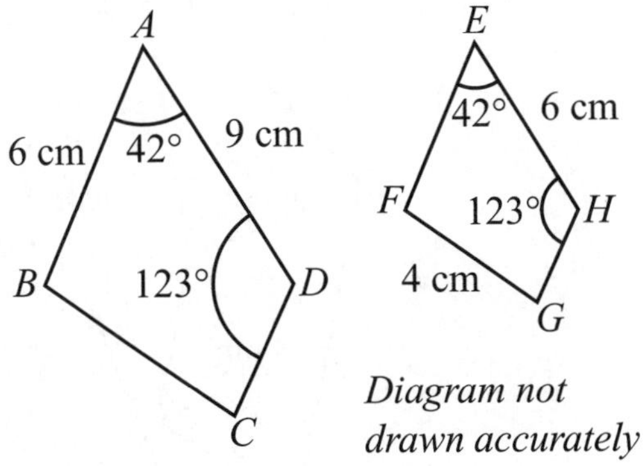

Diagram not drawn accurately

Find the lengths of *EF* and *BC*.

EF = ... cm

BC = ... cm

[Total 3 marks]

2 Cian wants to estimate the height of a flagpole in his local park. He finds that if he stands a horizontal distance of 63 m away from the flagpole and holds his index finger up in front of him it exactly covers the flagpole.

Cian's finger is 8 cm long and he holds it at a horizontal distance of 60 cm away from his body. Use this information to find an estimate for the height of the flagpole.

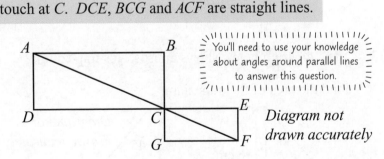

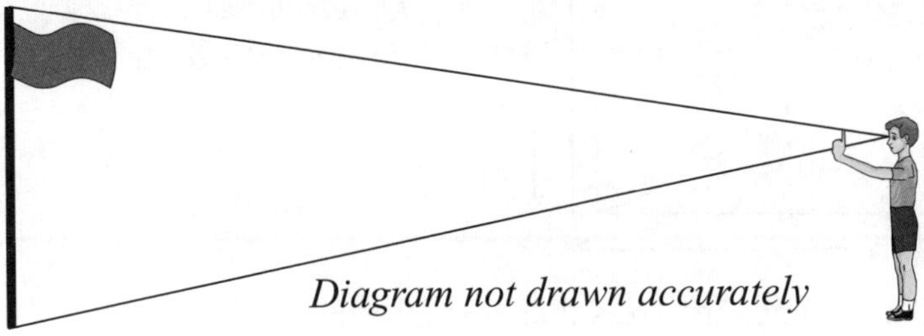

Diagram not drawn accurately

.... m

[Total 3 marks]

3 *ABCD* and *CEFG* are rectangles that touch at *C*. *DCE*, *BCG* and *ACF* are straight lines.

Explain how you can tell that triangles *ABC* and *CEF* are similar.

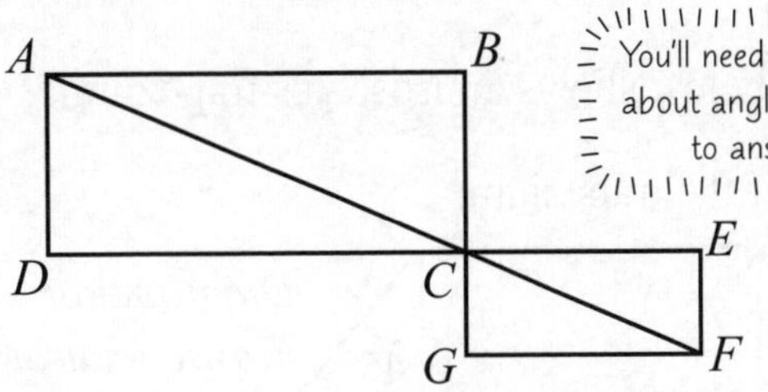

You'll need to use your knowledge about angles around parallel lines to answer this question.

Diagram not drawn accurately

[Total 3 marks]

Score: ☐ / 9

M3 Perimeter and Area

1 Find the total area of shape S, made up from a kite and a rhombus.

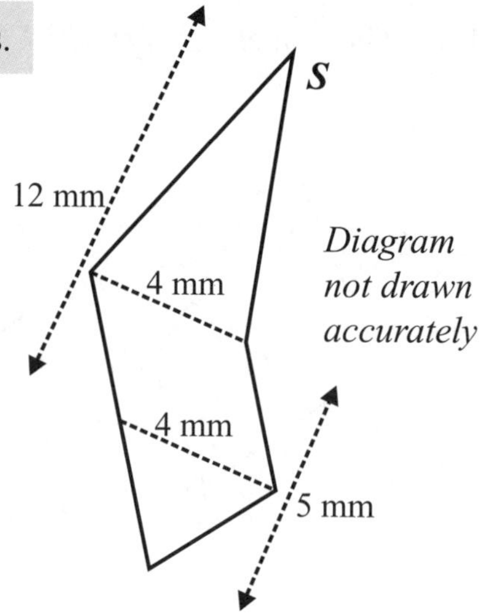

.... mm^2

[Total 5 marks]

2 Lynn is designing a garden. The diagram shows her design. Lynn's garden will be rectangular, with a semicircular flowerbed at one end, and a matching semicircular patio at the other end. The rest of the space will be taken up by a lawn.

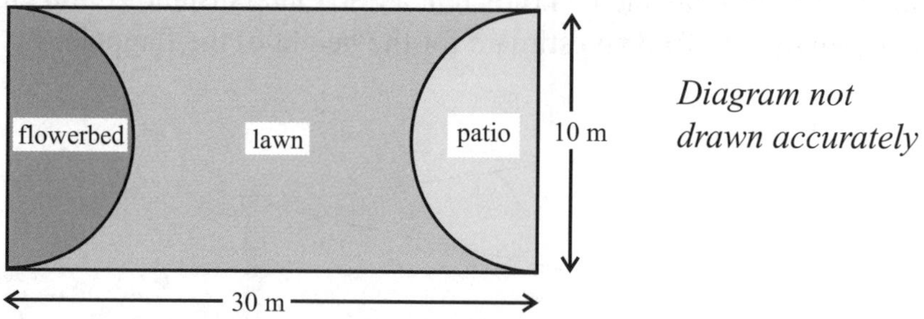

The grass seed that Lynn is planning to use comes in boxes that cost £7 each. Each box will cover 10 m^2. How much will it cost Lynn to plant the lawn?

£ ....

[Total 5 marks]

3 The diagram below shows an isosceles trapezium.

Find the area of the trapezium.

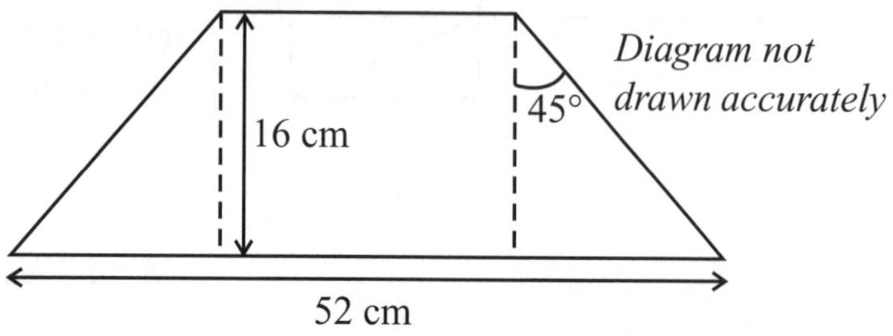

.... cm^2

[Total 3 marks]

4 Consider a square and a triangle. The sides of the square are x cm long. The base length and height of the triangle are equal, and are twice as long as the sides of the square. The area of the triangle is 9 cm² larger than the area of the square.

Find the perimeter of the square.

.... cm

[Total 5 marks]

5 Look at the sector shown in the diagram below.

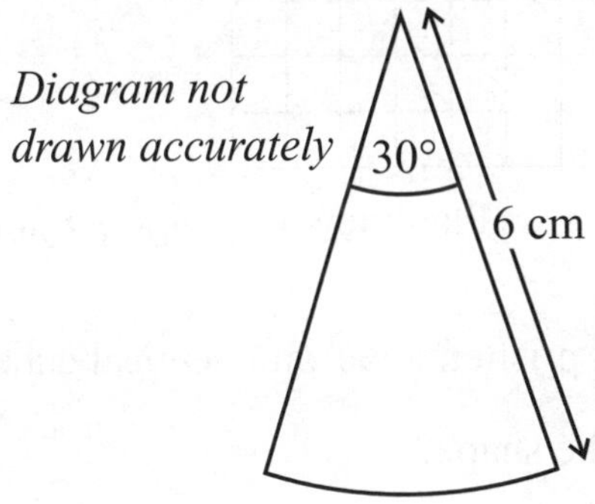

Find the perimeter and the area of the sector.
Give your answers to 3 significant figures.

Perimeter = ... cm

Area = ... cm²

[Total 5 marks]

6 An industrial rolling machine is made up of three identical cylinders of radius 9 cm. The ends of the rollers are surrounded by a strip of metal, as illustrated in the diagram below.

Find the length of the metal strip, giving your answer correct to 1 d.p.

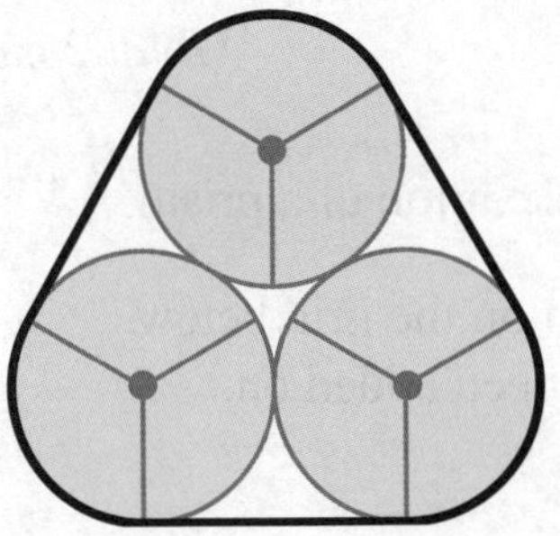

If you're struggling with the straight bits, try looking at the horizontal part first.

.... cm

[Total 4 marks]

Exam Practice Tip

Don't mix up radius and diameter. I know that sounds a bit obvious, but it's something that lots of people do in exams. The radius of a circle is half of its diameter. Think carefully about which one you're being given, and which one you need for a formula.

Score

27

M3 Plans and Elevations

1 The diagram below shows a solid made from identical cubes.
The side elevation of the solid is drawn on the adjacent grid.

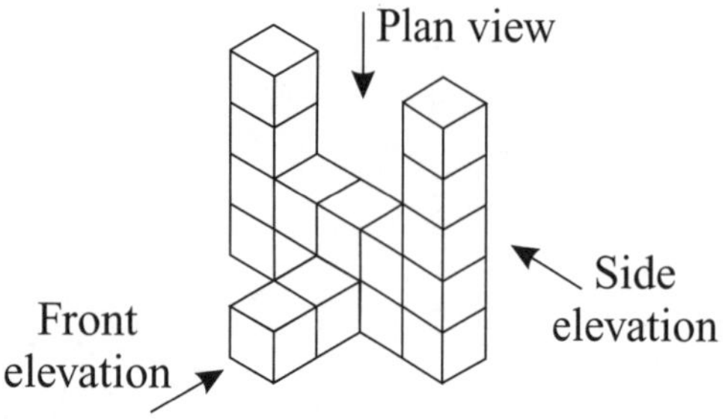

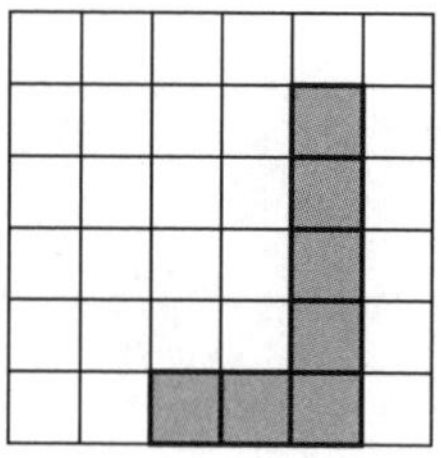

Side elevation

On the grids opposite, draw the front elevation and plan view of the solid.

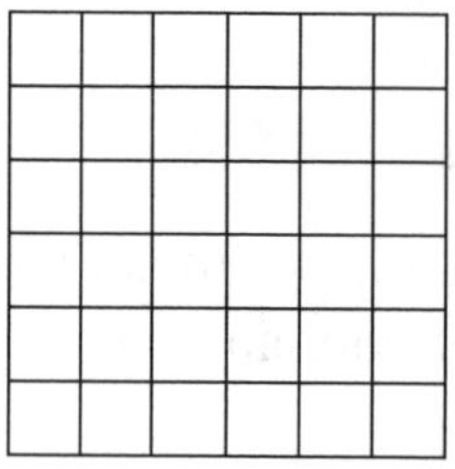

Front elevation

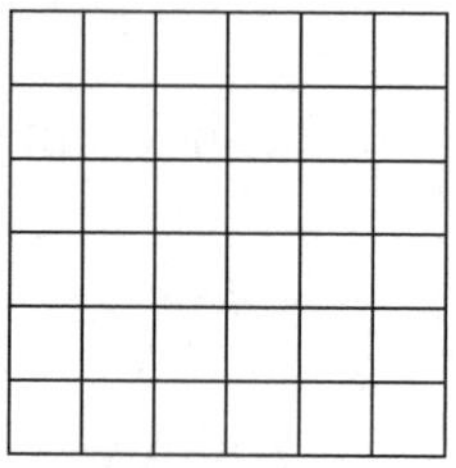

Plan view

[Total 3 marks]

2 Shown below are the plan and the front and side elevations of a prism made from identical cubes.

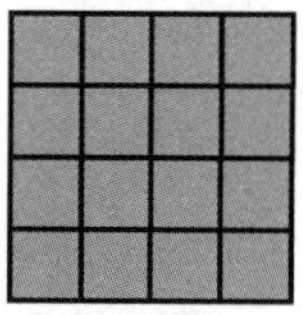

Plan view

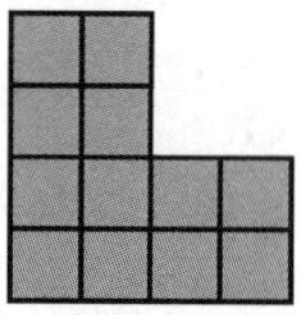

Front elevation

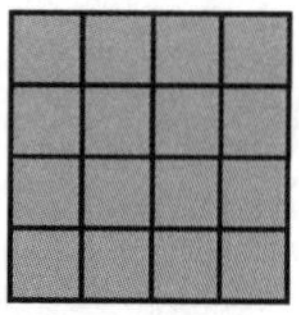

Side elevation

How many cubes make up the shape?
Show your working.

....

[Total 2 marks]

3 The diagram below shows the plan, the front elevation and the side elevation of a prism.

Plan view

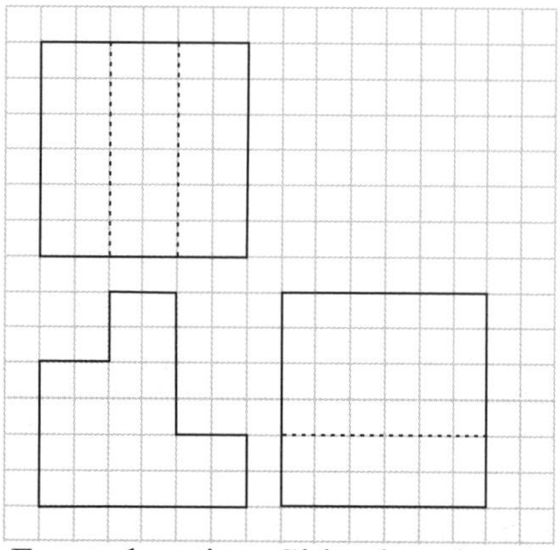

Front elevation Side elevation

Draw a sketch of the solid prism on the grid below.
The front elevation has already been added on.

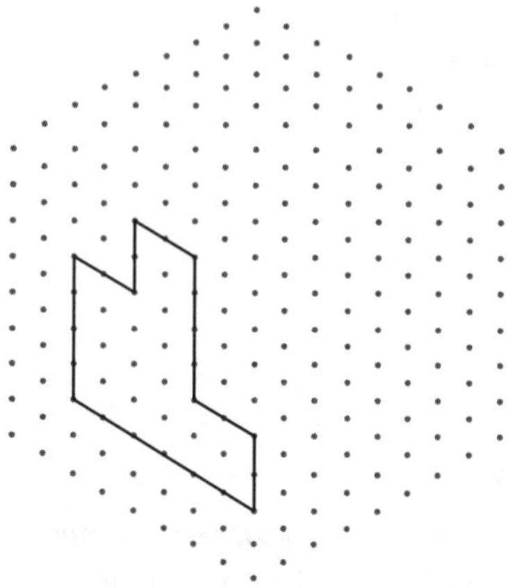

[Total 2 marks]

Score: $\frac{\quad}{7}$

3D Shapes — Surface Area & Volume (1)

M3

1 The diagram on the right shows Amy's new paddling pool. It has a diameter of 2 metres, and is 40 cm high.

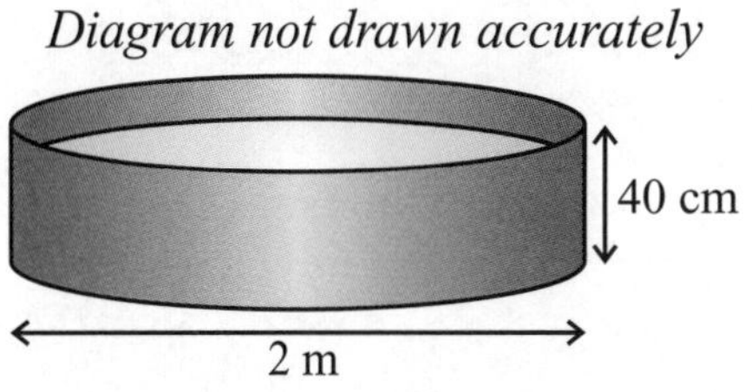

The instructions that came with the pool say that it should only be filled three-quarters full. What is the maximum volume of water that Amy can put in the pool?

.... m^3

[Total 4 marks]

2 The cross-section of a prism is a regular hexagon.

Each side of the hexagon has a length of 8 cm.
The distance from the centre of the hexagon to the midpoint of each side is 7 cm.
Calculate the volume of the prism.

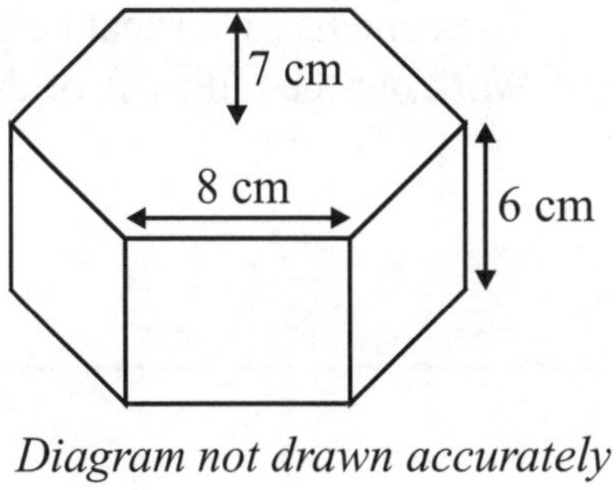

.... cm^3

[Total 3 marks]

3 The volume of the cone shown on the right is 113 cm^3 correct to 3 significant figures.

Calculate the radius of the base of the cone.

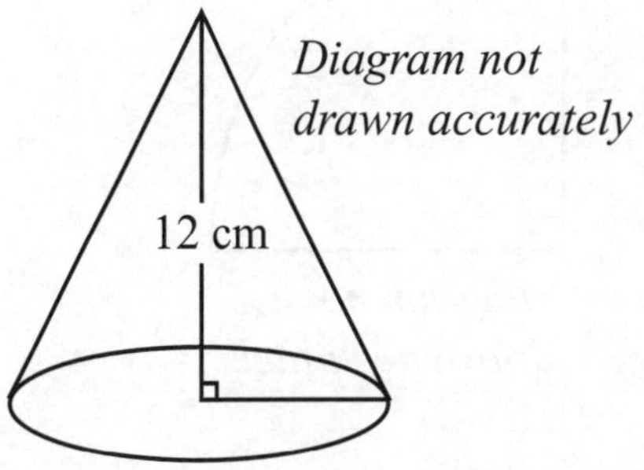

.... cm

[Total 2 marks]

4 A spherical ball has volume 478 cm^3.

Find the surface area of the ball, giving your answer correct to 1 d.p.

.... cm^2

[Total 4 marks]

5 The cone and sphere in the diagram below have the same volume.

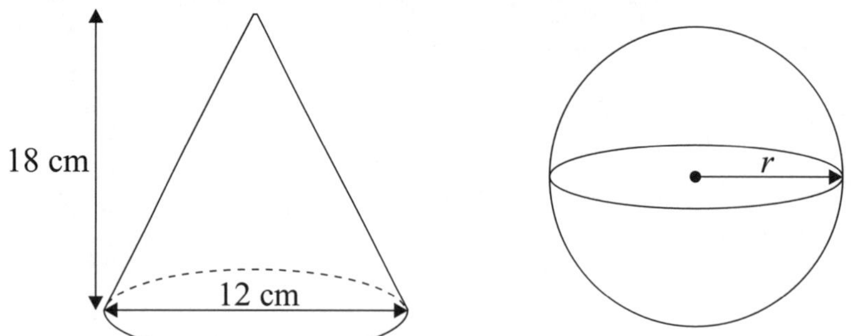

The cone has a vertical height of 18 cm and a base diameter of 12 cm.
Work out the radius, r, of the sphere. Give your answer to 3 significant figures.

.... cm

[Total 4 marks]

6 The curved surface of a cone is made from the net below, which has an area of 64 cm^2.

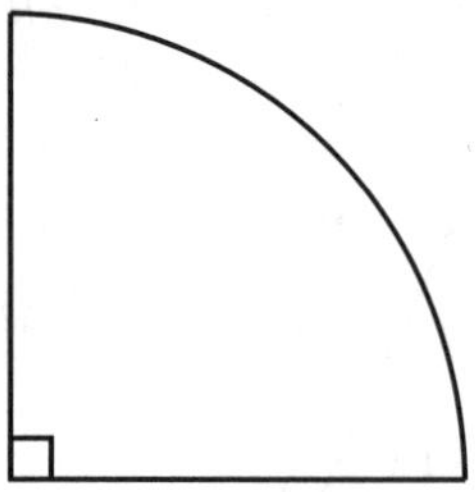

Diagram not drawn accurately

The cone has a circular base.
Find the radius of the circular base.

.... cm

[Total 5 marks]

Score: ____ / **22**

3D Shapes — Surface Area & Volume (2)

M4

1 The diagram below shows a fish tank containing a solid frustum-shaped ornament. Before the top of the cone was removed to form the frustum, the original cone reached the top of the tank.

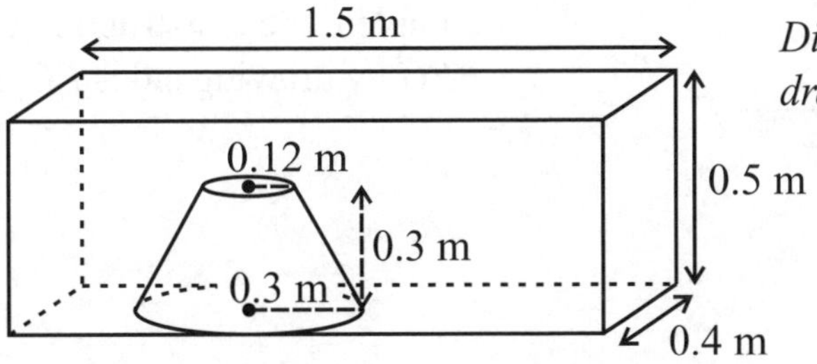

Diagram not drawn accurately

The tank is a cuboid, and the ornament is fixed in place.
What is the maximum volume of water that the tank can hold?
Give your answer in litres to 3 significant figures.

.... litres
[Total 6 marks]

2 A solid cone has radius 15 cm and height 36 cm. The top of the cone is removed to create a frustum two-thirds of the height of the original cone, shown in the diagram below.

Diagram not drawn accurately

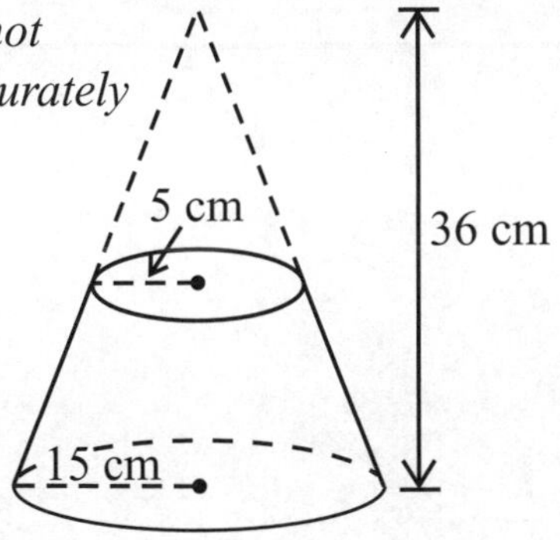

a) Find the volume of the frustum.
Give your answer to 2 decimal places.

.... cm^3
[3]

b) The slant height of the frustum is 26 cm, and the slant height of the original cone was 39 cm.
Find the surface area of the frustum. Give your answer to 2 decimal places.

.... cm^2
[4]

[Total 7 marks]

Score: ____ / 13

Loci and Construction

M7

1 *EFG* is an isosceles triangle. Sides *EG* and *FG* are both 4.5 cm long.

Side *EF* has been drawn here.

a) Showing all your construction lines, complete the construction of triangle *EFG* by drawing sides *EG* and *FG*.

[2]

b) Construct a perpendicular from point *G* to the line *EF*. Show all your construction lines.

[2]

[Total 4 marks]

2 Construct triangle *PQR* in the space below using the following information:

Side *PQ* = 7 cm. Side *QR* = 4 cm. Angle *PQR* = 65°.

[Total 3 marks]

3 A dog is tied to a beam *AB* by a lead which allows it to run a maximum of 2 m from the beam.

Shade the region on the diagram where the dog may run, using the scale shown.

Scale: 1 cm represents 1 m

[Total 2 marks]

4 ABC is a triangle.

Find and shade the region inside the triangle which is both closer to the line *AB* than the line *BC*, and also more than 6.5 cm from the point *C*.

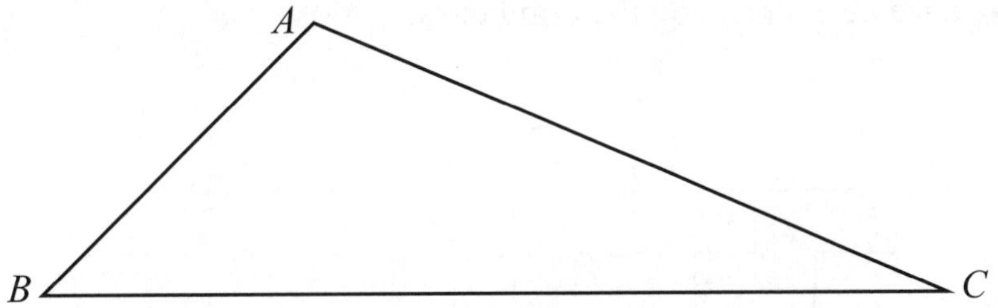

[Total 4 marks]

5 Hilary and Tony are deciding where they would like to put a pond in their garden.
Hilary wants the centre of the pond to be exactly 1 m from the garden wall *BC*.
Tony wants the centre of the pond to be exactly 2 m from the tree *F*.

Accurately complete the plan of the garden below by placing crosses in the positions that Hilary and Tony would both be happy for the centre of the pond to be.

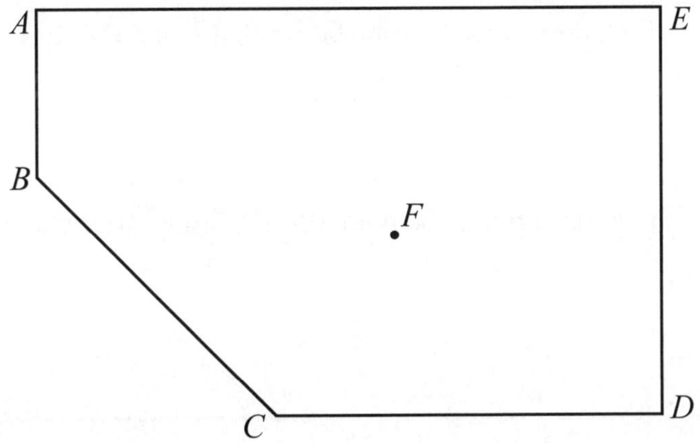

Scale: 1 cm represents 1 m

[Total 4 marks]

6 A town council are putting up a new visitor information board.
They want it to be placed within the area shown, closer to the park than to the library, but also closer to the station than to the park.

The diagram on the right shows a scale map of the town centre.

a) Shade in the region of the town where the board could be placed.

[5]

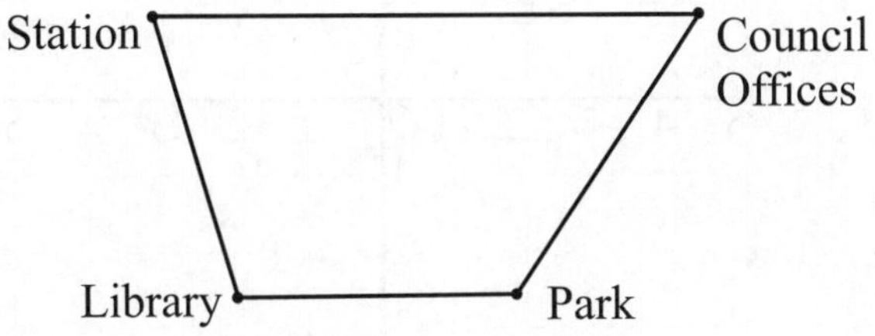

The council decides to place the board at the position closest to their offices.

b) Mark where they place the board with a cross on the diagram.

[1]

[Total 6 marks]

Exam Practice Tip

Even if you're not told that you need to use a ruler and compasses, you'll be expected to use them when you're asked to construct something. Make sure you don't rub out your construction lines — even if it doesn't ask for them in the question you might not get all the marks unless you show how you did your construction.

Score

23

M7 Translation, Rotation and Reflection

1 Shapes **F** and **G** have been drawn on the grid below.

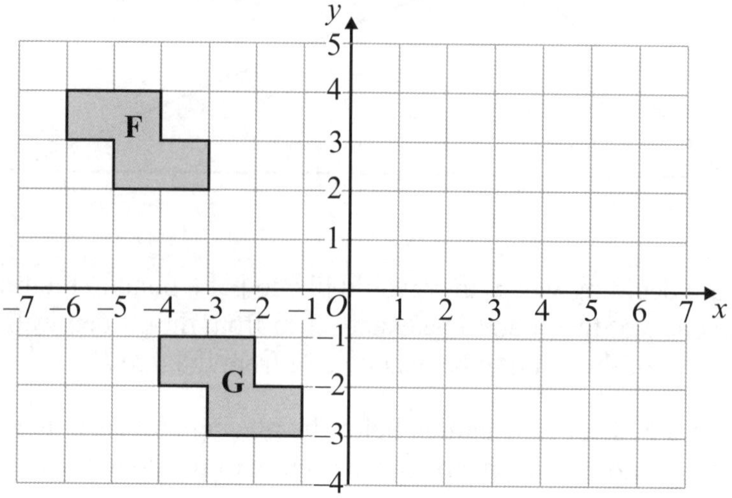

a) Write down the vector which describes the translation that maps **F** onto **G**.

....

[2]

b) Rotate shape **F** by 90° clockwise around the point (0, –2). Label your image **H**.

[2]

[Total 4 marks]

2 In the diagram below, **B** is an image of **A**.

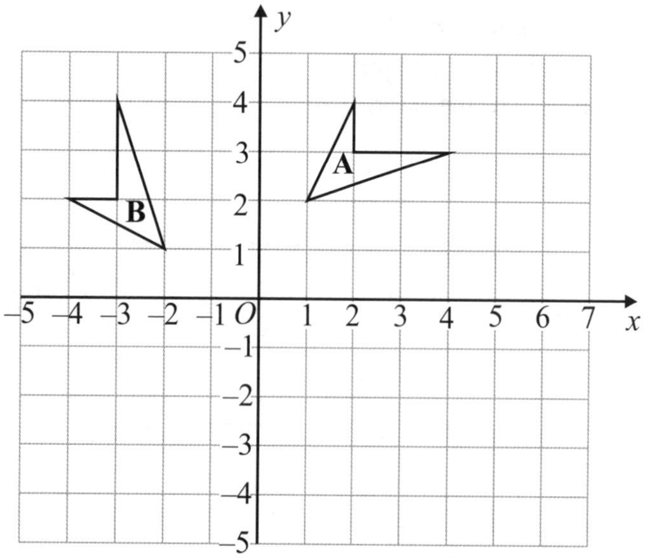

a) Describe fully the single transformation that maps **A** onto **B**.

....

....

....

....

[3]

b) Translate shape **B** by the vector $\begin{pmatrix}-1\\-3\end{pmatrix}$ and then reflect the new shape in the line $y = x$.
Label the image as **C**.

[4]

[Total 7 marks]

Score: ☐ / **11**

Enlargement (1)

M7

1 Triangle **A** has been drawn on the grid below.

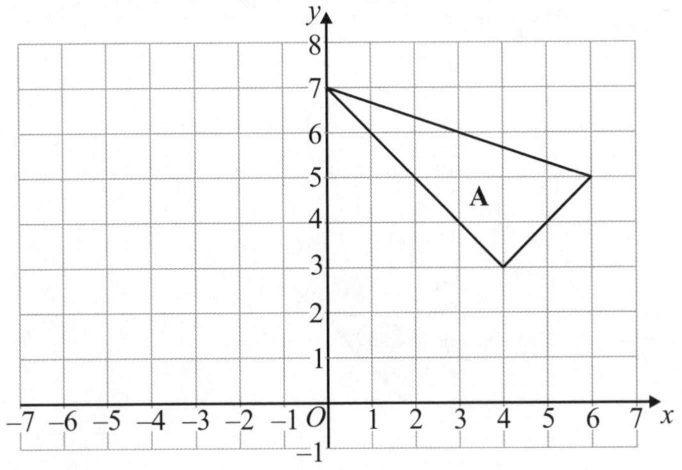

Enlarge triangle **A** by scale factor $\frac{1}{2}$ with centre of enlargement (–6, 1). Label your image **B**.

[Total 3 marks]

2 Triangle **R** has been drawn on the grid below.

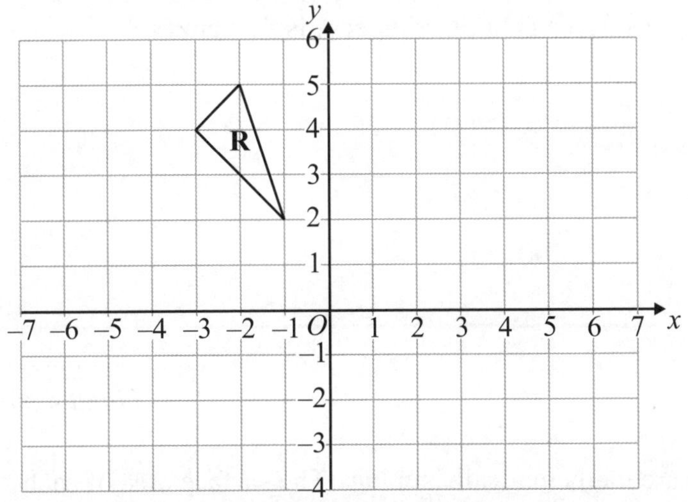

Reflect triangle **R** in the line $y = x$ and then enlarge it with centre (6, –3) and scale factor 3. Label the resulting shape **S**.

[Total 4 marks]

3 The radius of a tennis ball and the radius of a basketball are in the ratio 1 : 7.

Assuming both balls are spheres, work out the ratio of the volume of a tennis ball to the volume of a basketball.

....

[Total 1 mark]

4 A parallelogram has an area of 7 cm².

The parallelogram is enlarged with scale factor 3. Work out the area of the enlarged parallelogram.

.... cm^2

[Total 2 marks]

Score: ___ / **10**

M8

Enlargement (2)

1 A triangle has been drawn on the grid below.

Enlarge the triangle by a scale factor of –2 about the point **C**.

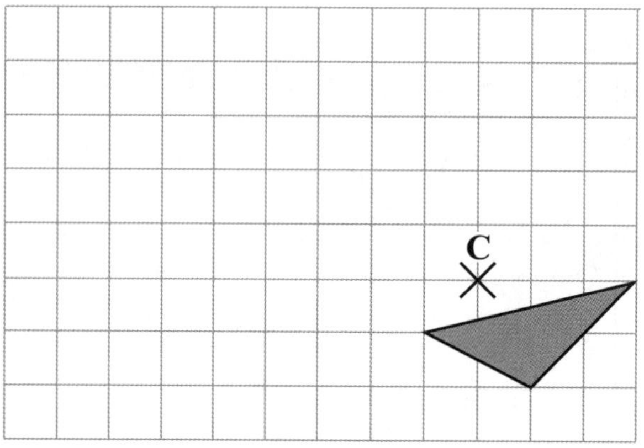

[Total 3 marks]

2 Cylinder B is an enlargement of cylinder A. The ratio of the volume of cylinder A to the volume of cylinder B is 27 : 64. The surface area of cylinder A is 81π cm².

Find the surface area of cylinder B.

.... cm²

[Total 4 marks]

3 **A**, **B** and **C** are three solid cones which are mathematically similar. The surface area of each cone is given below. The perpendicular height of **A** is 4 cm. The volume of **C** is 135π cm³.

Not to scale

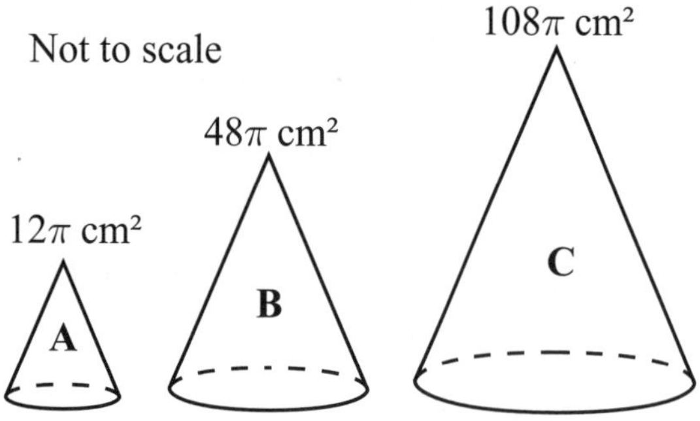

a) Calculate the volume of **A**.

.... cm³

[4]

b) Calculate the perpendicular height of **B**.

.... cm

[3]

[Total 7 marks]

Score: ☐ / **14**

Sampling and Data Collection (1)

M3

1 Leah is doing a questionnaire at her school to find out how many after-school activities other pupils participate in.

a) Design a question for Leah to include in her questionnaire. You should include suitable response boxes.

[2]

Leah asks pupils at an after school drama club to complete her questionnaire.

b) Write down **one** reason why this might not be a suitable sample.

....

[1]

[Total 3 marks]

2 Mario asked 50 people at a football match how they travelled there. He found that 22 of them travelled by car. There were 5000 people at the match altogether.

a) Use the information above to estimate the number of people who travelled to the match by car.

....

[3]

b) Suggest how Mario could get a more reliable estimate of the number of people who travelled to the match by car.

....

....

[1]

c) Daisy was at a different football match on the same day. She uses Mario's sample data to estimate that 374 of the 850 people at her match travelled there by car.
Explain the assumption Daisy has made and comment on the reliability of her estimate.

....

....

....

[2]

[Total 6 marks]

Exam Practice Tip

If you're asked about questionnaires in the exam, think about how the question is worded and how suitable the response boxes are. The question should be clear and mustn't lead someone to give a certain answer, and the boxes should cover all possibilities without overlapping. Think about whether the sample is unbiased, too.

Score

9

M4 Sampling and Data Collection (2)

1 The table below shows information on the ages of 800 teenagers.

Age (years)	13	14	15	16
Number of teenagers	248	192	176	184

Marissa wants to survey a sample of these teenagers, stratified by age.

a) Briefly describe a method she could use to take a sample of 100 of these teenagers, stratified by age.

....

....

[2]

b) Work out how many teenagers aged 14 should be in the sample.

Teenagers aged 14 = (total aged 14 ÷ total teenagers) × size of sample

= (.................. ÷ ....) × ....

= ....

....

[2]

[Total 4 marks]

2 The table below shows the number of students in two different schools.

School	Male	Female	Total
Appleborough School	435	487	922
Warringpool High	568	543	1111
Total	1003	1030	2033

Cheng takes a sample of 150 students, stratified by school and gender.
Work out how many female students from Appleborough School are in the sample.

You should answer with a whole number.

....

[Total 2 marks]

3 Dougie is investigating the heights of pupils in his school. He takes a sample of 75 pupils, stratified by year. The table below shows the number of pupils in each year.

Year	8	9	10	11	12
Number of pupils	167	162	150	125	116

Work out how many pupils from Year 12 are in the sample.

....

[Total 3 marks]

Score: /9

Venn Diagrams

M3

1 The Venn diagram below shows the percentages of female contestants (F) and singers (S) in a talent competition.

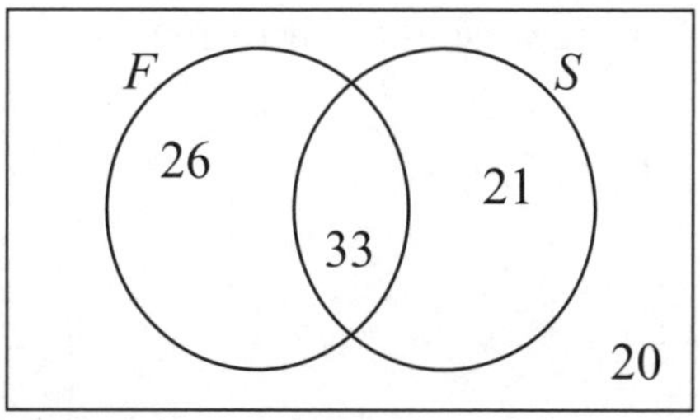

What fraction of the contestants are neither female nor singers?
Give your answer in its simplest form.

....
[Total 2 marks]

2 A cheese stall sells three different cheeses: Cheddar, Wensleydale and Stilton.
One afternoon the stall had 100 customers. Each customer bought at least one cheese.

28 customers bought Wensleydale. Of these, 12 customers also bought Stilton.
43 customers bought Cheddar. Of these, 10 also bought Wensleydale and 7 also bought Stilton.
5 customers bought all three cheeses.

a) Draw a Venn diagram to show this information.

[3]

b) How many customers bought Cheddar or Stilton?

....
[1]

c) Of those who bought Stilton, what fraction also bought Cheddar, but not Wensleydale?

....
[2]

[Total 6 marks]

Score: ___ / **8**

M3

Pie Charts

1 A survey was carried out in a local cinema to find out which flavour of popcorn people bought. The results are in the table below.

a) Draw and label a pie chart to represent the information.

Type of popcorn	Number sold
Plain	12
Salted	18
Sugared	9
Toffee	21

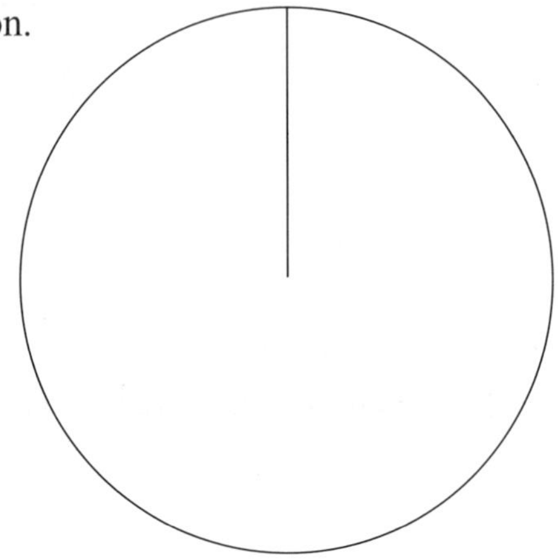

[4]

Another survey was carried out to find out which flavour of ice cream people bought. The results are shown in the pie chart below.

Chris compares the two pie charts and says,

"The results show that more people chose strawberry ice cream than toffee popcorn."

b) Explain whether or not Chris is right.

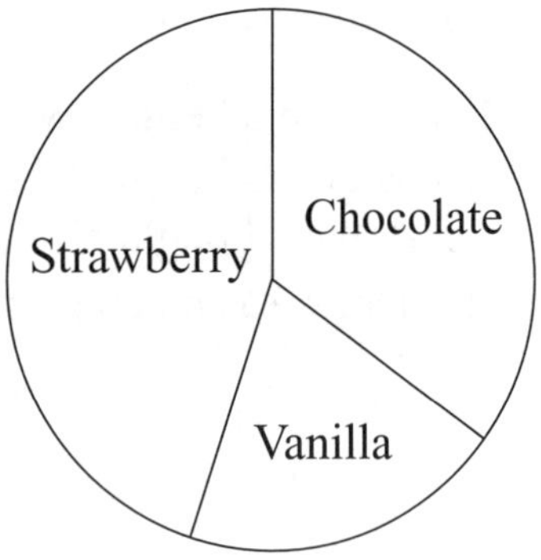

....

....

....

....

[1]

[Total 5 marks]

2 There are 80 students in Year 11. The pie chart below shows their favourite types of soup.

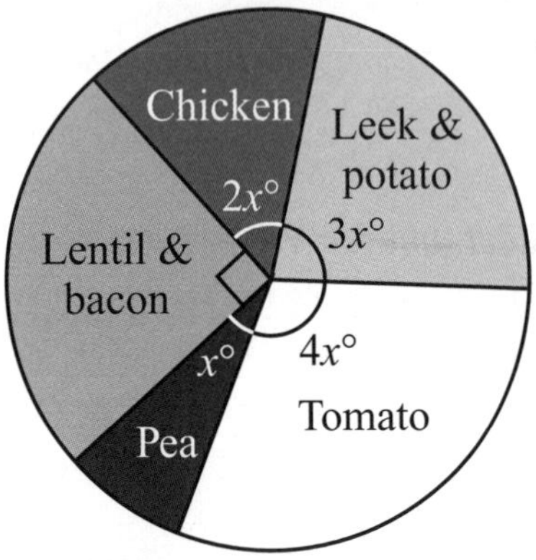

How many students chose leek & potato soup?

....

[Total 4 marks]

Score: ___ / **9**

Other Graphs and Charts

M3

1 The numbers of swallows seen in Eli's garden over three years are shown in the time series graph below.

Describe the overall trend in the numbers of swallows seen in Eli's garden over the 3-year period.

....

....

....

....

[Total 1 mark]

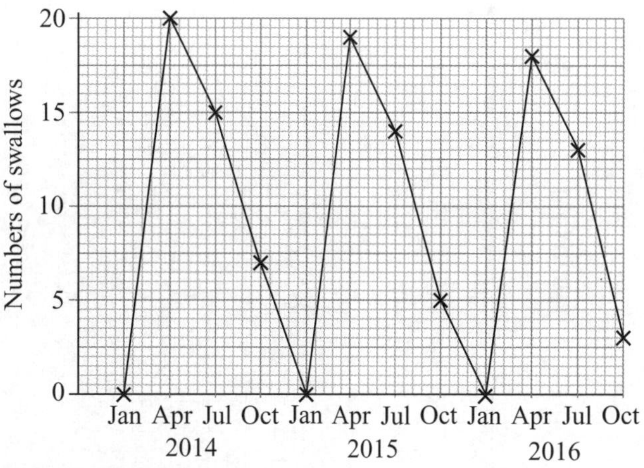

2 200 people were asked if they were right-handed or left-handed. The table below shows some information about the results.

	Left-handed	Right-handed	Total
Male	9	51	
Female		126	
Total	23		200

What fraction of females were left-handed? Give your answer in its simplest form.

....

[Total 4 marks]

3 The flow chart below shows how to convert miles to kilometres.

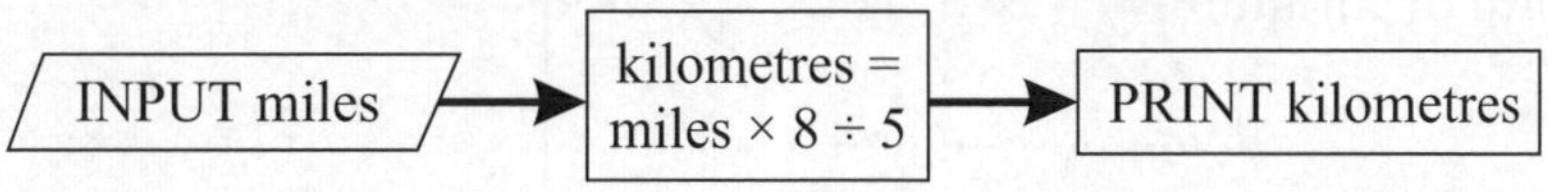

a) The flow chart does not have enough boxes. Identify the boxes that are missing.

....

[1]

b) Draw a flow chart below with this problem corrected.

[2]

[Total 3 marks]

Score: ___ / **8**

M3 Scatter Graphs

1 15 pupils in a class study both Spanish and Italian.
Their end of year exam results are shown on the scatter graph below.

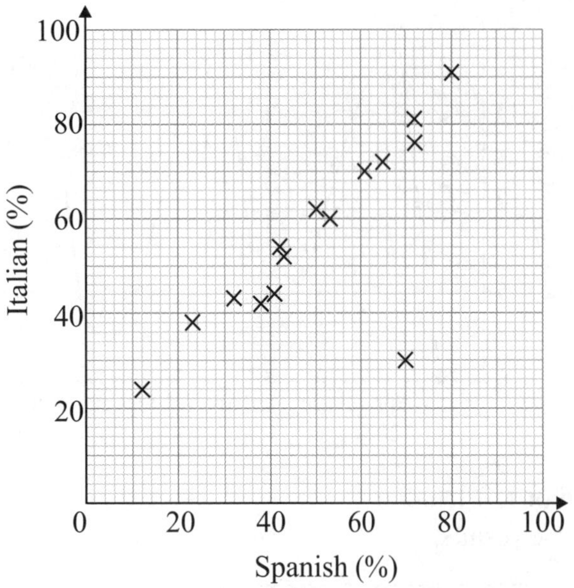

a) Circle the point that doesn't follow the trend. *[1]*

b) Describe the strength and type of correlation shown by the points that do follow the trend.

....

.... *[1]*

c) Draw a line of best fit for the data. *[1]*

[Total 3 marks]

2 A furniture company is comparing how much it spent on advertising in random months with the total sales value for that month. This information is shown on the graph below.

The table shows the data for three more months.

Amount spent on advertising (thousands of pounds)	0.75	0.15	1.85
Sales (thousands of pounds)	105	60	170

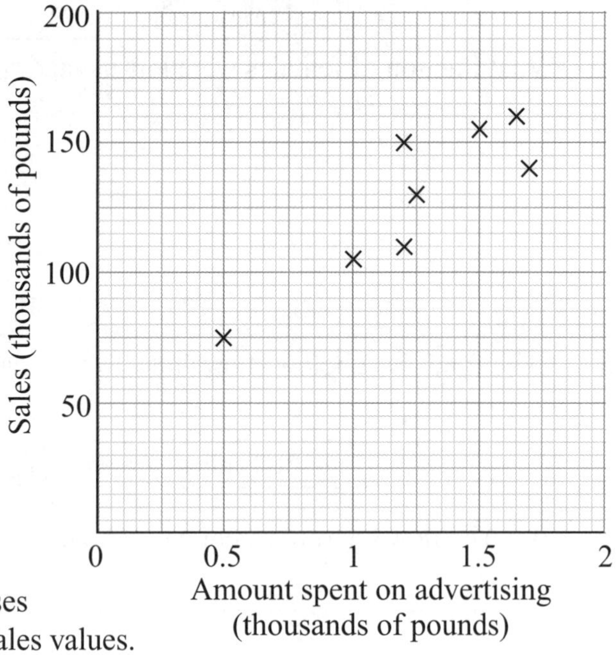

a) Plot this information on the scatter graph. *[1]*

b) Use your graph to estimate how much the company would be likely to have spent on advertising in a month where it sold £125 000 worth of furniture.

£ .... *[2]*

c) The company plans to increase its monthly spend on advertising to £3000. It uses the trend in the data above to predict future sales values. Comment on how reliable this prediction is likely to be.

....

.... *[2]*

[Total 5 marks]

Score: / **8**

Mean, Mode, Median and Range

M3

1 A bakery records the number of cookies it sells each day for ten days. The mean number is 17 and the median number is 15.

The next day the bakery sells 18 cookies.

a) Is the mean number sold over all eleven days higher than 17? Explain your answer.

....

[1]

b) Is the median number sold over all eleven days higher than 15? Explain your answer.

....

[1]

[Total 2 marks]

2 Conor has 6 pygmy goats. Their weights, in kg, are listed below.

32 23 31 28 36 26

a) Which three weights, from the list above, would have a range which is half the value of the median of the three weights? Write down the range and median with your answer.

.................., ..., ...

range = ..., median = ...

[2]

b) Two of the goats wander off and don't return. The mean weight of the herd is now 27.25 kg. Find the weights of the two goats who wandered off.

.... kg and .... kg

[3]

[Total 5 marks]

3 Show that the difference between the mean and the median of five consecutive integers is always zero.

Call the five consecutive integers n, n + 1, ..., ... and ....

Median = middle value = ...

$$\text{Mean} = \frac{n + (n + 1) + \ldots\ldots + \ldots\ldots + \ldots\ldots}{\ldots\ldots} = \frac{\ldots\ldots}{\ldots\ldots} = \ldots\ldots$$

Difference between mean and median = ...

[Total 3 marks]

Exam Practice Tip

Questions on the mean aren't usually as straightforward as calculating its value from a list of numbers. No, I'm afraid that won't cut the mustard. You have to figure out how to use the information you're given — e.g. if you know the mean and the number of values, you can easily find the total of all the values.

Score

10

M3 Frequency Tables — Finding Averages

1 The table shows the number of pets owned by each pupil in class 7F.

Number of pets	Frequency
0	8
1	3
2	5
3	8
4	4
5	1

a) How many pupils are there in class 7F?

....
[2]

b) Find the total number of pets owned by pupils in class 7F.

....
[2]

c) Work out the mean number of pets per pupil in class 7F.

....
[2]

[Total 6 marks]

2 For her GCSE homework, Vanessa collected information about the number of text messages pupils in her school sent one day. She recorded her results in the frequency table below.

Number of messages	Frequency
0	2
1	0
2	4
3	7
4	0
5	11
6	0
7	6
8	3
9	0
10	3

a) How many text messages were sent in total?

....
[2]

b) Use the table to calculate:

i) the mean number of text messages sent.

....
[2]

ii) the modal number of text messages sent.

....
[1]

iii) the median number of text messages sent.

....
[2]

[Total 7 marks]

Score: ☐ / **13**

Grouped Frequency Tables

M3

1 During a science experiment 10 seeds were planted and their growth measured to the nearest cm after 12 days. The results were recorded in the table below.

Growth in cm	Number of plants
$0 \leq x \leq 2$	2
$3 \leq x \leq 5$	4
$6 \leq x \leq 8$	3
$9 \leq x \leq 11$	1

Use the table to find:

a) the modal class,

....

[1]

b) the class which contains the median,

....

[1]

c) an estimate of the mean growth.

You can add columns to the table to help you.

.... cm

[4]

[Total 6 marks]

2 The table shows the times it took 32 pupils at a school to run a 200 m sprint.

Time (t seconds)	Frequency
$22 < t \leq 26$	4
$26 < t \leq 30$	8
$30 < t \leq 34$	13
$34 < t \leq 38$	6
$38 < t \leq 42$	1

a) Calculate an estimate for the mean time.

.... seconds

[4]

b) What percentage of pupils got a time of more than 30 seconds?

..........................%

[2]

c) Explain whether you could use the results in the table above to draw conclusions about how long it takes 16-year-old boys at the school to run 200 m.

....

[1]

[Total 7 marks]

Score: $\frac{}{13}$

M3 Averages and Spread

1 Liz sells earrings. The prices in pounds of 15 pairs of earrings are given below.

3 4 8 10 11 5 7 4 12 8 9 5 20 15 5

a) Draw an ordered stem and leaf diagram to show this information. You must include a key.

[3]

b) Liz reduces all her prices by 50p. Will the interquartile range of the new prices be less than, greater than or the same as the interquartile range of the old prices? Explain your answer.

....

....

[1]

[Total 4 marks]

2 Rachel and Harry record the distance they cycle each week for 26 weeks. The box plot below shows information about Rachel's cycling. The table gives information about Harry's cycling.

Rachel:

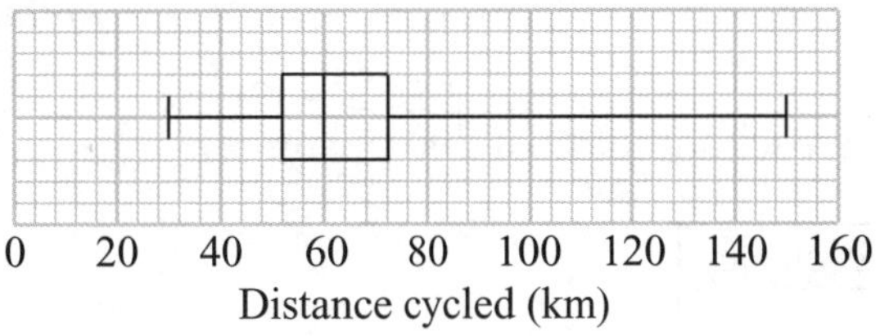

Harry's data	Distance cycled (km)
Shortest distance	0
Lower quartile	32
Median	50
Upper quartile	80
Furthest distance	128

a) Work out the interquartile range of the distances Rachel cycled.

.... km

[2]

b) Explain why the interquartile range might be a better measure of the spread of Rachel's distances than the range.

....

....

[1]

c) Use the grid opposite to draw a box plot showing Harry's data.

Harry:

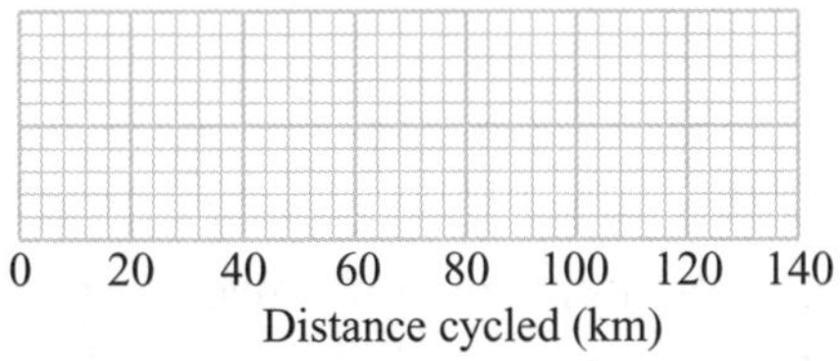

[2]

d) Rachel says that the distances she cycled were more consistent than the distances Harry cycled. Do you agree with her? Explain your answer.

....

....

[2]

[Total 7 marks]

3 A bakery records the number of loaves of bread it sells each week over an 11-week period. Their data is shown below:

31 33 31 40 45 46 42 31 29 38 42

Calculate the median and the interquartile range of the data. Show your working.

median .... IQR ....

[Total 5 marks]

4 Tom gives a puzzle to a sample of boys and girls. These box plots show information about the time it took the children to finish the puzzle.

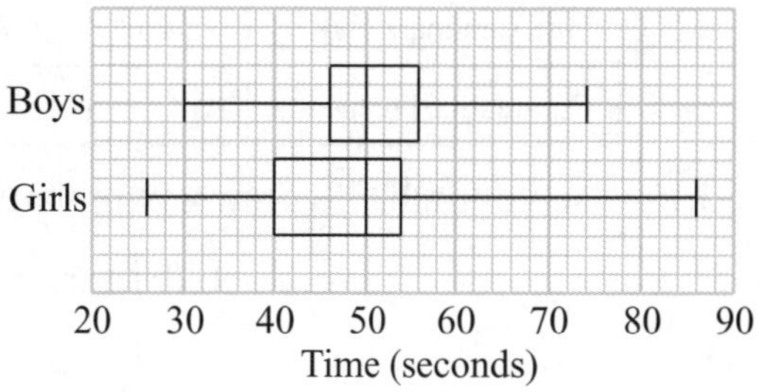

Compare the distributions of the times taken by the boys and the times taken by the girls.

....

....

....

[Total 2 marks]

5 The stem and leaf diagram below shows the amount of rainfall in mm that fell on an island during two different 15 day periods — one in June and the other in November.

Key (June)
2 | 1 = 12 mm of rain

June		November
9 8	0	1 2 2 7 9
5 2	1	2 3 5 5 8
9 8 6 3	2	0 2 2 3 5
8 8 7 4 1 0	3	
3	4	

Key (November)
0 | 1 = 1 mm of rain

Compare the rainfall on the island in June and November using the medians and interquartile ranges.

....

....

....

....

....

[Total 6 marks]

Exam Practice Tip

Even in maths, you sometimes have to answer questions in sentences — but don't forget to show values or calculations to support your answer. Use the number of marks as a guide as to how much detail to go into. E.g. if there are two marks available for comparing data sets, you need to make two comparisons.

Score

24

M3 Cumulative Frequency

1 120 pupils in a year group sit an examination at the end of the year.
Their results are given in the table below.

Exam mark (%)	$0 < x \leq 20$	$20 < x \leq 30$	$30 < x \leq 40$	$40 < x \leq 50$	$50 < x \leq 60$	$60 < x \leq 70$	$70 < x \leq 80$	$80 < x \leq 100$
Frequency	3	10	12	24	42	16	9	4

a) Complete the cumulative frequency table below.

Exam mark (%)	≤ 20	≤ 30	≤ 40	≤ 50	≤ 60	≤ 70	≤ 80	≤ 100
Cumulative Frequency								

[1]

b) Use your table to draw a cumulative frequency graph on the grid below.

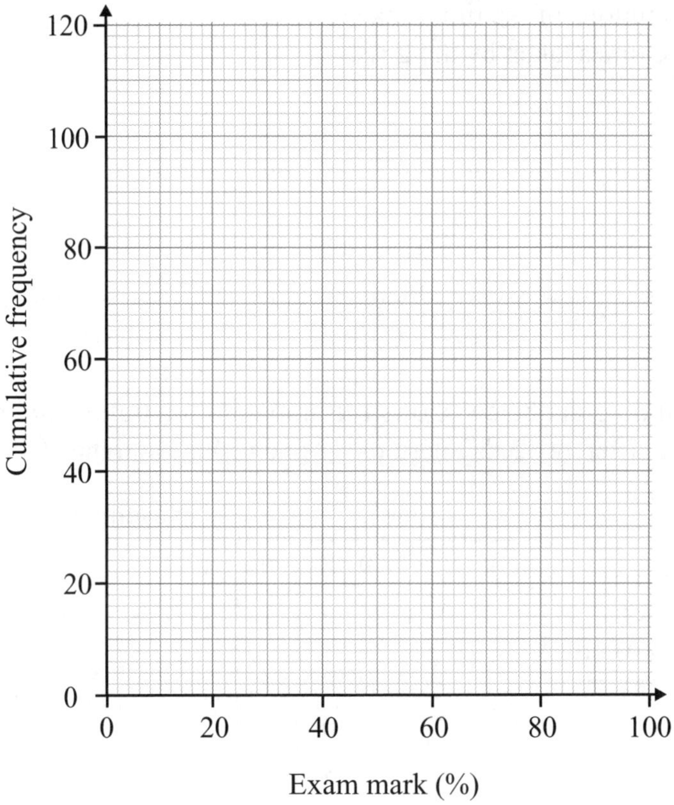

[3]

c) Use your graph to find an estimate for the median.

.... %

[1]

d) Use your graph to find an estimate for the interquartile range.

.... %

[2]

e) Each pupil received a grade based on their mark. Four times as many pupils achieved grade C or higher as those who got a lower grade. Estimate the lowest mark needed to get grade C.

.... %

[3]

[Total 10 marks]

2 The cumulative frequency graph below gives information about the length of time it takes to travel between Dunnagh and Trunloup on the main road each morning. The graph has been drawn using the data from a grouped frequency table.

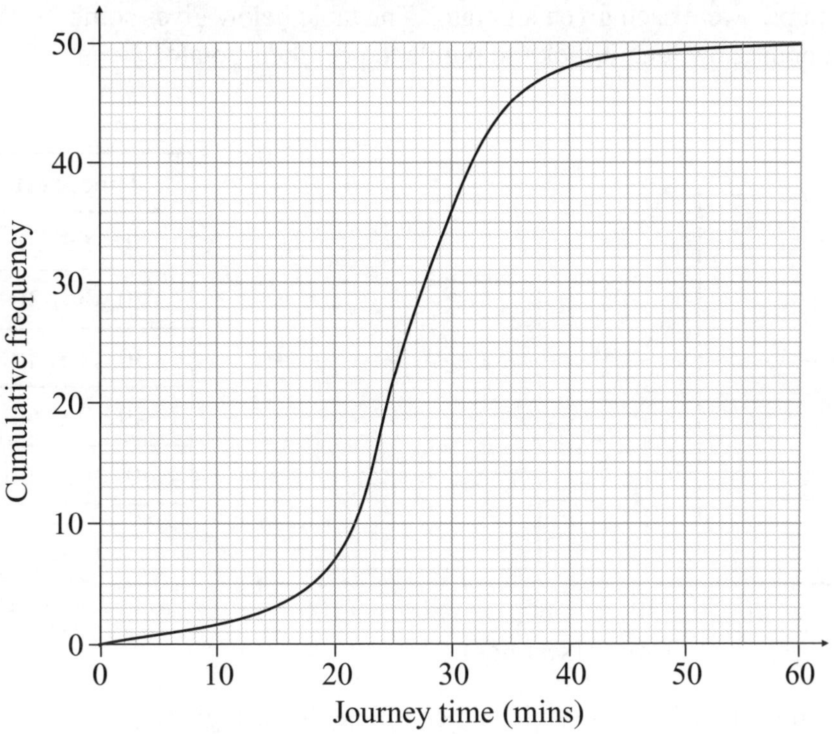

a) Use the graph to estimate:

i) the number of journeys that took between 27 and 47 minutes.

.... journeys

[2]

ii) the percentage of journeys that took longer than 40 minutes.

.... %

[2]

b) Explain why your answers to part a) above are only estimates.

....

....

[1]

The minimum journey time was 12 minutes and the maximum journey time was 52 minutes.

c) Using this information and the graph above, draw a box plot on the grid below to show the morning journey times between Dunnagh and Trunloup.

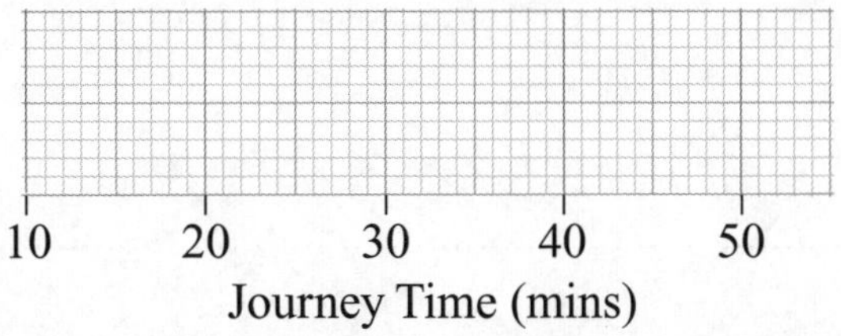

[3]

[Total 8 marks]

Score: ___ / **18**

M4 Histograms and Frequency Density

1 A group of pupils were each given a potato. The table below gives some information about how long it took the pupils to peel their potato.

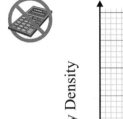

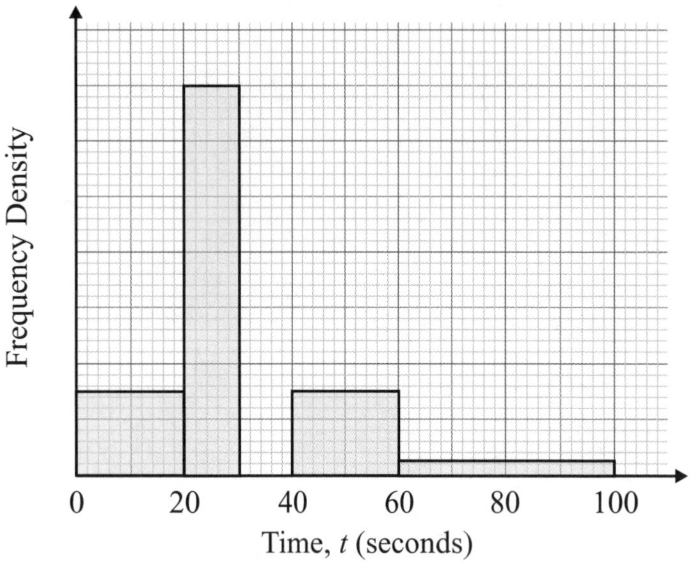

Time, t (s)	Frequency
$0 < t \leq 20$	15
$20 < t \leq 30$	
$30 < t \leq 40$	30
$40 < t \leq 60$	15
$60 < t \leq 100$	5

Don't forget to fill in the scale on the frequency density axis.

Fill in the missing entry from the table and complete the histogram.

[Total 3 marks]

2 The histogram shows how much time 270 children spent on the internet one evening.

A large sample of adults were asked how much time they spent on the internet on the same evening.
The mean time for the adults was 102 minutes.

Does the data shown support the hypothesis that, on average, adults used the internet for longer than children on this particular evening?

Make sure you show calculations to support your conclusion.

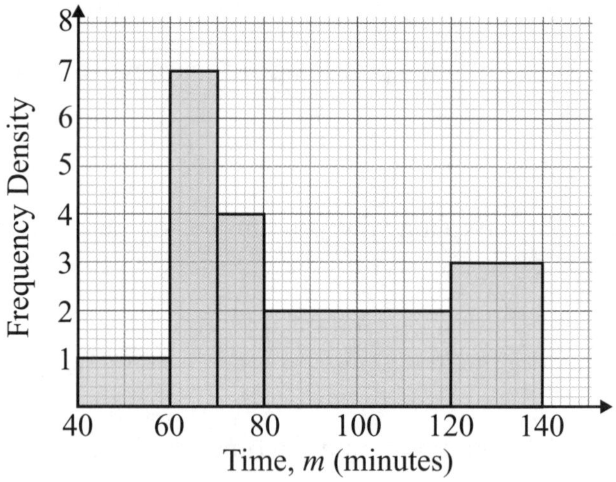

....

....

....

....

[Total 4 marks]

3 The histogram shows information about the weights, w kg, of 100 newborn lambs at a farm.

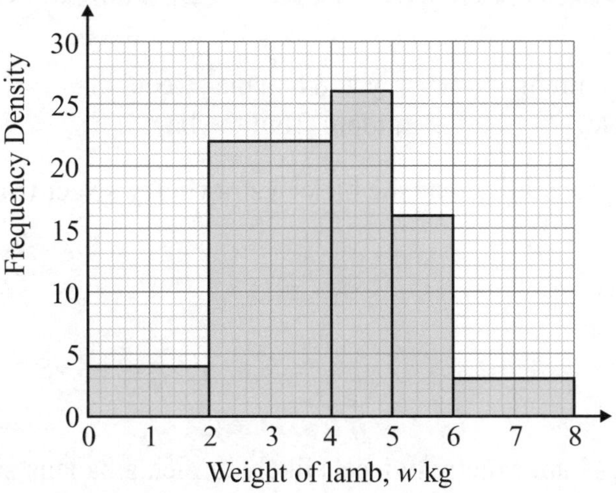

a) Calculate an estimate of the percentage of lambs weighing more than 3.5 kg.

.... %

[3]

b) This table shows information about the weights of the newborn lambs at a different farm.

Weight, w kg	$0 < w \leq 2$	$2 < w \leq 4$	$4 < w \leq 5$	$5 < w \leq 6$	$6 < w \leq 8$
Frequency	4	28	30	28	10

Draw a histogram on the grid to show this data.

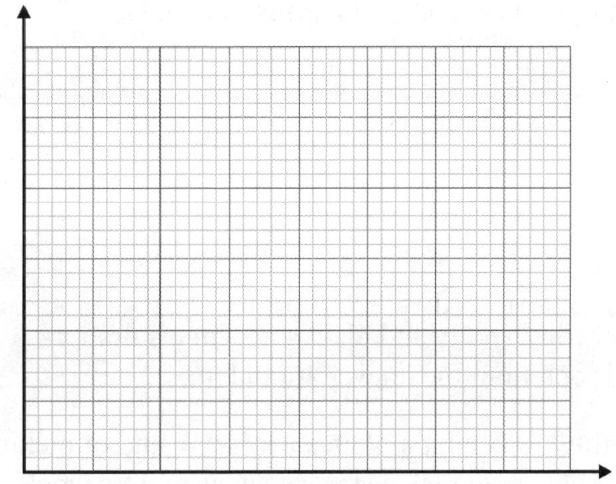

[3]

c) Compare the weights of newborn lambs for the two farms.

....

....

[1]

This question is only worth 1 mark, so you don't need to do any complicated calculations.

[Total 7 marks]

Exam Practice Tip

Histograms aren't the nicest things, but there's a good way to deal with them: learn the formula for frequency density (and then learn it again). Crack that, and you'll be able to find the frequency represented by any bar. Then you can just turn the histograms you're given into grouped frequency tables. Much better.

Score

14

M7 Probability Basics

1 Ailbhe has a bag containing strawberry and banana sweets in the ratio 2 : 5. She picks a sweet at random from the bag.

a) What is the probability that she picks a strawberry sweet from the bag?

....

[1]

b) Ailbhe says, "I am exactly twice as likely to pick a banana sweet as a strawberry sweet". Is she correct? Explain your answer.

....

....

[2]

[Total 3 marks]

2 There are p counters in a bag. n of the counters are blue and the rest are red. One counter is picked out at random.

Work out the probability that the counter picked is red.
Give your answer as a fraction in terms of p and n.

....

[Total 2 marks]

3 Arthur has stripy, spotty and plain socks in his drawer. He picks a sock from the drawer at random.

The probability of picking a plain sock is 0.4, and of picking a spotty sock is y.
He is twice as likely to pick a stripy sock as a spotty sock.
Find the value of y. Give your answer as a decimal.

P(stripy sock) = ... y

.... + y + ... = 1

.... = 0.6

y = ...

y = ...

[Total 3 marks]

Score: $\frac{\quad}{8}$

Counting Outcomes

M7

1 Alvar has a fair six sided dice and a set of five cards numbered 2, 4, 6, 8 and 10. He rolls the dice and chooses a card at random. Alvar adds the number on the dice to the number on the card to calculate his total score.

Find the probability that Alvar will score more than 4.

....

[Total 3 marks]

2 A shop sells three different meal deals. The possible meal deal options are:
- sandwich and drink
- sandwich and snack
- sandwich, snack and drink

There are 5 different sandwiches, 8 different drinks and 4 different snacks.
How many possible meal deal combinations are there?

....

[Total 3 marks]

3 Trish spins 5 fair spinners, each with sides numbered 1-4. She writes down, in order, the number that each spinner lands on to generate a 5 digit number.

a) How many different possibilities are there for the 5 digit number she generates?

....

[1]

b) What is the probability of Trish generating a 5 digit number not containing a 1?

....

[2]

[Total 3 marks]

4 A row of six disco lights all flash at the same time.
Each light randomly flashes either red, blue, green or yellow.

What is the probability that, in one flash, no lights are green or yellow?

....

[Total 3 marks]

Score: ___ / **12**

M7 Probability Experiments

1 Suda has a six-sided dice. The sides are numbered 1 to 6.

Suda rolls the dice 50 times. Her results are shown in the table below.

Number	1	2	3	4	5	6
Relative Frequency	0.32	0.12	0.24	0.14	0.06	0.12

a) How many times did she roll a 6?

....

[2]

b) Is Suda's dice fair? Explain your answer.

....

....

[2]

c) She rolls the dice another 50 times. Should she expect the same results? Explain your answer.

....

....

[1]

[Total 5 marks]

2 Eimear has a bag containing a large number of counters.
Each counter is numbered either 1, 2, 3, 4 or 5.

She selects one counter from the bag at random, makes a note of its number, and then puts it back in the bag. Eimear does this 100 times. Her results are shown in the table below.

Number on counter	1	2	3	4	5
Frequency	23	25	22	21	9
Relative Frequency					

a) Complete the table, giving the relative frequencies of each counter being selected.

[1]

b) Eimear's friend Elvin says that he thinks that the bag contains the same number of counters with each number. Do you agree? Give a reason for your answer.

....

[1]

c) Using Eimear's results, estimate the probability of selecting an odd number when one counter is picked from the bag at random.

....

[2]

[Total 4 marks]

3 Danielle thinks she can predict if a fair coin will land showing heads or tails.

a) She makes a prediction and flips the coin. She repeats this 8 times.
The results are shown in the table below.

Prediction	H	H	T	H	T	H	H	H
Outcome	H	T	H	H	T	H	H	T

i) How many predictions would you expect to be correct if she was just guessing?

....

[1]

ii) Do you think Danielle can predict the flip of a coin? Explain your answer.

....

....

[1]

Danielle flipped the coin another 100 times and predicted the outcome of each flip.
She predicted it would land showing heads 39 times. It landed on tails 53 times.
Of the times it landed on tails, 3 more of her predictions were correct than were wrong.

b) i) Complete the frequency tree below to show these results.

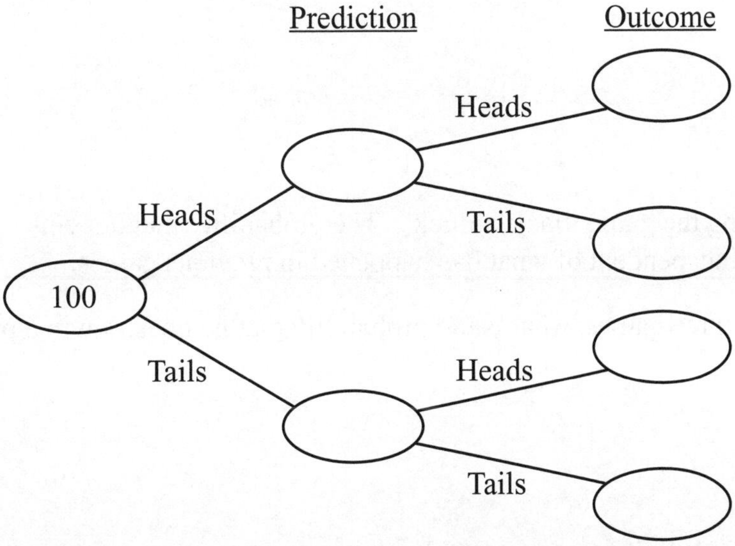

[3]

ii) Work out the relative frequency of Danielle predicting the outcome correctly.

....

[2]

c) Are the results from the experiment in part a) or part b) more reliable? Explain your answer.

....

....

[1]

[Total 8 marks]

Score: $\frac{}{17}$

M7 The AND / OR Rules

1 A biased 5-sided spinner is numbered 1-5.

The probability that the spinner will land on each of the numbers 1 to 5 is given in this table.

Number	1	2	3	4	5
Probability	0.3	0.15	0.2	0.25	0.1

a) What is the probability of the spinner landing on a multiple of 3 or a square number?

....

[2]

b) The spinner is spun twice.
What is the probability that it lands on a 2 on the second spin, but not on the first?

....

[2]

[Total 4 marks]

2 Shaun is playing the game 'hook-a-duck'. The probability that he wins a prize is 0.3, independent of what has happened in previous games.

a) If he plays three games, what is the probability that he doesn't win a prize?

....

[1]

b) Shaun says, "If I play two games, I have a better than even chance of winning a prize". Is he correct? Explain your answer.

....

....

....

[2]

[Total 3 marks]

Exam Practice Tip

You can't just use the AND / OR rules mindlessly — you need to do a bit of thinking about the events before you start any questions. If you're using the OR rule you need to check if the events can happen at the same time or not. If you're using the AND rule you'll have to check that the events are independent.

Score ____ / 7

Tree Diagrams (1)

M7

1 Jo and Heather are meeting for coffee. The probability that Jo will wear burgundy trousers is $\frac{2}{5}$, while there is a one in four chance that Heather will wear burgundy trousers. The two events are independent.

a) Complete the tree diagram below.

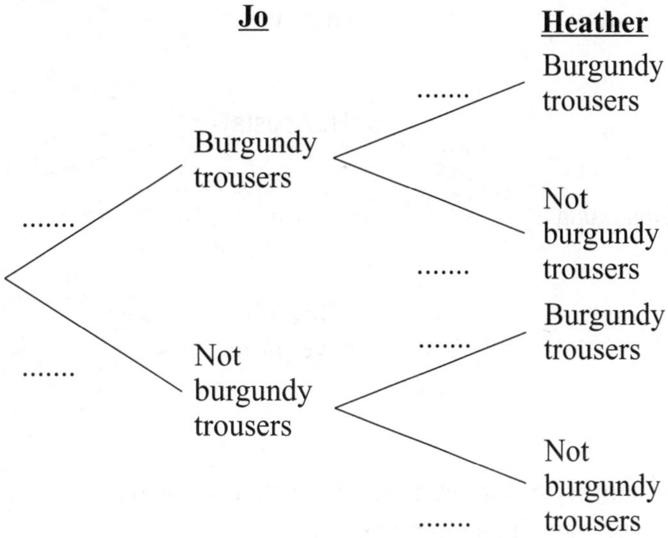

[2]

b) What is the probability that neither of them wear burgundy trousers?

....

[2]

[Total 4 marks]

2 Paul and Jen play a game where they roll a fair dice. If it lands on a factor of 6 then Paul gets a point, otherwise Jen gets a point. The winner is the person who gets the most points.

a) If they roll the dice twice, what is the probability that it will be a draw?

....

[3]

b) If they roll the dice three times, what is the probability that Paul wins?

....

[3]

[Total 6 marks]

Exam Practice Tip

To find the probability of an end result from a tree diagram, just multiply along the branches. If you want the total probability of more than one end result, add up the relevant probabilities (and remember that sometimes it's easier to find the probability of the thing you want not happening, then subtracting from 1).

Score

10

M8 Tree Diagrams (2)

1 The probability that Gemma has pasta for dinner depends on whether she had pasta the previous day. The probability that she will have pasta for dinner is 0.3 if she had it the previous day and 0.8 if she didn't have it the previous day.

a) Gemma had pasta today. Complete the tree diagram below.

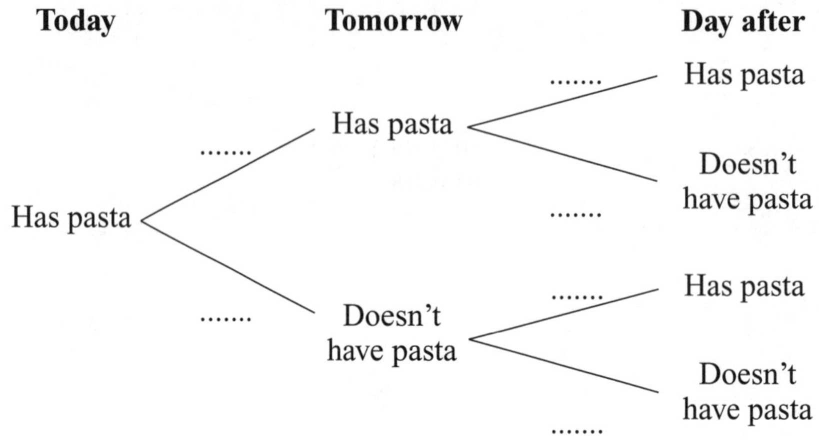

[2]

b) What is the probability of Gemma having pasta on exactly one of the next two days if she had pasta today?

....

[2]

[Total 4 marks]

2 A box of chocolates contains 12 chocolates. 7 are milk chocolate and 5 are white chocolate. Two chocolates are chosen at random without replacement.

a) If the first chocolate chosen is a milk chocolate, what is the probability that the second chocolate chosen is also a milk chocolate?

....

[1]

b) Calculate the probability of at least one milk chocolate being chosen.

....

[2]

c) Calculate the probability that one milk chocolate and one white chocolate are chosen in any order.

....

[2]

[Total 5 marks]

Score: ___ / 9

Answers

Section One — Number

Page 3: Types of Number and BODMAS (1)

1 $\frac{197.8}{\sqrt{0.01+0.23}} = \frac{197.8}{\sqrt{0.24}} = \frac{197.8}{0.489897948...}$

$= 403.757559... = 403.76$ (2 d.p.)

[2 marks available — 2 marks for answer correct to 2 decimal places, otherwise 1 mark for unrounded answer]

2 $\sqrt{\frac{12.71+137.936}{\cos 50° \times 13.2^2}} = \sqrt{\frac{150.646}{0.642787609... \times 174.24}}$

$= \sqrt{1.34506182...}$

$= 1.1597680...$

$= 1.16$ (2 d.p.)

[2 marks available — 2 marks for answer correct to 2 decimal places, otherwise 1 mark for unrounded answer]

3 E.g. $6 = \sqrt{3x+2y}$, so $36 = 3x + 2y$
Try different values of x and see what y-value each one gives:
$x = 2$: $3x = 6$, so $2y = 36 - 6 = 30$, so $y = 15$
$x = 4$: $3x = 12$, so $2y = 36 - 12 = 24$, so $y = 12$
[2 marks available — 1 mark for each correct pair of x and y values]
The only other possible solution is x = 6, y = 9 (you'll get full marks if you got this solution instead).

4 $(4 + 28 \div 7)^2 \div (2 \times 4^2)$
$= (4 + 4)^2 \div (2 \times 16)$ ***[1 mark]***
$= 8^2 \div 32$ ***[1 mark]***
$= 64 \div 32 = 2$ ***[1 mark]***

Reciprocal $= 1 \div 2 = \frac{1}{2}$ ***[1 mark]***
[4 marks available in total — as above]

Page 4: Types of Number and BODMAS (2)

1 Irrational numbers: π, 0.6π, and $\sqrt{3}$.
[2 marks available — 2 marks for all three correct irrational numbers, lose 1 mark for one missing or a rational number included]
Don't be fooled — $\sqrt{16}$ = 4, which is rational.

2 a) $\sqrt{5^2 - 5 \times 3} = \sqrt{25 - 15} = \sqrt{10}$
— the expression is irrational.
[2 marks available — 1 mark for $\sqrt{25-15}$, 1 mark for $\sqrt{10}$ and correctly stating this is irrational]

b) $\frac{\sqrt{6}}{4\sqrt{10 - 2 \times 2}} = \frac{\sqrt{6}}{4\sqrt{6}} = \frac{1}{4}$
— the expression is rational.
[2 marks available — 1 mark for $\frac{\sqrt{6}}{4\sqrt{6}}$, 1 mark for $\frac{1}{4}$ and correctly stating this is rational]

3 a) Perimeter = circumference = 9π, which is irrational. ***[1 mark]***

b) Use Pythagoras: $a^2 + b^2 = c^2$
c^2 (longest side) $= 5^2 + 12^2$
$= 25 + 144 = 169$
so $c = \sqrt{169} = 13$
Lengths of all sides are rational, so perimeter is rational.
[3 marks available — 1 mark for a correct method to find the length of longest side, 1 mark for correct calculation of the length of longest side as $\sqrt{169}$ or 13, 1 mark for a correct explanation that the perimeter is rational]

Page 5: Multiples, Factors and Prime Factors

1 a)

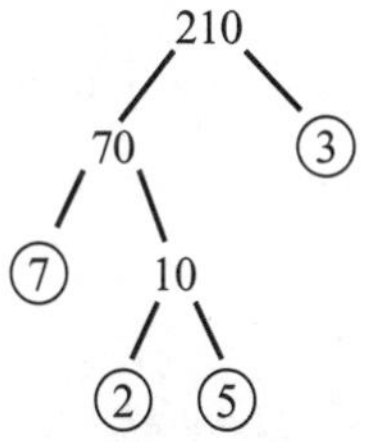

$210 = 2 \times 3 \times 5 \times 7$
[2 marks available — 1 mark for a correct method, 1 mark for all prime factors correct.]

b) Write 105 as a product of its prime factors:

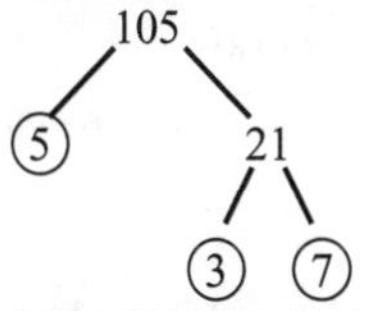

$105 = 3 \times 5 \times 7$
Now square it: $105^2 = 3^2 \times 5^2 \times 7^2$
[2 marks available — 1 mark for a correct method, 1 mark for all prime factors correct]

2 E.g. 4 (even) has three factors (1, 2 and 4). 81 (odd) has five factors (1, 3, 9, 27 and 81).
[2 marks available — 1 mark for each correct example of odd and even square numbers with a suitable number of factors.]
These aren't the only square numbers that would work here — any pair where the odd number has more factors than the even number would get you the marks.

3 Common multiples of 6 and 7:
42, 84, 126, 168, 210, 252, ... ***[1 mark]***
Factors of 252: 1, 2, 3, 4, 6, 7, 9, 12, 14, 18, 21, 28, 36, 42, 63, 84, 126, 252
Factors of 420: 1, 2, 3, 4, 5, 6, 7, 10, 12, 14, 15, 20, 21, 28, 30, 35, 42, 60, 70, 84, 105, 140, 210, 420 ***[1 mark for both sets of factors]***
Common factors of 252 and 420:
1, 2, 3, 4, 6, 7, 12, 14, 21, 28, 42, 84
[1 mark]
So $x = 84$ ***[1 mark]***
[4 marks available in total — as above]
You could also narrow the choice down to 84 and 126 straight away as these are the only common multiples in the range you're given — then try dividing 252 and 420 by these numbers to see which is a common factor.

Page 6: LCM and HCF

1 a) Factors of 54 are:
1, 2, 3, 6, 9, 18, 27, 54
Factors of 72 are:
1, 2, 3, 4, 6, 8, 9, 12, 18, 24, 36, 72
So the HCF is 18 ***[1 mark]***

b) Multiples of 54 are:
54, 108, 162, 216, 270, ...
Multiples of 72 are:
72, 144, 216, 288, ...
So the LCM is 216 ***[1 mark]***

2 a) LCM $= 3^7 \times 7^3 \times 11^2$ ***[1 mark]***

b) HCF $= 3^4 \times 11$ ***[1 mark]***

3 a) LCM $= 2^8 \times 5^3 \times 7$
[2 marks available — 2 marks for the correct answer, otherwise 1 mark for a common multiple of all three numbers]

b) HCF $= 2^5$
[2 marks available — 2 marks for the correct answer, otherwise 1 mark for a common factor of all three numbers]

Pages 7-8: Fractions

1 65% = 0.65, $\frac{2}{3} = 0.666...$, $\frac{33}{50} = 0.66$
So order is 0.065, 65%, $\frac{33}{50}$, $\frac{2}{3}$
[2 marks available — 2 marks for all four numbers in the correct order, otherwise 1 mark for writing the numbers in the same form (either decimals, percentages or fractions)]

2 a) $3\frac{1}{2} + 2\frac{3}{5} = \frac{7}{2} + \frac{13}{5} = \frac{35}{10} + \frac{26}{10}$

$= \frac{35 + 26}{10} = \frac{61}{10}$

or $6\frac{1}{10}$

[3 marks available — 1 mark for writing as improper fractions, 1 mark for writing over a common denominator, 1 mark for the correct answer]

b) $3\frac{3}{4} - 2\frac{1}{3} = \frac{15}{4} - \frac{7}{3} = \frac{45}{12} - \frac{28}{12}$

$= \frac{45 - 28}{12} = \frac{17}{12}$

or $1\frac{5}{12}$

[3 marks available — 1 mark for writing as improper fractions, 1 mark for writing over a common denominator, 1 mark for the correct answer]

If you've used a different method in Q2, but still shown your working, and ended up with the same final answer, then you still get full marks.

3 $1 - \frac{2}{15} - \frac{5}{12} = 1 - \frac{8}{60} - \frac{25}{60} = \frac{27}{60} = \frac{9}{20}$

[3 marks available — 1 mark for writing over a common denominator, 1 mark for doing the subtraction correctly and 1 mark for simplifying to find the correct answer]

4 a) $1\frac{2}{3} \times \frac{9}{10} = \frac{5}{3} \times \frac{9}{10} = \frac{45}{30} = \frac{3}{2} = 1\frac{1}{2}$

[3 marks available — 1 mark for multiplying the two fractions together, 1 mark for an equivalent fraction, 1 mark for the correct final answer]

b) $3\frac{1}{2} \div 1\frac{2}{5} = \frac{7}{2} \div \frac{7}{5} = \frac{7}{2} \times \frac{5}{7} = \frac{35}{14} = \frac{5}{2} = 2\frac{1}{2}$

[3 marks available — 1 mark for taking the reciprocal and multiplying the two fractions together, 1 mark for an equivalent fraction, 1 mark for the correct final answer]

5 a) $17\frac{1}{2} \times \frac{1}{5} = \frac{35}{2} \times \frac{1}{5} = \frac{35}{10} = \frac{7}{2}$ ***[1 mark]*** tonnes of flour used to make cheese scones.

Then $\frac{7}{2}$ out of 25 $= \frac{7}{2} \div 25 = \frac{7}{50}$

[1 mark]

[2 marks available in total — as above]

b) $\frac{7}{50} = \frac{14}{100} = 14\%$ ***[1 mark]***

6 a) $\frac{7}{40} = \begin{array}{r} 0.\ 1\ \ 7\ \ 5\ \ 0 \\ 40\overline{)\,7.{}^{7}0{}^{30}0{}^{20}0{}^{0}0} \end{array} = 0.175$

[2 marks available — 1 mark for a correct division method, 1 mark for the correct answer]

b) $\frac{10}{11} = \begin{array}{r} 0\ 0.\ \ 9\ \ 0\ \ 9\ \ 0 \\ 11\overline{)\,1{}^{1}0.{}^{10}0{}^{1}0{}^{10}0{}^{1}0} \end{array} = 0.\dot{9}\dot{0}$

[3 marks available — 1 mark for a correct division method, 1 mark for continuing until there is a pattern, 1 mark for the correct answer]

c) $\frac{7}{33} = \begin{array}{r} 0.\ 2\ 1\ 2\ 1 \\ 33\overline{)\,7.{}^{7}0{}^{4}0{}^{7}0{}^{4}0} \end{array} = 0.\dot{2}\dot{1}$

[3 marks available — 1 mark for a correct division method, 1 mark for continuing until there is a pattern, 1 mark for the correct answer]

Page 9: Recurring Decimals into Fractions

1 a) Let $r = 0.\dot{7}$, so $10r = 7.\dot{7}$ ***[1 mark]***

$10r - r = 7.\dot{7} - 0.\dot{7}$

$9r = 7$

$r = \frac{7}{9}$ ***[1 mark]***

[2 marks available in total — as above]

b) Let $r = 0.\dot{2}\dot{6}$, so $100r = 26.\dot{2}\dot{6}$ ***[1 mark]***

$100r - r = 26.\dot{2}\dot{6} - 0.\dot{2}\dot{6}$

$99r = 26$

$r = \frac{26}{99}$ ***[1 mark]***

[2 marks available in total — as above]

c) Let $r = 1.\dot{3}\dot{6}$, so $100r = 136.\dot{3}\dot{6}$ ***[1 mark]***

$100r - r = 136.\dot{3}\dot{6} - 1.\dot{3}\dot{6}$

$99r = 135$

$r = \frac{135}{99}$ ***[1 mark]***

$r = \frac{15}{11}$ or $1\frac{4}{11}$ ***[1 mark]***

[3 marks available in total — as above]

2 Let $10r = 5.\dot{9}\dot{0}$, so $1000r = 590.\dot{9}\dot{0}$ ***[1 mark]***

$990r = 585$ ***[1 mark]***

$r = \frac{585}{990} = \frac{13}{22}$ ***[1 mark]***

[3 marks available in total — as above]

Page 10: Rounding Numbers

1 a) 58.4 seconds ***[1 mark]***

b) 60 seconds ***[1 mark]***

2 11.00 ***[1 mark]***

3 $\frac{4.32^2 - \sqrt{13.4}}{16.3 + 2.19} = 0.8113466...$ ***[1 mark]***

$= 0.811$ (3 s.f.) ***[1 mark]***

[2 marks available in total — as above]

4 a) 1750 m ***[1 mark]***

b) 16.34 °C is the highest value given to 4 s.f. that would round to 16.3 °C. ***[1 mark]***

Page 11: Estimating

1 a) $\frac{215.7 \times 44.8}{460} \approx \frac{200 \times 40}{500} = \frac{8000}{500} = 16$

[3 marks available — 1 mark for correctly rounding 1 number to 1 significant figure, 1 mark for correctly rounding the other 2 numbers to 1 significant figure, 1 mark for correct answer]

b) The answer to a) will be smaller than the exact answer, because in the rounded fraction the numerator is smaller and denominator is larger compared to the exact calculation.

[1 mark for 'smaller than the exact answer' and correct reasoning]

2 $\sqrt{\frac{2321}{19.673 \times 3.81}} \approx \sqrt{\frac{2000}{20 \times 4}}$

[1 mark for rounding sensibly]

$= \sqrt{\frac{100}{4}} = \sqrt{25}$

[1 mark for either expression]

$= 5$ ***[1 mark]***

[3 marks available in total — as above]

You might have a different answer if you've rounded differently — as long as your rounding is sensible, you'll get the marks.

3 $V = \frac{1}{3}\pi(10)^2 \times 24 \approx \frac{1}{3} \times 3 \times 10^2 \times 20$

$= 100 \times 20 = 2000 \text{ cm}^3$

[2 marks available — 1 mark for rounding numbers sensibly, 1 mark for a suitable answer using rounded numbers]

4 108 is between $10^2 = 100$ and $11^2 = 121$ ***[1 mark]***

It is closer to 100 so the square root is closer to 10 than 11, e.g. 10.4 ***[1 mark for an estimate between 10.2-10.5]***

[2 marks available in total — as above]

Page 12: Bounds (1)

1 a) 54.05 cm ***[1 mark]***

b) lower bound for the width of the paper = 23.55 cm ***[1 mark]***

lower bound for the perimeter = (54.05 cm × 2) + (23.55 cm × 2) = 155.2 cm ***[1 mark]***

[2 marks available in total — as above]

2 upper bound for x = 57.5 mm ***[1 mark]***

upper bound for y = 32.5 mm ***[1 mark]***

upper bound for area =

57.5 mm × 32.5 mm = 1868.75 mm^2

= 1870 mm^2 to 3 s.f. ***[1 mark]***

[3 marks available in total — as above]

3 Upper bound of $x = 2.25$ ***[1 mark]***

So upper bound of $4x + 3 = 4 \times 2.25 + 3 = 12$

Lower bound of $x = 2.15$ ***[1 mark]***

So lower bound of $4x + 3 = 4 \times 2.15 + 3 = 11.6$

Written as an interval, this is $11.6 \leq 4x + 3 < 12$

[2 marks — 1 for both bounds correct, 1 mark for expressing as an inequality correctly]

[4 marks available in total — as above]

4 lower bound for volume = $0.935 \times 0.605 \times 0.205 = 0.11596...$ m^3
upper bound for volume = $0.945 \times 0.615 \times 0.215 = 0.12495...$ m^3
Both the upper bound and lower bound round to 0.12 m^3 to 2 d.p. (or 2 s.f.) so the volume to 2 d.p. is 0.12 m^3.
[4 marks available — 1 mark for the correct upper and lower bounds for the dimensions, 1 mark for the correct lower bound for volume, 1 mark for the correct upper bound for volume, 1 mark for rounding to a suitable number of decimal places (or significant figures) to obtain the final answer]

Page 13: Bounds (2)

1 Lower bound of difference = 13.65 – 8.35 ***[1 mark]*** = 5.3 litres ***[1 mark]***
[2 marks available in total — as above]

2 Upper bound of area = 5.25 cm^2 ***[1 mark]***
Lower bound of height = 3.15 cm ***[1 mark]***
$2 \times (5.25 \div 3.15) = 3.33$ to 2 d.p. ***[1 mark]***
[3 marks available — as above]

3 speed = distance ÷ time
lower bound for distance = 99.5 m
upper bound for time = 12.55 s
[1 mark for both]
lower bound for speed
$= \frac{99.5}{12.55}$ m/s = 7.928... m/s ***[1 mark]***
lower bound for speed to 2 s.f. = 7.9 m/s
lower bound for speed to 1 s.f. = 8 m/s
upper bound for distance = 100.5 m
lower bound for time = 12.45 s
[1 mark for both]
upper bound for speed
$= \frac{100.5}{12.45}$ m/s = 8.072... m/s ***[1 mark]***
upper bound for speed to 2 s.f. = 8.1 m/s
upper bound for speed to 1 s.f. = 8 m/s
The lower bound to 2 s.f. does not equal the upper bound to 2 s.f., but the lower bound to 1 s.f. does equal the upper bound to 1 s.f. So Ridhi's speed is 8 m/s to 1 significant figure.
[1 mark for comparing bounds to reach correct answer to 1 s.f.]
[5 marks available in total — as above]

Pages 14-15: Standard Form

1 a) 6.482×10^8 ***[1 mark]***
b) 2.45×10^{-5} ***[1 mark]***

2 a) $A = 4.834 \times 10^9 = 4\,834\,000\,000$ ***[1 mark]***
b) $B \times C = (2.7 \times 10^5) \times (5.8 \times 10^3)$
$= (2.7 \times 5.8) \times (10^5 \times 10^3)$
$= 15.66 \times 10^8$ ***[1 mark]***
$= 1.566 \times 10^9$ ***[1 mark]***
[2 marks available in total — as above]
c) C, B, A (5.8×10^3, 2.7×10^5, 4.834×10^9) ***[1 mark]***

3 time (s) = distance (miles) ÷ speed (miles/s)
$= (9.3 \times 10^7) \div (1.86 \times 10^5)$ seconds ***[1 mark]***
$= 5 \times 10^2$ seconds ***[1 mark]***
[2 marks available in total — as above]

4 $A = (5 \times 10^5) + (5 \times 10^3) + (5 \times 10^2) + (5 \times 10^{-2})$
$= 500\,000 + 5000 + 500 + 0.05$ ***[1 mark]***
$= 505\,500.05$ ***[1 mark]***
[2 marks available in total — as above]

5 4.5 billion = 4 500 000 000 = 4.5×10^9 and 150 million = 150 000 000 = 1.5×10^8 ***[1 mark]***
$(4.5 \times 10^9) \div (1.5 \times 10^8) =$
$(4.5 \div 1.5) \times (10^9 \div 10^8)$ ***[1 mark]***
$= 3 \times 10^1 = 30$ ***[1 mark]***.
So the ratio is 1 : 30 ***[1 mark]***
[4 marks available in total — as above]

6 a) number of tablets = dose (grams) ÷ dose per tablet (grams)
$= (4 \times 10^{-4}) \div (8 \times 10^{-5})$ ***[1 mark]***
$= (4 \div 8) \times (10^{-4} \div 10^{-5})$
$= 0.5 \times 10^1$ ***[1 mark]***
$= 5$ ***[1 mark]***
[3 marks available in total — as above]
b) new dose = 4×10^{-4} grams + 6×10^{-5} grams ***[1 mark]***
$= 4 \times 10^{-4}$ grams + 0.6×10^{-4} grams ***[1 mark]***
$= (4 + 0.6) \times 10^{-4}$ grams
$= 4.6 \times 10^{-4}$ grams per day ***[1 mark]***
[3 marks available in total — as above]
You could have done this one by turning 4×10^{-4} into 40×10^{-5} and adding it to 6×10^{-5} instead.

7 Total weight of ship and passengers = $7.59 \times 10^7 + 2.1 \times 10^5$
$= 7.611 \times 10^7$ kg ***[1 mark]***
$(2.1 \times 10^5) \div (7.611 \times 10^7) = 0.002759...$ ***[1 mark]***
$0.002759 \times 100 = 0.28$ % (to 2 d.p.) ***[1 mark]***
[3 marks available in total — as above]

Page 16: Different Number Systems

1

64	32	16	8	4	2	1
1	0	1	1	0	1	1

1011011 as a decimal number = 64 + 0 + 16 + 8 + 0 + 2 + 1 = 91 ***[1 mark]***

2

32	16	8	4	2	1
0	1	0	1	0	0
20 – 32 = –12	20 – 16 = 4	4 – 8 = –4	4 – 4 = 0	0 – 2 = –2	0 – 1 = –1

20 in binary = 10100 ***[1 mark]***

3 a)

32	16	8	4	2	1
0	1	1	0	0	1
25 – 32 = –7	25 – 16 = 9	9 – 8 = 1	1 – 4 = –3	1 – 2 = –1	1 – 1 = 0

11001 ***[1 mark]***

b)

16	8	4	2	1
1	0	1	1	0

10110 as a decimal number = 16 + 4 + 2 = 22 ***[1 mark]***

Section Two — Ratio, Proportion and Percentages

Pages 17-19: Ratios

1 Longest – shortest = 7 – 5 = 2 parts = 9 cm ***[1 mark]***
1 part = 9 ÷ 2 = 4.5 cm
Original piece of wood is 5 + 6 + 6 + 7 = 24 parts ***[1 mark]***
So, the original piece of wood is 24 × 4.5 = 108 cm ***[1 mark]***
[3 marks available in total — as above]

2 a) $3\frac{3}{4} : 1\frac{1}{2} = 4 \times 3\frac{3}{4} : 4 \times 1\frac{1}{2}$
$= 15 : 6$ ***[1 mark]***
$= 5 : 2$ ***[1 mark]***
[2 marks available in total — as above]
b) 5 + 2 = 7 parts
1 part: 2800 ml ÷ 7 = 400 ml
Yellow paint = 400 ml × 5 = 2000 ml
Blue paint = 400 ml × 2 = 800 ml
[2 marks available — 1 mark for finding the amount of 1 part, 1 mark for finding the correct amounts for both yellow and blue paint]
If your answer to part a) was incorrect, but your answers to part b) were correct for your incorrect ratio, you still get the marks for part b).

3 Catrin, Ariana, Nasir and Simone shared the money in the ratio 1 : 2 : 4 : 8 ***[1 mark for 1 : 2 : 4 : 8 or an equivalent ratio (order may be different)]***
660 ÷ (1 + 2 + 4 + 8) = 44 ***[1 mark]***
Simone got £44 × 8 = £352 ***[1 mark]***
[3 marks available in total — as above]
You could answer this question using a formula — if you let x be the amount of money that Catrin gets, then x + 2x + 4x + 8x = £660.

4 a) $\frac{2}{9}$ as much milk is used as ice cream ***[1 mark]***
b) 1 part: 801 ÷ 9 = 89 ml ***[1 mark]***
9 + 2 = 11 parts
89 × 11 = 979 ml ***[1 mark]***
[2 marks available in total — as above]

c) E.g.
Find a point on the graph:
When ice cream = 900 ml,
milk = $900 \times \frac{2}{9} = 200$ ml

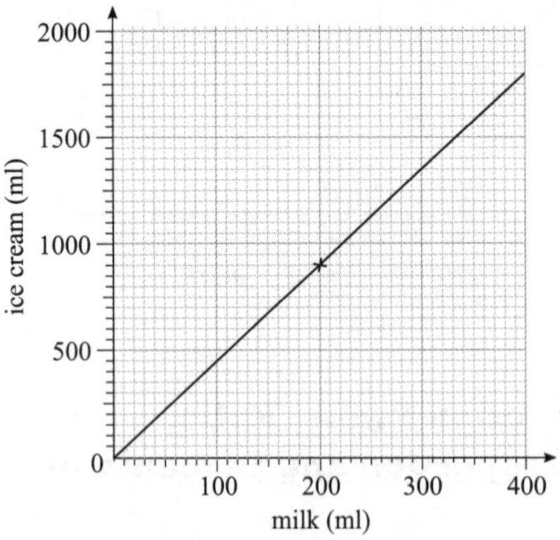

[2 marks available — 1 mark for plotting any point on the line correctly, 1 mark for a straight line that passes through that point and (0, 0)]

5 16 kg of Mr Appleseed's Supercompost contains:
$\frac{4}{8} \times 16 = 8$ kg of soil.
$\frac{3}{8} \times 16 = 6$ kg of compost.
$\frac{1}{8} \times 16 = 2$ kg of grit.
Soil costs £8 ÷ 40 = £0.20 per kg.
Compost costs £15 ÷ 25 = £0.60 per kg.
Grit costs £12 ÷ 15 = £0.80 per kg.
16 litres of Mr Appleseed's Supercompost costs:
(8 × 0.2) + (6 × 0.6) + (2 × 0.8) = £6.80
Profit: £10 – £6.80 = £3.20
[5 marks available — 1 mark for the correct mass of one ingredient, 1 mark for the correct masses for the other two ingredients, 1 mark for working out the price per kg for each ingredient, 1 mark for the total cost of 16 kg of Supercompost, 1 mark for the correct answer]

6 $x - 5 : y - 3 = 5 : 8$ and $x + 5 : y + 7 = 5 : 7$
[1 mark]
$\frac{x-5}{y-3} = \frac{5}{8}$ and $\frac{x+5}{y+7} = \frac{5}{7}$ ***[1 mark]***
$8(x - 5) = 5(y - 3)$ and $7(x + 5) = 5(y + 7)$
Expand and simplify to give:
$8x - 5y = 25$ [1] and $7x - 5y = 0$ [2]
[1 mark]
[1] – [2]: $x = 25$ ***[1 mark]***
Sub into [1]: $(8 \times 25) - 5y = 25$
$5y = 175$,
so $y = 35$ ***[1 mark]***
Solution: $x = 25$, $y = 35$
[5 marks available in total — as above]

7 Call the number of black olives b and the number of green olives g.
$b : g = 5 : 11$ and $b - 3 : g - 1 = 3 : 7$
[1 mark for both]
$\frac{b}{g} = \frac{5}{11}$ and $\frac{b-3}{g-1} = \frac{3}{7}$ ***[1 mark for both]***
$11b = 5g$ and $7(b - 3) = 3(g - 1)$
$11b - 5g = 0$ [1] and $7b - 3g = 18$ [2]
[1 mark]
[1] × 3: $33b - 15g = 0$ [3]
[2] × 5: $35b - 15g = 90$ [4]
[1 mark for both]
[4] – [3]: $2b = 90$
$b = 45$ ***[1 mark]***
Sub into [1]:
$(11 \times 45) - 5g = 0$
$5g = 495$, so $g = 99$ ***[1 mark]***
Solution: $b = 45$, $g = 99$
[6 marks available in total — as above]
You might have started with $\frac{b}{b+g} = \frac{5}{16}$ and $\frac{b-3}{b+g-4} = \frac{3}{10}$ and used these to form simultaneous equations instead.

Page 20: Direct and Inverse Proportion (1)

1 1 t-shirt will take: 3 m² ÷ 5 = 0.6 m² of cotton ***[1 mark]***
85 t-shirts will take: 0.6 m² × 85 = 51 m² of cotton ***[1 mark]***
1 m² of cotton costs: £5.50 ÷ 2 = £2.75
[1 mark]
51 m² of cotton costs £2.75 × 51 = £140.25
[1 mark]
[4 marks available in total — as above]
There are other methods you could use to get this answer — as long as it's right, and your working makes sense, you'll get the marks.

2 a) 1 litre of petrol will keep 8 go-karts going for:
20 ÷ 12 = 1.666... minutes ***[1 mark]***
18 litres of petrol will keep 8 go-karts going for:
1.666... × 18 = 30 minutes ***[1 mark]***
18 litres of petrol will keep 1 go-kart going for:
30 × 8 = 240 minutes ***[1 mark]***
18 litres of petrol will keep 6 go-karts going for:
240 ÷ 6 = 40 minutes ***[1 mark]***
[4 marks available in total — as above]
Again, you might have done this in a slightly different way.

b) In 1 minute, 8 go-karts will use
12 ÷ 20 = 0.6 litres ***[1 mark]***
In 45 minutes, 8 go-karts will use
0.6 × 45 = 27 litres ***[1 mark]***
27 litres of petrol cost:
£1.37 × 27 = £36.99 ***[1 mark]***
[3 marks available in total — as above]

3 $h \propto S^2$, so $h = kS^2$ ***[1 mark]***
When $h = 35$ and $S = 50$, $35 = k \times 50^2$,
so $k = 35 \div 50^2 = 0.014$ ***[1 mark]***
So $h = 0.014S^2$
$h = 0.014S^2$ so when $S = 40$,
$h = 0.014 \times 40^2 = 22.4$ ***[1 mark]***
[3 marks available in total — as above]

Page 21: Direct and Inverse Proportion (2)

1

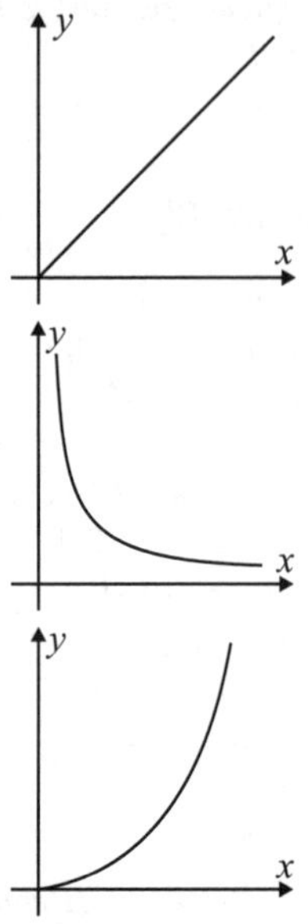

[3 marks available — 1 mark for each correct graph]

2 $f \propto \frac{1}{d^2}$, so $f = \frac{k}{d^2}$ ***[1 mark]***
When $d = 100$ and $f = 20$, $20 = \frac{k}{100^2}$,
so $k = 20 \times 100^2 = 200\,000$ ***[1 mark]***
$f = \frac{200\,000}{d^2}$
When $d = 800$, $f = \frac{200\,000}{800^2} = 0.3125$
[1 mark]
[3 marks available in total — as above]

3 a) 2 farmers will shear 30 sheep in 60 minutes, so 1 farmer will shear 30 sheep in 60 × 2 = 120 minutes
[1 mark]
1 farmer will shear 1 sheep in
120 ÷ 30 = 4 minutes ***[1 mark]***
1 farmer will shear 1 × (80 ÷ 4) =
20 sheep in 80 minutes ***[1 mark]***
3 farmers will shear 20 × 3 =
60 sheep in 80 minutes ***[1 mark]***
[4 marks available in total — as above]
This is another one where you don't have to do it exactly how it's shown here. Remember to make your working clear, though.

b) 1 farmer will shear 1 sheep in 4 minutes, so if $t = ks$ then $t = 4s$ ***[1 mark]***
The time taken is indirectly proportional to the number of farmers, so $t = \frac{4s}{f}$ ***[1 mark]***
[2 marks available in total — as above]
Check your answer by putting in the numbers from the question and your answer to part a) to make sure the formula works.

Pages 22-24: Percentages

1 20% = 20 ÷ 100 = 0.2 so multiplier = 1 + 0.2 = 1.2
£927 × 1.2 = £1112.40
[2 marks available — 1 mark for a correct method, 1 mark for the correct answer]

2 For every 2 grapes there are 5 cherries so there are $\frac{2}{5}$ = 40% as many grapes as cherries. ***[1 mark]***

3 £15 714 = 108%
£15 714 ÷ 108 = £145.50 = 1% ***[1 mark]***
£145.50 × 100 = 100% ***[1 mark]***
= £14 550 ***[1 mark]***
[3 marks available in total — as above]

4 £41 865 – £10 000 = £31 865
20% = 20 ÷ 100 = 0.2
20% of £31 865 = 0.2 × £31 865 = £6373 ***[1 mark]***
£45 000 – £41 865 = £3135
40% = 40 ÷ 100 = 0.4
40% of £3135 = 0.4 × £3135 = £1254 ***[1 mark]***
£6373 + £1254 = £7627
(£7627 ÷ £45 000) × 100 ***[1 mark]***
= 16.948... = 16.9% (1 d.p.) ***[1 mark]***
[4 marks available in total — as above]

5 12% = 12 ÷ 100 = 0.12 so multiplier = 1 – 0.12 = 0.88
After one month: 17 500 × 0.88 = 15 400
After two months: 15 400 × 0.88 = 13 552
After three months:
13 552 × 0.88 = 11 925.76
= 11 900 to the nearest hundred
[3 marks available — 1 mark for finding the multiplier, 1 mark for applying the multiplier three times, 1 mark for the correct answer]
You could also use the 'handy formula' for harder compound percentage change questions to solve this one.

6 £32 is a 60% profit so £32 = 160% of cost price ***[1 mark]***
1% of cost price = £32 ÷ 160 = £0.20 ***[1 mark]***
He wants an 88% profit = 188% of cost price
188% = £0.20 × 188 = £37.60 ***[1 mark]***
[3 marks available in total — as above]

7 a) Original price = £180, change in price = £5.40
Percentage increase = $\frac{£5.40}{£180}$ × 100
= 3%
[2 marks available — 1 mark for using the correct formula, 1 mark for the correct answer]

b) Buying tickets in 1 transaction:
(3 × £180) + £5.40 = £545.40
Buying tickets in 3 transactions:
(£180 + £5.40) × 3 = £556.20
Decrease in cost = £556.20 – £545.40 = £10.80 ***[1 mark]***
You could have found this by working out that the extra charges they avoided = 2 × £5.40 = £10.80. As long as your method's clear and makes sense, you'll get marks for it.
Percentage decrease = $\frac{£10.80}{£556.20}$ × 100 ***[1 mark]***
= 1.9417... % = 1.94% (2 d.p.)
[1 mark]
[3 marks available in total — as above]
Careful here — the percentage saving is actually a percentage change, where the change is the saving and the original amount is the cost of the three separate transactions.

c) Amount borrowed = £180 + £5.40 = £185.40 ***[1 mark]***
APR = 18% = 0.18 so multiplier = 1.18 ***[1 mark]***
Amount to pay back = 185.40 × 1.18 = 218.772
= £218.77 ***[1 mark]***
[3 marks available in total — as above]

8 A ratio of 3 : 7 means that 3 out of 10 = 30% of the customers were children.
60% of 30% = 0.6 × 30% = 18% were blond-haired children.
100% – 30% = 70% were adults.
20% of 70% = 0.2 × 70% = 14% were blond-haired adults.
So, 18% + 14% = 32% of the customers had blond hair.
[4 marks available — 1 mark for finding the total number of parts in the ratio, 1 mark for finding blond-haired children percentage, 1 mark for finding blond-haired adults percentage, 1 mark for the correct answer]

9 a) Original area of triangular face = $\frac{1}{2} \times x \times x = 0.5x^2$ cm²
Area after increase = $\frac{1}{2} \times 1.15x \times 1.15x$
$= 0.66125x^2$ cm²
[1 mark]
Change in area = $0.66125x^2 - 0.5x^2 = 0.16125x^2$ cm² ***[1 mark]***
Percentage increase = $\frac{0.16125x^2}{0.5x^2}$ × 100 ***[1 mark]*** = 32.25% ***[1 mark]***
[4 marks available in total — as above]
Alternatively, you could have found the new area by doing $0.5 \times 1.15x \times 1.15x = 1.15^2 \times 0.5x^2 = 1.3225 \times$ original area, which means the percentage change is 32.25%.

b) Let ay cm be the length of the new prism.
Volume of new prism = $0.66125x^2 \times ay$ ***[1 mark]***
Volume of original prism = $0.5x^2y$ cm³
The prisms have the same volume so:
$0.66125x^2 \times ay = 0.5x^2y$ ***[1 mark]***
$a = \frac{0.5x^2y}{0.66125x^2y}$
a = 0.7561... ***[1 mark]***
So the length of the new prism is (0.7561... × y) cm
(1 – 0.7561) × 100 ***[1 mark]***
= 24.3856...%
= 24.4% decrease (1 d.p.) ***[1 mark]***
[5 marks available in total — as above]
In both parts of this question, you had to cancel some variables in the fraction. Remember, variables can cancel out just like numbers — if you've got the same variable on the top and bottom of the fraction, you can make it disappear as if by magic.

Pages 25-26: Compound Growth and Decay

1 Multiplier = 1 + 0.06 = 1.06 ***[1 mark]***
In 3 years she will owe:
£750 × (1.06)³ = £893.262
= £893.26 (to the nearest penny) ***[1 mark]***
[2 marks available in total — as above]

2 a) Multiplier = 1 – 0.08 = 0.92 ***[1 mark]***
Population after 15 years = 2000 × (0.92)¹⁵ = 572.59... ≈ 573 fish ***[1 mark]***
[2 marks available in total — as above]
It'll take more than 15 years for the population to get down to 572 fish, so you need to round up (the population hasn't dropped to 572 yet so there are still 573).

b) Find how the population changes each year:
$2000 \times 0.92 = 1840$
$2000 \times 0.92^2 = 1692.8$
$2000 \times 0.92^3 = 1557.376$
$2000 \times 0.92^4 = 1432.78592 < 1500$
Population is less than 1500 after 4 years.
[3 marks available — 1 mark for the correct method of calculating 2000×0.92^n for increasing values of n, 1 mark for at least three values correctly calculated, 1 mark for correct answer]

3 $5000 \times 0.16 = 800$ trees are planted in 2013 ***[1 mark]***
A maximum of $800 \times 0.75 = 600$ trees are cut down
At the end of 2013 there is a minimum of $5000 + (800 - 600) = 5200$ pine trees ***[1 mark]***
$5200 \times 0.16 = 832$ trees are planted in 2014 ***[1 mark]***
A maximum of $832 \times 0.75 = 624$ trees are cut down
At the end of 2014 there is a minimum of $5200 + (832 - 624) = 5408$ pine trees ***[1 mark]***
[4 marks available in total — as above]
If you used a different method here, you'd still get full marks if you got the final answer right.

4 a) Compound Collector Account:
Multiplier = 1 + 0.055 = 1.055 ***[1 mark]***
£10 000 × $(1.055)^5$ = £13 069.60 (2 d.p.) ***[1 mark]***
Simple Saver Account:
6.2% of £10 000 = 0.062 × £10 000 = £620 ***[1 mark]***
5 × £620 = £3100
£10 000 + £3100 = £13 100 so the Simple Saver Account will have the biggest balance after 5 years. ***[1 mark]***
[4 marks available in total — as above]

b) E.g. He might want to deposit more money during the 5 years and he can't with the Simple Saver Account. ***[1 mark]***

5 £2704 = £2500 × $(\text{Multiplier})^2$ ***[1 mark]***
$\frac{£2704}{£2500} = (\text{Multiplier})^2$
Multiplier $= \sqrt{\frac{£2704}{£2500}} = 1.04$ ***[1 mark]***
Interest rate = 1.04 – 1 = 0.04 = 4% ***[1 mark]***
[3 marks available in total — as above]

6 Multiplier = 1 – 0.25 = 0.75 ***[1 mark]***
If N_0 is the original amount,
$N_0 \times (0.75)^{35-31} = 2\,000\,000$ ***[1 mark]***
$N_0 = 2\,000\,000 \div 0.75^4 = 6\,320\,987.654...$
= £6 300 000 (to the nearest £100 000) ***[1 mark]***
[3 marks available in total — as above]

Section Three — Algebra

Page 27: Algebra Basics

1 Area $= 20 \times a \times b = 20ab$ cm² ***[1 mark]***

2
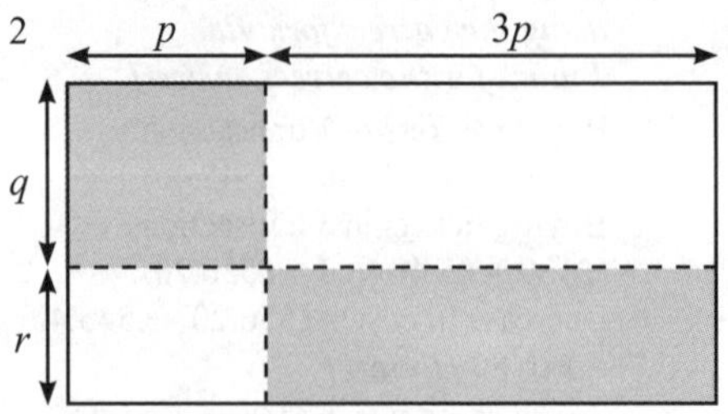

[1 mark]

3 Height $= 7 \times (f + g) + 9 \times (h - g) + 5 \times 2h$ ***[1 mark]***
$= 7f + 7g + 9h - 9g + 10h$
$= 7f - 2g + 19h$ cm ***[1 mark]***
[2 marks available in total — as above]

4 Perimeter of rectangle =
$4x + 3 + 4x + 3 + 5x - 9 + 5x - 9$
$= 18x - 12$ cm ***[1 mark]***.
So perimeter of hexagon $= 18x - 12$ cm.
Hexagon side length $= (18x - 12) \div 6$ ***[1 mark]***
$= 3x - 2$ cm ***[1 mark]***.
[3 marks available in total — as above]

Page 28: Multiplying Out Brackets

1 a) $5p(6 - 2p) = 30p - 10p^2$
[2 marks available — 1 mark for each term]

b) $(2t - 5)(3t + 4) = (2t \times 3t) + (2t \times 4) + (-5 \times 3t) + (-5 \times 4)$
$= 6t^2 + 8t - 15t - 20$ ***[1 mark]***
$= 6t^2 - 7t - 20$ ***[1 mark]***
[2 marks available in total — as above]

2 $4(5x - 7) + 6(4 - 2x) = 20x - 28 + 24 - 12x$
$= 8x - 4 = 4(2x - 1)$
So $a = 4$, $b = 2$ and $c = -1$
[3 marks available — 1 mark for each correct value]

3 Area = ½ × base × height
$= \frac{1}{2}(3x + 5y)(2x - 4y)$ ***[1 mark]***
$= \frac{1}{2} \times (6x^2 - 2xy - 20y^2)$ ***[1 mark]***
$= 3x^2 - xy - 10y^2$ ***[1 mark]***
[3 marks available in total — as above]
You could have instead multiplied (2x – 4y) by ½ first of all. The area would then just be (3x + 5y)(x – 2y), which is a bit simpler to multiply out.

4 a) It means the relationship is an identity, so it is true for all values of a and b. ***[1 mark]***

b) $2(3 - x)(6 - 2x) = (6 - 2x)(6 - 2x)$
$= (6 - 2x)^2$ ***[1 mark]***
$= 6^2 - 2 \times 6 \times 2x + (2x)^2$ ***[1 mark]***
$= 36 - 24x + 4x^2$ $(= 4x^2 - 24x + 36)$ ***[1 mark]***
[3 marks available in total — as above]

Page 29: Factorising

1 a) $7y - 21y^2 = 7(y - 3y^2) = 7y(1 - 3y)$
[2 marks available — 1 mark for each correct factor]

b) $2v^3w + 8v^2w^2 = 2(v^3w + 4v^2w^2)$
$= 2v^2w(v + 4w)$
[2 marks available — 1 mark for each correct factor]

2 a) $x^2 - 16 = x^2 - 4^2 = (x + 4)(x - 4)$
[1 mark]

b) $x^2 - 121y^2 = (x + 11y)(x - 11y)$
[1 mark]

c) $9n^2 - 4m^2 = (3n)^2 - (2m)^2$
$= (3n + 2m)(3n - 2m)$
[2 marks available — 1 mark for each correct factor]

3 $x^3 - 25x = x(x^2 - 25) = x(x + 5)(x - 5)$
[3 marks available — 1 mark for each correct factor]

Page 30: Powers

1 $\frac{1}{25}$ ***[1 mark]***

2 a) $a^5 \times a^{-3} = a^{5+(-3)} = a^2$ ***[1 mark]***

b) $(d^9)^2 = d^{9 \times 2} = d^{18}$ ***[1 mark]***
so $\frac{(d^9)^2}{d^4} = \frac{d^{18}}{d^4} = d^{18-4} = d^{14}$ ***[1 mark]***
[2 marks available in total — as above]

3 a) $3^0 = 1$ ***[1 mark]***

b) $\left(\frac{5}{4}\right)^{-2} = \left(\frac{4}{5}\right)^2$ ***[1 mark]***
$= \frac{16}{25}$ ***[1 mark]***
[2 marks available in total — as above]

4 a) $3a^3 \times 2ab^2 = (3 \times 2) \times (a^3 \times a) \times b^2$
$= 6a^4b^2$
[2 marks available — 1 mark for correct working, 1 mark for the correct answer]

b) $\frac{4a^5b^3}{2ab^2} = (4 \div 2) \times (a^5 \div a) \times (b^3 \div b^2)$
$= 2a^4b$
[2 marks available — 1 mark for correct working, 1 mark for the correct answer]

c) $\left(\frac{3a^2b^2 \times (b^{-1})^2}{2a^3}\right)^{-2} = \left(\frac{3b^{2-2}}{2a^{3-2}}\right)^{-2} = \left(\frac{3}{2a}\right)^{-2}$
$= \left(\frac{2a}{3}\right)^2 = \frac{4a^2}{9}$
[3 marks available — 1 mark for correct working to simplify the fraction within the brackets, 1 mark for correct simplification of fraction within the brackets, 1 mark for correct answer]
You don't need to work this out exactly the way it's shown here — as long as each step and the final answer are right, you'll get full marks. Make sure you use the BODMAS rules, though.

Page 31: Powers and Roots

1 $y^{-3} = \frac{1}{y^3}$, $y^1 = y$, $y^0 = 1$, $y^{\frac{1}{3}} = \sqrt[3]{y}$,
so the correct order is...
y^{-3} y^0 $y^{\frac{1}{3}}$ y^1 y^3
[2 marks available — 2 marks for all 5 in the correct order, otherwise 1 mark for any 4 in the correct relative order.]
If you can't identify which term is the smallest just by looking at them, try substituting a value for y into all the expressions and working out the answer. Then it'll be easy to tell which is the smallest.

2 $8^{\frac{4}{3}} = (8^{\frac{1}{3}})^4 = (2)^4 = 16$
[2 marks available — 1 mark for correct working, 1 mark for the correct final answer.]

3 a) $(64x^2)^{\frac{1}{3}} = \sqrt[3]{64} \times x^{(2\times\frac{1}{3})} = 4x^{\frac{2}{3}}$
[2 marks available — 1 mark for correct working, 1 mark for the correct final answer]

b) $\left(\frac{4}{y}\right)^{-\frac{1}{2}} = \left(\frac{y}{4}\right)^{\frac{1}{2}} = \sqrt{\frac{y}{4}} = \frac{\sqrt{y}}{2}$
[2 marks available — 1 mark for correct working, 1 mark for the correct final answer]

4 $(9a^4)^{\frac{1}{2}} = \sqrt{9a^4} = 3a^2$ ***[1 mark]***
$\frac{2ab^2}{6a^3b} = \frac{2}{6} \times \frac{a}{a^3} \times \frac{b^2}{b} = \frac{1}{3} \times \frac{1}{a^2} \times b$
$= \frac{b}{3a^2}$ ***[1 mark]***
so $(9a^4)^{\frac{1}{2}} \times \frac{2ab^2}{6a^3b} = 3a^2 \times \frac{b}{3a^2} = b$
[1 mark]
[3 marks available in total — as above]

5 $64^{\frac{1}{3}} = \sqrt[3]{64} = 4$ ***[1 mark]***
$4^{-2} = \frac{1}{4^2} = \frac{1}{16}$ ***[1 mark]***
so $64^{\frac{1}{3}} \times 4^{-2} = 4 \times \frac{1}{16} = \frac{4}{16} = \frac{1}{4}$ or 0.25
[1 mark]
[3 marks available in total — as above]

Page 32: Manipulating Surds

1 $(2+\sqrt{3})(5-\sqrt{3}) =$
$(2 \times 5) + (2 \times -\sqrt{3}) + (\sqrt{3} \times 5)$
$+ (\sqrt{3} \times -\sqrt{3})$
$= 10 - 2\sqrt{3} + 5\sqrt{3} - 3$
$= 7 + 3\sqrt{3}$
[2 marks available — 1 mark for correct working, 1 mark for the correct answer]

2 a) $\frac{\sqrt{54}}{\sqrt{3}} = \sqrt{54 \div 3} = \sqrt{18} = \sqrt{9} \times \sqrt{2} = 3\sqrt{2}$
[1 mark]

b) $2\sqrt{50} = 2\sqrt{25 \times 2} = 2 \times 5\sqrt{2}$
$= 10\sqrt{2}$
$(\sqrt{2})^3 = \sqrt{2} \times \sqrt{2} \times \sqrt{2}$
$= (\sqrt{2})^2 \times \sqrt{2} = 2\sqrt{2}$
So $2\sqrt{50} - (\sqrt{2})^3 = 10\sqrt{2} - 2\sqrt{2}$
$= 8\sqrt{2}$
[2 marks available — 2 marks for the correct answer, otherwise 1 mark for correctly simplifying either surd]

3 $\sqrt{396} = \sqrt{36 \times 11} = 6\sqrt{11}$ ***[1 mark]***
$\frac{22}{\sqrt{11}} = \frac{22\sqrt{11}}{11} = 2\sqrt{11}$ ***[1 mark]***
$\sqrt{44} = \sqrt{4 \times 11} = 2\sqrt{11}$
So $\frac{220}{\sqrt{44}} = \frac{220}{2\sqrt{11}} = \frac{220\sqrt{11}}{22} = 10\sqrt{11}$
[1 mark]
So $\sqrt{396} + \frac{22}{\sqrt{11}} - \frac{220}{\sqrt{44}} =$
$6\sqrt{11} + 2\sqrt{11} - 10\sqrt{11}$
$= -2\sqrt{11}$ ***[1 mark]***
[4 marks available in total — as above]

4 a) $\frac{33}{\sqrt{11}} = \frac{33 \times \sqrt{11}}{\sqrt{11} \times \sqrt{11}} = \frac{33\sqrt{11}}{11} = 3\sqrt{11}$
[1 mark]

b) $\frac{1+\sqrt{7}}{3-\sqrt{7}} = \frac{(1+\sqrt{7})(3+\sqrt{7})}{(3-\sqrt{7})(3+\sqrt{7})}$ ***[1 mark]***
$= \frac{3+\sqrt{7}+3\sqrt{7}+7}{9-7}$ ***[1 mark]***
$= \frac{10+4\sqrt{7}}{2}$ ***[1 mark]***
$= 5 + 2\sqrt{7}$ ***[1 mark]***
[4 marks available in total — as above]

Pages 33-34: Solving Equations

1 Let the number of points Felix scores be x. Then Poppy scores $2x$ points and Alexi scores $(2x + 25)$ points,
so $x + 2x + (2x + 25) = 700$ ***[1 mark]***
$5x + 25 = 700$
$5x = 675$ ***[1 mark]***
$x = 135$ ***[1 mark]***
So Felix scores 135 points, Poppy scores $2 \times 135 = 270$ points and Alexi scores $(2 \times 135) + 25$ points $= 295$ points.
[1 mark]
[4 marks available in total — as above]

2 $\frac{5}{4}(2c - 1) = 3c - 2$
$5(2c - 1) = 4(3c - 2)$ ***[1 mark]***
$(5 \times 2c) + (5 \times -1) = (4 \times 3c) + (4 \times -2)$
$10c - 5 = 12c - 8$
$12c - 10c = 8 - 5$ ***[1 mark]***
$2c = 3$ so $c = \frac{3}{2}$ or 1.5 ***[1 mark]***
So one side of the triangle measures
$3(1.5) - 2 = 2.5$ cm ***[1 mark]***
[4 marks available in total — as above]

3 If Neil worked h hours, Liam worked $(h + 30)$ hours.
$360 \div 4.5 = 80$
$80 = h + (h + 30) = 2h + 30$
$50 = 2h$, so $h = 25$
Neil worked 25 hours and Liam worked $(25 + 30) = 55$ hours.
[3 marks available — 1 mark for forming an equation for the total number of hours, 1 mark for solving the equation to find h, 1 mark for finding the number of hours each boy worked]

4 a) $\frac{28 - z}{4} = 5$
$28 - z = 20$
$z = 28 - 20$
$z = 8$
[2 marks available — 1 mark for multiplying both sides by 4, 1 mark for correct answer]

b) $5x^2 = 180$
$x^2 = 36$ ***[1 mark]***
$x = \pm 6$ ***[1 mark]***
[2 marks available in total — as above]

c) $\frac{8 - 2x}{3} + \frac{2x + 4}{9} = 12$
$\frac{3 \times 9(8 - 2x)}{3} + \frac{3 \times 9(2x + 4)}{9}$
$= 3 \times 9 \times 12$
$9(8 - 2x) + 3(2x + 4) = 324$
$72 - 18x + 6x + 12 = 324$
$18x - 6x = 72 + 12 - 324$
$12x = -240$ so $x = -20$
[4 marks available — 2 marks for rearranging to remove the fractions, 1 mark for rearranging to get all x-terms on one side, 1 mark for correct answer]

d) $\frac{3 - 5x}{2} - \frac{4x - 7}{5} = -\frac{21}{3}$
$\frac{2 \times 5(3 - 5x)}{2} - \frac{2 \times 5(4x - 7)}{5}$
$= -7 \times 2 \times 5$
$5(3 - 5x) - 2(4x - 7) = -70$
$15 - 25x - 8x + 14 = -70$
$15 + 14 + 70 = 25x + 8x$
$33x = 99$ so $x = 3$
[4 marks available — 2 marks for rearranging to remove the fractions, 1 mark for rearranging to get all x-terms on one side, 1 mark for correct answer]

5 If one number is x, the other number is $3x$.
$3x^2 = 147$ ***[1 mark]***,
so $x^2 = 49$, which means that $x = 7$ (as $x > 0$) ***[1 mark]*** and $3x = 21$ ***[1 mark]***,
so Hassan is thinking of 7 and 21.
[3 marks available in total — as above]

Page 35: Trial and Improvement

1 E.g.

x	$x^3 + 4x$	
2	$2^3 + (4 \times 2) = 8 + 8 = 16$	Too small
3	$3^3 + (4 \times 3) = 27 + 12 = 39$	Too big
2.5	$2.5^3 + (4 \times 2.5) = 25.625$	Too big
2.3	$2.3^3 + (4 \times 2.3) = 21.367$	Too small
2.4	$2.4^3 + (4 \times 2.4) = 23.424$	Too small
2.45	$2.45^3 + (4 \times 2.45) = 24.506...$	Too big

So the solution is between $x = 2.4$ and $x = 2.45$, so to 1 d.p. the solution is $x = 2.4$
[4 marks available — 1 mark for any trial between 2 and 3, 1 mark for any trial between 2.4 and 2.5 inclusive, 1 mark for a different trial between 2.43 and 2.45 inclusive, 1 mark for the correct final answer]

2 E.g.

x	$x^2(x + 1)$	Notes
3	36	too small
4	80	too big
3.5	55.125	too small
3.7	64.343	too big
3.6	59.616	too small
3.65	61.949...	too small

The solution is between $x = 3.7$ and $x = 3.65$, so to 1 d.p. the solution is $x = 3.7$

[4 marks available — 1 mark for any trial between the initial values chosen, 2 further marks for correct next steps in the trial and improvement method, 1 mark for the correct final answer]

Pages 36-37: Rearranging Formulas

1 a) $y = \frac{x-2}{3}$, so $3y = x - 2$ and $x = 3y + 2$

[2 marks available — 1 mark for multiplying both sides by 3, 1 mark for the correct answer.]

b) When $y = 5$, $x = (3 \times 5) + 2$
$= 15 + 2 = 17$

[2 marks available — 1 mark for correct substitution, 1 mark for the correct answer.]

2 a) $V = \frac{1}{3}Ah$, so $3V = Ah$ and $h = \frac{3V}{A}$

[2 marks available — 1 mark for multiplying both sides by 3, 1 mark for the correct answer.]

b) When $V = 18$ and $A = 12$,
$h = \frac{3 \times 18}{12} = \frac{54}{12} = 4.5$ cm

[2 marks available — 1 mark for correct substitution, 1 mark for the correct answer.]

3 a) $F = \frac{9}{5}C + 32$,
so $\frac{9}{5}C = F - 32$ and $C = \frac{5}{9}(F - 32)$

[2 marks available — 1 mark for subtracting 32 from each side, 1 mark for the correct answer.]

b) When $F = 41$, $C = \frac{5}{9}(41 - 32) = \frac{5}{9}(9)$
$= 5$ °C

[2 marks available — 1 mark for correct substitution, 1 mark for the correct answer.]

4 $s = \frac{1}{2}gt^2$, so $gt^2 = 2s$ ***[1 mark]***,
$t^2 = \frac{2s}{g}$ ***[1 mark]***,
$t = \sqrt{\frac{2s}{g}}$ ***[1 mark]***

[3 marks available in total — as above]

5 $a + y = \frac{b-y}{a}$, so...
$a(a + y) = b - y$ ***[1 mark]***, $a^2 + ay = b - y$,
$ay + y = b - a^2$ ***[1 mark]***, $y(a + 1) = b - a^2$ ***[1 mark]***,
$y = \frac{b-a^2}{a+1}$ ***[1 mark]***

[4 marks available in total — as above]

6 $x = \sqrt{\frac{(1+n)}{(1-n)}}$, so $x^2 = \frac{(1+n)}{(1-n)}$ ***[1 mark]***,
$x^2(1 - n) = 1 + n$,
$x^2 - x^2n = 1 + n$ ***[1 mark]***,
$x^2 - 1 = n + x^2n$ ***[1 mark]***,
$x^2 - 1 = n(1 + x^2)$ ***[1 mark]***,
$n = \frac{x^2-1}{1+x^2}$ ***[1 mark]***

[5 marks available in total — as above]

7 a) The amount that Pearse paid is given by $\frac{2}{3}T$ ***[1 mark]***
The amount that Marek paid is $4.5 + 0.5d$
If Marek paid twice as much as Pearse, then $4.5 + 0.5d = 2 \times \frac{2}{3}T$,
so $4.5 + 0.5d = \frac{4T}{3}$ ***[1 mark]***

[2 marks available in total — as above]

b) $4.5 + 0.5d = \frac{4T}{3}$, so $0.5d = \frac{4T}{3} - 4.5$
and $d = 2(\frac{4T}{3} - 4.5) = \frac{8T}{3} - 9$
When $T = 22.5$, $d = \frac{8 \times 22.5}{3} - 9$
$= 51$ miles

[3 marks available — 1 mark for correctly rearranging the equation, 1 mark for correctly substituting T = 22.5, 1 mark for the correct answer.]

Page 38: Factorising Quadratics (1)

1 $x^2 + 9x + 18 = (x + 3)(x + 6)$

[2 marks available — 1 mark for correct numbers in brackets, 1 mark for correct signs]

The brackets can be either way around — $(x + 6)(x + 3)$ is also correct.

2 $y^2 - 4y - 5 = (y + 1)(y - 5)$

[2 marks available — 1 mark for correct numbers in brackets, 1 mark for correct signs]

3 a) $x^2 - 9x + 20 = (x - 4)(x - 5)$

[2 marks available — 1 mark for correct numbers in brackets, 1 mark for correct signs]

b) $x - 4 = 0$ or $x - 5 = 0$
$x = 4$ or $x = 5$

[1 mark for both solutions correct]

4 $x^2 + 4x - 12 = 0$
$(x + 6)(x - 2) = 0$

[1 mark for correct numbers in brackets, 1 mark for correct signs]

$x + 6 = 0$ or $x - 2 = 0$
$x = -6$ or $x = 2$

[1 mark for both solutions]
[3 marks available in total — as above]

5 Let the two consecutive even numbers be $2n$ and $2n + 2$.
$2n(2n + 2) = 288$ ***[1 mark]***
$4n^2 + 4n = 288$
$4n^2 + 4n - 288 = 0$
$n^2 + n - 72 = 0$
$(n + 9)(n - 8) = 0$ ***[1 mark]***,
so $n = -9$ or $n = 8$.
The numbers are positive, so $n = 8$ ***[1 mark]***.
The larger of the two numbers is $2(8) + 2 = 18$ ***[1 mark]***.

[4 marks available in total — as above]

Page 39: Factorising Quadratics (2)

1 a) $2x^2 + x - 28 = (2x - 7)(x + 4)$

[2 marks available — 1 mark for correct numbers in brackets, 1 mark for correct signs]

b) $5x^2 - 19x + 18 = (5x - 9)(x - 2)$

[2 marks available — 1 mark for correct numbers in brackets, 1 mark for correct signs]

2 a) $3x^2 + 16x - 12 = 0$
$(3x - 2)(x + 6) = 0$

[1 mark for correct numbers in brackets, 1 mark for correct signs]

$3x - 2 = 0$ or $x + 6 = 0$
$x = \frac{2}{3}$ or $x = -6$

[1 mark for both solutions]
[3 marks available in total — as above]

b) $2x^2 - 7x + 3 = -3$
$2x^2 - 7x + 6 = 0$
$(2x - 3)(x - 2) = 0$

[1 mark for correct numbers in brackets, 1 mark for correct signs]

$2x - 3 = 0$ or $x - 2 = 0$
$x = \frac{3}{2}$ or $x = 2$

[1 mark for both solutions]
[3 marks available in total — as above]

3 a) The area of the square is $(x + 3)(x + 3)$
$= x^2 + 6x + 9$ ***[1 mark]***.
The area of the triangle is
$\frac{1}{2}(2x + 2)(x + 3)$
$= \frac{1}{2}(2x^2 + 6x + 2x + 6)$
$= \frac{1}{2}(2x^2 + 8x + 6)$
$= x^2 + 4x + 3$ ***[1 mark]***
So the area of the whole shape is
$x^2 + 6x + 9 + x^2 + 4x + 3$
$= 2x^2 + 10x + 12$ ***[1 mark]***
$2x^2 + 10x + 12 = 60$,
so $2x^2 + 10x - 48 = 0$ ***[1 mark]***

[4 marks available in total — as above]

b) $2x^2 + 10x - 48 = 0$
$(2x - 6)(x + 8) = 0$ ***[1 mark]***
$2x - 6 = 0$ or $x + 8 = 0$
$x = 3$ or $x = -8$

[1 mark for both solutions]

A length can't have a negative value so the answer must be $x = 3$ ***[1 mark]***

[3 marks available in total — as above]

Page 40: The Quadratic Formula

1 a = 1, b = 5 and c = 3

$x = \frac{-5 \pm \sqrt{5^2 - 4 \times 1 \times 3}}{2 \times 1} = \frac{-5 \pm \sqrt{13}}{2}$

$x = -0.70$ or $x = -4.30$

[3 marks available — 1 mark for correct substitution, 1 mark for each correct solution]

2 a = 2, b = –7 and c = 2

$x = \frac{-(-7) \pm \sqrt{(-7)^2 - 4 \times 2 \times 2}}{2 \times 2}$

$= \frac{7 \pm \sqrt{33}}{4}$

$x = 3.19$ or $x = 0.31$

[3 marks available — 1 mark for correct substitution, 1 mark for each correct solution]

3 a = 3, b = –2 and c = –4

$x = \frac{-(-2) \pm \sqrt{(-2)^2 - 4 \times 3 \times -4}}{2 \times 3}$

$= \frac{2 \pm \sqrt{52}}{6} = \frac{2 \pm 2\sqrt{13}}{6}$

$x = 1.54$ or $x = -0.869$ (3 s.f.)

[3 marks available — 1 mark for correct substitution, 1 mark for each correct solution]

4 $(x + 3)(3x + 3) = 30$

$3x^2 + 12x + 9 = 30$

$3x^2 + 12x - 21 = 0$

$x^2 + 4x - 7 = 0$

a = 1, b = 4 and c = –7

$x = \frac{-4 \pm \sqrt{4^2 - 4 \times 1 \times -7}}{2 \times 1} = \frac{-4 \pm \sqrt{44}}{2}$

$= \frac{-4 \pm 2\sqrt{11}}{2} = -2 \pm \sqrt{11}$

Lengths cannot be negative,

so $x = -2 + \sqrt{11}$.

So the longer side is $3(-2 + \sqrt{11}) + 3$

= 6.9 cm (1 d.p.)

[5 marks available — 1 mark for setting up the quadratic equation, 1 mark for the correct substitution, 1 mark for solving the quadratic equation, 1 mark for choosing the correct value of x, 1 mark for the correct answer]

Page 41: Algebraic Fractions (1)

1 a) $\frac{6-2x}{4} - \frac{5-6x}{6} = \frac{3(6-2x)}{3 \times 4} - \frac{2(5-6x)}{2 \times 6}$

$= \frac{18-6x}{12} - \frac{10-12x}{12}$

$= \frac{18-6x-10+12x}{12} = \frac{8+6x}{12} = \frac{3x+4}{6}$

[3 marks available — 1 mark for making the denominators the same, 1 mark for collecting like terms, 1 mark for simplifying the fraction to give the final answer]

b) $\frac{2}{p} + \frac{4q}{r} = \frac{2r}{pr} + \frac{4qp}{rp}$

$= \frac{2r + 4pq}{pr}$

$= \frac{2(r + 2pq)}{pr}$

[2 marks available — 1 mark for making the denominators the same, 1 mark for the correct final answer]

c)

$\frac{2x+6}{3} + \frac{4-2x}{5} - \frac{x-5}{4}$

$= \frac{5 \times 4(2x+6)}{3 \times 5 \times 4} + \frac{3 \times 4(4-2x)}{3 \times 5 \times 4} - \frac{3 \times 5(x-5)}{3 \times 5 \times 4}$

$= \frac{40x+120}{60} + \frac{48-24x}{60} - \frac{15x-75}{60}$

$= \frac{40x+120+48-24x-15x+75}{60} = \frac{x+243}{60}$

[2 marks available — 1 mark for making the denominators the same, 1 mark for the correct final answer]

2 a) $\frac{3x-12}{x^2-16} = \frac{3(x-4)}{(x+4)(x-4)} = \frac{3}{x+4}$

[3 marks available — 1 mark for correctly factorising the denominator, 1 mark for correctly factorising the numerator, 1 mark for the correct answer]

b) $\frac{x^2-4}{x^2+8x+12} = \frac{(x+2)(x-2)}{(x+2)(x+6)} = \frac{x-2}{x+6}$

[3 marks available — 1 mark for correctly factorising the denominator, 1 mark for correctly factorising the numerator, 1 mark for the correct answer]

3 a) $\frac{x^2}{3x} \times \frac{6}{x+1} = \frac{6x^2}{3x(x+1)} = \frac{2x}{x+1}$

[2 marks available — 1 mark for correct multiplication, 1 mark for the correct answer]

b) $\frac{10x}{3+x} \div \frac{4}{5(3+x)} = \frac{10x}{3+x} \times \frac{5(3+x)}{4} =$

$\frac{50x(3+x)}{4(3+x)} = \frac{50x}{4} = \frac{25x}{2}$

[3 marks available — 1 mark for converting to a multiplication, 1 mark for correct multiplication, 1 mark for correct answer]

Page 42: Algebraic Fractions (2)

1 $\frac{4x^2+10x-6}{16x^2-4} = \frac{(4x-2)(x+3)}{(4x-2)(4x+2)} = \frac{x+3}{4x+2}$

[3 marks available — 1 mark for correctly factorising the denominator, 1 mark for correctly factorising the numerator, 1 mark for the correct answer]

2 $\frac{2}{3} + \frac{m-2n}{m+3n} = \frac{2(m+3n)}{3(m+3n)} + \frac{3(m-2n)}{3(m+3n)} =$

$\frac{2(m+3n)+3(m-2n)}{3(m+3n)}$

$= \frac{2m+6n+3m-6n}{3(m+3n)} = \frac{5m}{3(m+3n)}$

[3 marks available — 1 mark for finding the common denominator, 1 mark for a correct method for addition, 1 mark for the correct final answer]

3 $\frac{3}{x} + \frac{2x}{x+4} = \frac{3(x+4)+x(2x)}{x(x+4)} =$

$\frac{2x^2+3x+12}{x(x+4)}$

[3 marks available — 1 mark for putting over a common denominator, 1 mark for adding numerators, 1 mark for correctly simplifying]

4 First simplify the fractions on the left-hand side:

$\frac{3}{x-5} + \frac{2}{x-1} =$

$\frac{3(x-1)}{(x-5)(x-1)} + \frac{2(x-5)}{(x-5)(x-1)}$

$= \frac{3(x-1)+2(x-5)}{(x-5)(x-1)} = \frac{3x-3+2x-10}{(x-5)(x-1)}$

$= \frac{5x-13}{(x-5)(x-1)}$

Now solve the equation:

$\frac{5x-13}{(x-5)(x-1)} = 1$

$5x - 13 = (x-5)(x-1) = x^2 - 6x + 5$

$x^2 - 11x + 18 = 0$

$(x-9)(x-2) = 0$

$x - 9 = 0$ or $x - 2 = 0$

$x = 9$ or $x = 2$

[6 marks available — 1 mark for finding the common denominator, 1 mark for a correct method for adding the fractions, 1 mark for the simplified fraction, 1 mark for rearranging to give a quadratic, 1 mark for a correct method to solve the quadratic, 1 mark for finding both solutions]

5 $\frac{1}{x+2} + \frac{x+3}{x-2} - \frac{4}{x}$

$= \frac{x(x-2)}{x(x-2)(x+2)} + \frac{x(x+2)(x+3)}{x(x+2)(x-2)}$

$- \frac{4(x+2)(x-2)}{x(x+2)(x-2)}$

$= \frac{x^2-2x}{x(x^2-4)} + \frac{x(x^2+5x+6)}{x(x^2-4)} - \frac{4(x^2-4)}{x(x^2-4)}$

$= \frac{x^2-2x+x^3+5x^2+6x-4x^2+16}{x^3-4x}$

$= \frac{x^3+2x^2+4x+16}{x^3-4x}$

[4 marks available — 1 mark for correctly multiplying top and bottom of the first fraction by x(x – 2), 1 mark for correctly multiplying top and bottom of the second fraction by x(x + 2), 1 mark for correctly multiplying top and bottom of the third fraction by (x + 2)(x – 2), 1 mark for collecting like terms correctly]

Page 43: Simultaneous Equations (1)

1 $x + 3y = 11 \xrightarrow{\times 3} 3x + 9y = 33$ ***[1 mark]***

$$\begin{array}{ll} 3x + 9y = 33 & x + 3y = 11 \\ \underline{3x + y = 9\ -} & x + (3 \times 3) = 11 \\ 8y = 24 & x = 11 - 9 \\ y = 3 \textit{ [1 mark]} & x = 2 \textit{ [1 mark]} \end{array}$$

[3 marks available in total — as above]

For all the simultaneous equation questions, you could have eliminated the other variable and/or substituted into the other equation to the one shown here — you'd get the marks either way.

2 $2x + 3y = 12 \xrightarrow{\times 5} 10x + 15y = 60$
[1 mark]
$5x + 4y = 9 \xrightarrow{\times 2} 10x + 8y = 18$ ***[1 mark]***

$$\begin{array}{ll} 10x + 15y = 60 & 2x + 3y = 12 \\ \underline{10x + 8y = 18\ -} & 2x = 12 - (3 \times 6) \\ 7y = 42 & 2x = -6 \\ y = 6 \textit{ [1 mark]} & x = -3 \textit{ [1 mark]} \end{array}$$

[4 marks available in total — as above]

3 Let f be the number of chocolate frogs and m be the number of sugar mice.
$4f + 3m = £3.69$ and $6f + 2m = £3.96$
$4f + 3m = £3.69 \xrightarrow{\times 2} 8f + 6m = £7.38$
[1 mark]
$6f + 2m = £3.96 \xrightarrow{\times 3} 18f + 6m = £11.88$
[1 mark]

$$\begin{array}{ll} 18f + 6m = £11.88 & 4f + 3m = £3.69 \\ \underline{8f + 6m = £7.38\ -} & 3m = £3.69 - (4 \times 0.45) \\ 10f = £4.50 & 3m = £1.89 \\ f = £0.45 & m = £0.63 \\ \textit{[1 mark]} & \textit{[1 mark]} \end{array}$$

So a bag with 2 chocolate frogs and 5 sugar mice would cost
$(2 \times 0.45) + (5 \times 0.63) = £4.05$ ***[1 mark]***
[5 marks available in total — as above]

Page 44: Simultaneous Equations (2)

1 $x^2 + y = 4$, so $y = 4 - x^2$
$4x - 1 = 4 - x^2$ ***[1 mark]***
$x^2 + 4x - 5 = 0$ ***[1 mark]***
$(x + 5)(x - 1) = 0$ ***[1 mark]***
$x = -5$ or $x = 1$ ***[1 mark]***
When $x = 1$, $y = (4 \times 1) - 1 = 3$
When $x = -5$, $y = (4 \times -5) - 1 = -21$
So the solutions are $x = 1, y = 3$ and $x = -5, y = -21$ ***[1 mark]***
[5 marks available in total — as above]

2 $y = x + 6$, so $2x^2 + (x + 6)^2 = 51$ ***[1 mark]***
$2x^2 + x^2 + 12x + 36 = 51$
$3x^2 + 12x - 15 = 0$ ***[1 mark]***
$(3x - 3)(x + 5) = 0$ ***[1 mark]***
$x = 1$ or $x = -5$ ***[1 mark]***
When $x = 1$, $y = 1 + 6 = 7$
When $x = -5$, $y = -5 + 6 = 1$
So the solutions are $x = 1, y = 7$ and $x = -5, y = 1$ ***[1 mark]***
[5 marks available in total — as above]

3 $y = x^2 + 3x - 1$ and $y = 2x + 5$ so $x^2 + 3x - 1 = 2x + 5$ ***[1 mark]***
$x^2 + x - 6 = 0$
$(x + 3)(x - 2) = 0$ ***[1 mark]***
$x = -3$ or $x = 2$ ***[1 mark]***
When $x = -3$, $y = (2 \times -3) + 5 = -6 + 5 = -1$
When $x = 2$, $y = (2 \times 2) + 5 = 9$
So the lines intersect at $(-3, -1)$ and $(2, 9)$
[1 mark]
Change in $x = 2 - (-3) = 5$
Change in $y = 9 - (-1) = 10$
[1 mark for both]
$\sqrt{10^2 + 5^2} = \sqrt{125} = 5\sqrt{5}$, so $k = 5$
[1 mark]
[6 marks available in total — as above]

Page 45: Inequalities

1 $-4 \leq 2x < 8$ ***[1 mark]***

2 $4x + 1 > x - 5$, so $3x > -6$ ***[1 mark]***
and $x > -2$ ***[1 mark]***
[2 marks available in total — as above]

3 $5n - 3 \leq 17$, so $5n \leq 20$, so $n \leq 4$
[1 mark]
$2n + 6 > 8$, so $2n > 2$, so $n > 1$
[1 mark]
Putting these together gives $1 < n \leq 4$, so the possible integer values of n are 2, 3 and 4 ***[1 mark]***
[3 marks available in total — as above]

4 a) $5 - 3x > 7 - x$, so $-2 > 2x$ ***[1 mark]***
and $x < -1$ ***[1 mark]***
[2 marks available in total — as above]

b)

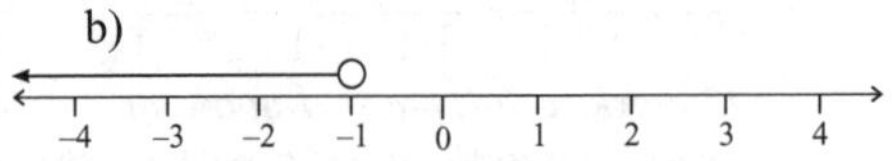

[1 mark]
The circle shouldn't be coloured in — if it was it'd be $x \leq -1$.

5 $2n + (2n + 2) + (2n + 4) < 1000$ ***[1 mark]***
$6n + 6 < 1000$
$6n < 994$
$n < 165.666...$ ***[1 mark]***
So the largest possible values of the numbers are obtained when $n = 165$, which gives 330, 332 and 334 ***[1 mark]***.
[3 marks available in total — as above]

Page 46: Graphical Inequalities

1 a)

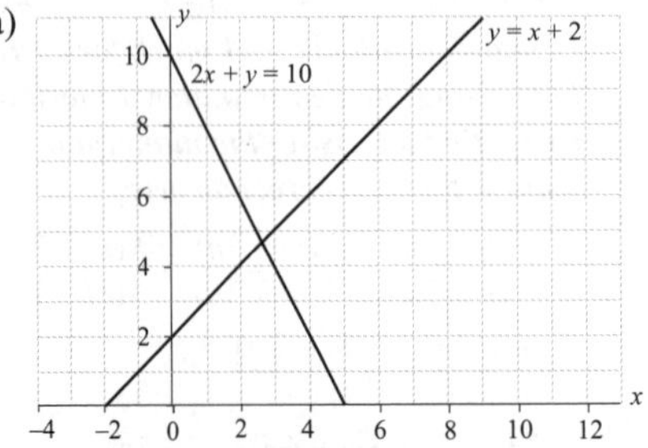

[2 marks available — 1 mark for correctly drawing 2x + y = 10, 1 mark for correctly drawing y = x + 2]

b)

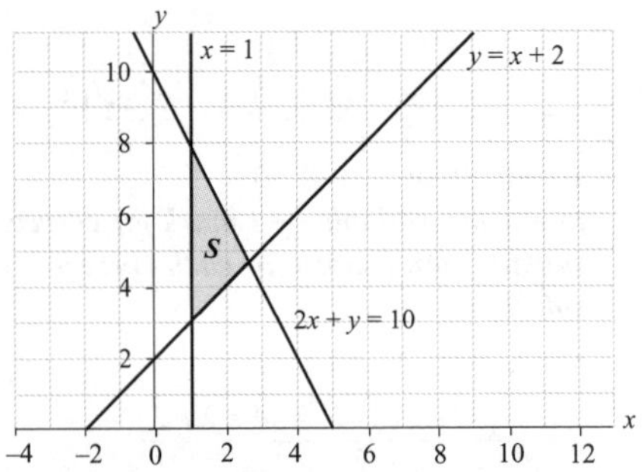

[2 marks available — 2 marks for correctly shaded area, lose 1 mark if the wrong side of one line is shaded]

2

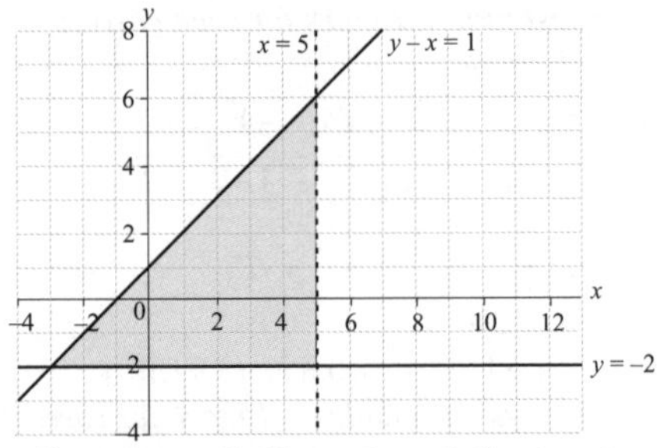

[4 marks available — 1 mark for drawing each line correctly, 1 mark for shading the correct area]

3 a) $y \geq 2$ ***[1 mark]***, $x + y \leq 8$ ***[1 mark]*** *and* $y \leq x$ ***[1 mark]***
[3 marks available in total — as above]

b) $y - x$ is lowest when y is low and x is high. From the graph, the lowest value of y is 2 and the highest value of x is 6, so the lowest possible value of $y - x = 2 - 6 = -4$
[2 marks available — 1 mark for correct reasoning, 1 mark for the correct answer]

Pages 47-49: Sequences

1 The first term in this sequence is $(3 \times 1) + 2 = 5$
The second term in this sequence is $(3 \times 2) + 2 = 8$
The third term in this sequence is $(3 \times 3) + 2 = 11$
So the first 3 terms in this sequence are 5, 8 and 11.
[2 marks available — 1 mark for first term correct, 1 mark for both second and third terms correct]

2 a) 3 8 13 18 (+5 +5 +5)
The common difference is 5, so the next two terms in the sequence will be $18 + 5 = 23$ and $23 + 5 = 28$. ***[1 mark]***

b) The common difference is 5 so $5n$ is in the formula.

$5n$: 5 10 15 20

↓-2 ↓-2 ↓-2 ↓-2

term: 3 8 13 18

You have to subtract 2 to get to the term, so the expression for the nth term is $5n - 2$.

[2 marks available — 2 marks for correct expression, otherwise 1 mark for finding 5n.]

c) Substituting $n = 30$ into the expression for the nth term:

$5n - 2 = (5 \times 30) - 2 = 148$ ***[1 mark]***

3 a) 3 7 11 15 19

$+4$ $+4$ $+4$ $+4$

The common difference is 4 so $4n$ is in the formula.

$4n$: 4 8 12 16 20

↓-1 ↓-1 ↓-1 ↓-1 ↓-1

term: 3 7 11 15 19

You have to subtract 1 to get to the term, so the expression for the nth term is $4n - 1$.

[2 marks available — 2 marks for correct expression, otherwise 1 mark for finding 4n.]

b) All multiples of 4 are even numbers, and an even number minus 1 is always an odd number. So all the terms in this sequence will be odd numbers. ***[1 mark]***

502 is an even number, so 502 cannot be in the sequence. ***[1 mark]***

[2 marks available in total — as above]

You could also show this by solving $4n - 1 = 502$ to give $n = 125.75$. As n is not an integer, 502 can't be in the sequence.

4 a) First week = 9 + 6 = 15 lessons

Subsequent weeks = 7 lessons per week, so the common difference is 7 and the rule contains $7n$.

$15 - 7 = 8$, so the rule is $7n + 8$

[3 marks available — 1 mark for working out the number of lessons in the first week, 1 mark for a correct method to find the common difference, 1 mark for a correct method to find the nth term given the common difference]

b) Number of drumming lessons in six weeks $= 6 + 5 \times 2 = 16$ ***[1 mark]***

Total number of lessons in six weeks $= 7(6) + 8 = 42 + 8 = 50$

Fraction $= \frac{16}{50}\left(= \frac{8}{25}\right)$ ***[1 mark]***

[2 marks available in total — as above]

5 Numerators: 1 5 9 13 17

$+4$ $+4$ $+4$ $+4$

The common difference is 4 so $4n$ is in the formula.

$4n$: 4 8 12 16 20

↓-3 ↓-3 ↓-3 ↓-3 ↓-3

term: 1 5 9 13 17

You have to subtract 3 to get to the term, so the expression for the nth term is $4n - 3$.

Denominators: 3 12 21 30 39

$+9$ $+9$ $+9$ $+9$

The common difference is 9 so $9n$ is in the formula.

$9n$: 9 18 27 36 45

↓-6 ↓-6 ↓-6 ↓-6 ↓-6

term: 3 12 21 30 39

You have to subtract 6 to get to the term, so the expression for the nth term is $9n - 6$.

Overall, the nth term is $\frac{4n - 3}{9n - 6}$

[4 marks available — 2 marks for the correct numerator, otherwise 1 mark for 4n, and 2 marks for the correct denominator, otherwise 1 mark for 9n]

6 a) To get from one term to the next, you have to multiply by $\sqrt{2}$, so the next term is $4\sqrt{2}$ and the next one is $4\sqrt{2} \times \sqrt{2} = 8$.

[2 marks available — 1 mark for each correct term]

b) $(\sqrt{2})^n$ ***[1 mark]***

7 a) 5 12 31 68

$+7$ $+19$ $+37$

The sequence goes up by a much larger amount each time so compare to n^3 (1, 8, 27, 64, ...) ***[1 mark]***

To get from n^3 to the sequence you add 4, so the nth term of the sequence is $n^3 + 4$ ***[1 mark]***.

[2 marks available in total — as above]

b) The next term is the 5th term

Next term $= (5)^3 + 4 = 125 + 4 = 129$

[1 mark]

8 a) Number of grey squares as a sequence: 1, 5, 9, 13, ...

Common difference = 4, so $4n$ is in the formula.

To get from $4n$ to each term, you have to subtract 3, so the expression for the nth term is $4n - 3$.

[2 marks available — 2 marks for correct expression, otherwise 1 mark for finding 4n]

b) Assume Giles makes the nth and $(n + 1)$th patterns.

He uses $4n - 3$ grey squares in the nth pattern and $4(n + 1) - 3 = 4n + 4 - 3 = 4n + 1$ grey squares in the $(n + 1)$th pattern ***[1 mark]***.

He uses 414 grey squares in total, so $(4n - 3) + (4n + 1) = 414$ ***[1 mark]***

$8n - 2 = 414$

$8n = 416$

$n = 52$

So Giles has made the 52nd and 53rd patterns ***[1 mark]***.

[3 marks available in total — as above]

c) Total number of squares:

1 7 17 31

$+6$ $+10$ $+14$

The sequence goes up by a larger amount each time so compare to n^2 (1, 4, 9, 16, ...) ***[1 mark]***

The sequence 1, 7, 17, 31, ... is similar to $2n^2$ ***[1 mark]***.

$2n^2$: 2, 8, 18, 32, ...

To get from $2n^2$ to the sequence you subtract 1, so the nth term of the sequence is $2n^2 - 1$ ***[1 mark]***.

[3 marks available in total — as above]

Section Four — Graphs

Page 50: Straight Line Graphs (1)

1

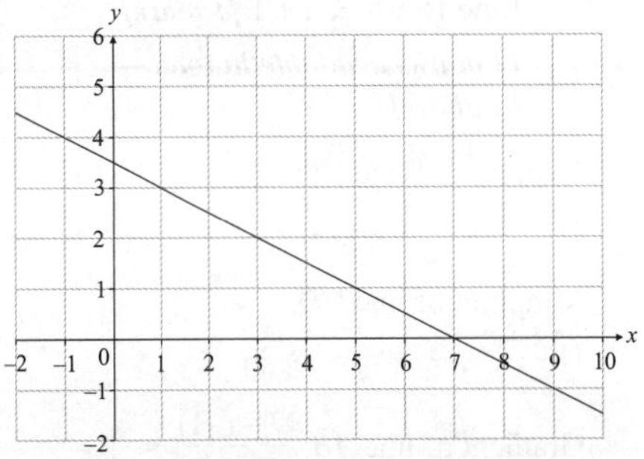

[3 marks available — 1 mark for plotting any point on the line (e.g. (0, 3.5)), 1 mark for plotting a second correct point (e.g. (7, 0)), 1 mark for the correct line extending between x = –2 and x = 10]

To draw these graphs, you could either create a table of values and plot the points, or you could set y = 0 and x = 0 and join up the points.

2 a) Using $y = mx + c$, where m is the gradient, and c is the y-intercept:

$m = \frac{(7 - (-3))}{(5 - 0)} = 2$ ***[1 mark]***

When $x = 0$, $y = -3$, so $c = -3$ ***[1 mark]***

So, $y = 2x - 3$ ***[1 mark]***

[3 marks available in total — as above]

b) Using gradient from part a), $m = 2$
When $x = 2$, $y = 10$, so $10 = (2 \times 2) + c$
i.e. $c = 6$ ***[1 mark]***
So, $y = 2x + 6$ ***[1 mark]***
[2 marks available in total — as above]

c) The average of the x-coordinates = $\frac{5+0}{2} = 2.5$
The average of the y-coordinates = $\frac{-3+7}{2} = 2$
Coordinates of $P = (2.5, 2)$.
[2 marks available — 1 mark for each coordinate]

Page 51: Straight Line Graphs (2)

1 a) $2a + 4 = 2c$, so $a + 2 = c$
Substitute values $a + 2 = c$ and $b - 6 = d$ into point (c, d):
$(c, d) = (a + 2, b - 6)$
Gradient of **S** = $\frac{b-6-b}{a+2-a} = \frac{-6}{2} = -3$
[3 marks available — 1 mark for correctly substituting values into a point, 1 mark for finding change in y over change in x, 1 mark for correct answer]

b) Gradient = $\frac{1}{3}$ ***[1 mark]***
So $y = \frac{1}{3}x + c$.
Substitute (6, 3) into the equation:
$3 = \frac{1}{3} \times 6 + c$
$c = 1$
Line **R**: $y = \frac{1}{3}x + 1$ ***[1 mark]***
[2 marks available in total — as above]

2 Midpoint of line AB:
$\left(\frac{5+1}{2}, \frac{7-1}{2}\right) = (3, 3)$
Midpoint of line CD:
$\left(\frac{13+3}{2}, \frac{4-2}{2}\right) = (8, 1)$
Gradient of line AB: $\frac{7-(-1)}{5-1} = \frac{8}{4} = 2$
Gradient of perpendicular = $-\frac{1}{2}$
Gradient of the line joining the midpoints of AB and CD:
Gradient = $\frac{1-3}{8-3} = \frac{-2}{5}$
$\frac{-1}{2} \neq \frac{-2}{5}$, therefore Sakura is incorrect.
[5 marks available — 1 mark for a correct method to find both midpoints, 1 mark for both midpoints correct, 1 mark for a correct method to find both gradients, 1 mark for both gradients correct, 1 mark for comparing gradients to show that the lines aren't perpendicular]

Pages 52-53: Quadratic Graphs

1 a) (1.5, –0.25) ***[1 mark]***
If your y-coordinate is between –0.23 and –0.28 you'll get the marks.

b) $a = 2$ ***[1 mark]***

2 a) Calculate points to plot, e.g. by making a table of values:

x	0	1	2	3	4	5	6	7	8
y	–35	0	25	40	45	40	25	0	–35

[1 mark for calculating 2 or 3 correct points, or 2 marks for calculating at least 4 correct points]

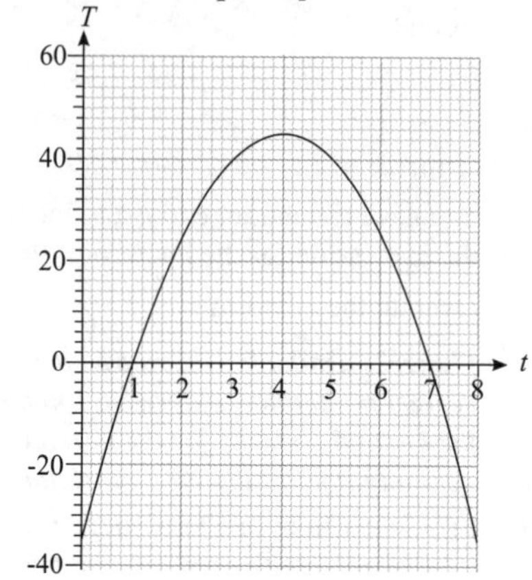

[1 mark for at least 4 points correctly plotted and 1 mark for a smooth curve through all the points]
[4 marks available in total — as above]

b) $t = 4$ ***[1 mark]***

c) Read off the values from the graph where $T = 20$: $t = 1.8$, $t = 6.2$
[2 marks available — 1 mark for each solution (allow answers ±0.2)]

3 To find intersections with the x-axis, solve $x^2 - 4x + 3 = 0$:
$(x - 3)(x - 1) = 0$ so $x = 1$, $x = 3$
So the x-intercepts are (1, 0) and (3, 0)
Use symmetry and the x-intercepts to find the turning point:
$x = \frac{3+1}{2} = 2$
$y = (2)^2 - 4(2) + 3 = 4 - 8 + 3 = -1$
The coordinates are (2, –1)
[4 marks available — 1 mark for a correct method to find the x-intercepts, 1 mark for correct x-intercepts, 1 mark for each correct coordinate of the turning point]

4 To find intersections with the x-axis, solve $2x^2 + 10x - 12 = 0$:
$x^2 + 5x - 6 = 0$
$(x + 6)(x - 1) = 0$ so $x = -6$, $x = 1$
So the x-intercepts are (–6, 0) and (1, 0)
[1 mark for a correct method to find the x-intercepts, 1 mark for correct x-intercepts]

To find where the graph crosses the y-axis, substitute $x = 0$ into the equation:
$y = 0 + 0 - 12 = -12$
So the y-intercept is (0, –12) ***[1 mark]***
Use symmetry and the x-intercepts to find the turning point of the curve:
$x = \frac{1+(-6)}{2} = -2.5$ ***[1 mark]***
$y = 2(-2.5)^2 + 10(-2.5) - 12 = -24.5$
[1 mark]
So the turning point lies at (–2.5, –24.5)

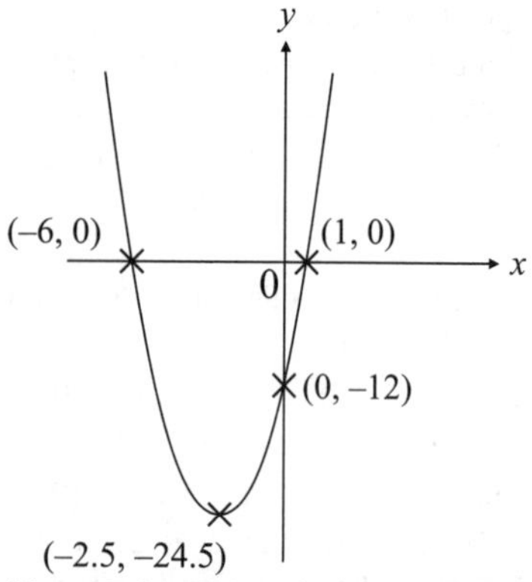

[1 mark for drawing a smooth curve in a sensible position on the axes, with the x- and y-intercepts and turning point correctly labelled]
[6 marks available in total — as above]

Page 54: Harder Graphs (1)

1 a)

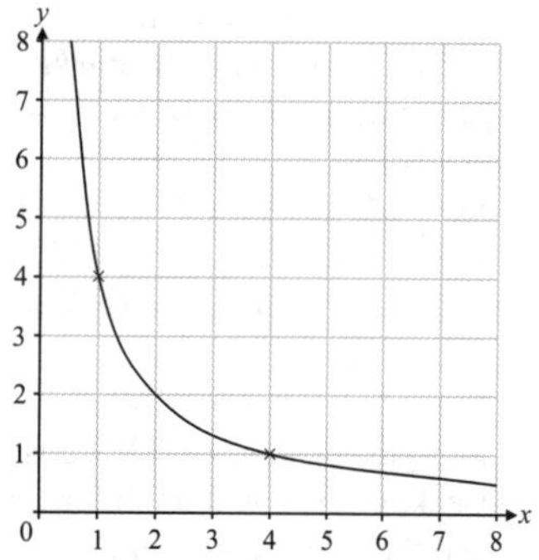

[2 marks available — 1 mark for a curve passing through (4, 1) and approaching x = 0 but not touching it, 1 mark for a curve passing through (1, 4) and approaching y = 0 but not touching it]

b)

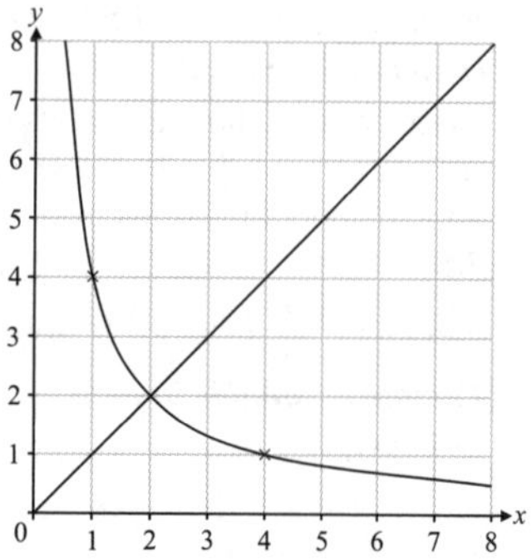

By plotting $y = x$ and reading off where it intersects the curve, the coordinates are (2, 2) ***[1 mark]***
You could also find the values of x and y by substituting $y = x$ into $y = \frac{4}{x}$.

2 Calculate points to plot, e.g. by making a table of values:

x	–3	–2	–1	0	1	2	3
y	–6	2	0	–6	–10	–6	12

[1 mark for a calculating 2 or 3 correct points or 2 marks for calculating at least 4 correct points]

Sketch:

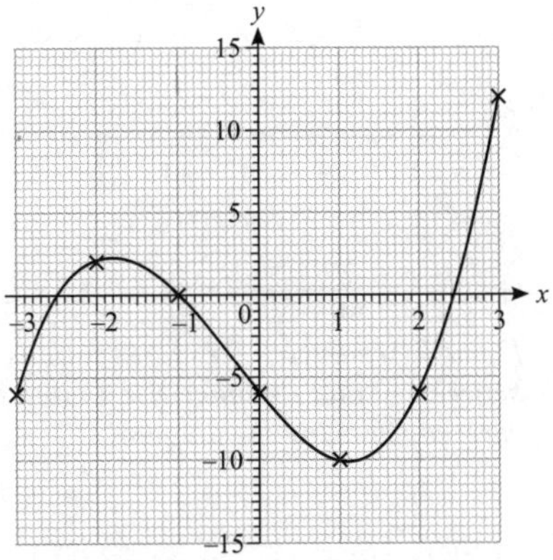

[1 mark for at least 4 points plotted correctly, 1 mark for a smooth line through all points]
[4 marks available in total — as above]

Page 55: Harder Graphs (2)

1 a) B ***[1 mark]***
b) C ***[1 mark]***
c) A ***[1 mark]***

2 a) Use the points from the graph:
(0, 800): $800 = xy^0$, so $x = 800$ ***[1 mark]***
(2, 12 800): $12\,800 = xy^2 = 800y^2$ ***[1 mark]***
$y^2 = 12\,800 \div 800 = 16$,
so $y = 4$ ***[1 mark]***
[3 marks available in total — as above]

b) Substitute $t = -2$ into the equation:
$C = 800 \times 4^{-2}$ ***[1 mark]***
$C = £50$ ***[1 mark]***
[2 marks available in total — as above]

Page 56: Circle Graphs

1 a) No, the curve will not pass through the origin. It is a circle equation, centred at (0, 0) with radius 4.
[1 mark for correct answer with suitable explanation or graph]

b) On the x-axis, $y = 0$, so
$x^2 + 0^2 = 16$
$x^2 = 16$
$x = -4, x = 4$ ***[1 mark]***

2 The line from the origin to the point (–4, –3) is a radius, so has gradient $\frac{0 - -3}{0 - -4} = \frac{3}{4}$, so the tangent at this point has gradient $-\frac{4}{3}$ as a tangent meets a radius at 90°.
The tangent passes through the point (–4, –3),
so $-3 = -\frac{4}{3}(-4) + c = \frac{16}{3} + c$, so $c = -\frac{25}{3}$
The equation of the tangent at (–4, –3) is
$y = -\frac{4}{3}x - \frac{25}{3}$
[3 marks available — 1 mark for finding the gradient of the radius, 1 mark for finding the gradient of the tangent, 1 mark for the correct answer]

3

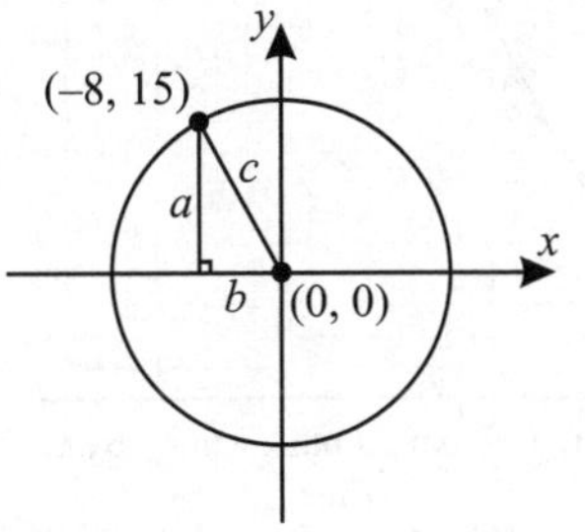

Radius goes from (–8, 15) to (0, 0)
Use Pythagoras' theorem to find length of radius:
$c^2 = a^2 + b^2$
$c^2 = 15^2 + 8^2$ ***[1 mark]***
$c^2 = 225 + 64 = 289$ ***[1 mark]***
$c = 17$ so the radius = 17 units ***[1 mark]***
The equation is $x^2 + y^2 = 289$ ***[1 mark]***
[4 marks available in total — as above]

Page 57: Solving Equations Using Graphs (1)

1 a) Calculate points to plot, e.g. by making a table of values:

x	–4	–3	–2	–1	0	1	2
y	3	–2	–5	–6	–5	–2	3

[1 mark for calculating 2 or 3 correct points, or 2 marks for calculating at least 4 correct points]

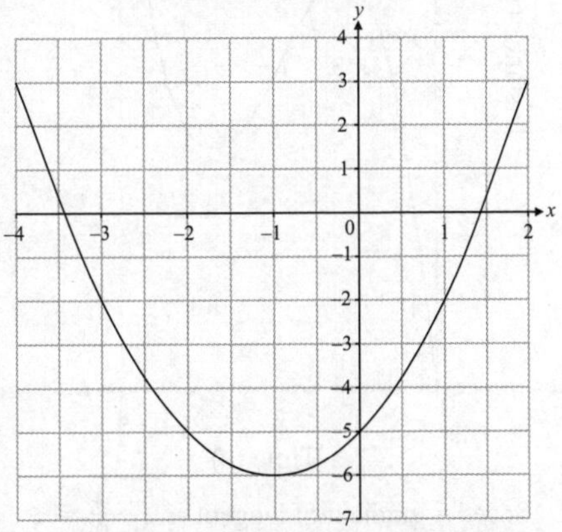

[1 mark for plotting at least four points correctly, 1 mark for a smooth curve through these points]
[4 marks available in total — as above]

b)

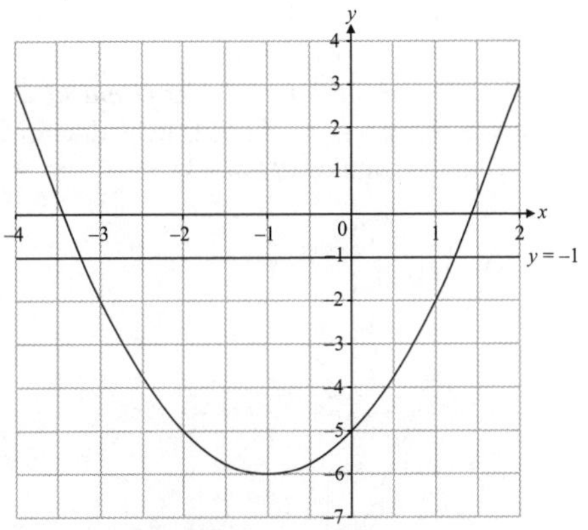

$x \approx -3.2$ and $x \approx 1.2$
[2 marks available — 1 mark for drawing the line y = –1, 1 mark for estimating both a solution between –3 and –3.4 and a solution between 1 and 1.4]

c) Draw line $x + y + 5 = 0$ on the graph:
$y = -x - 5$ in the form $y = mx + c$

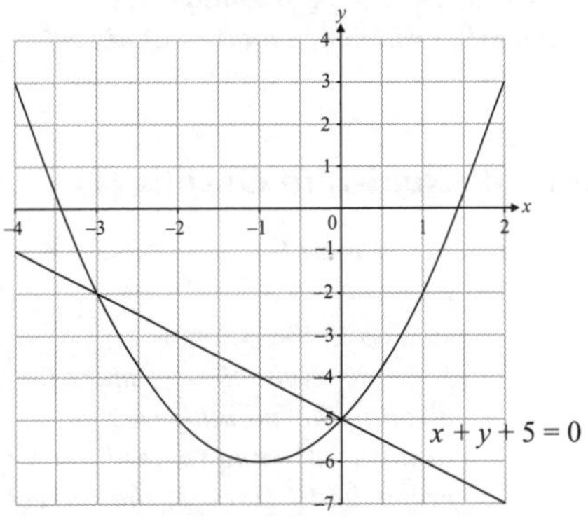

[2 marks for drawing the line correctly, otherwise 1 mark for a straight line passing through one correct point]
The coordinates are (–3, –2) and (0, –5) ***[1 mark for each]***
[4 marks available in total — as above]

Page 58: Solving Equations Using Graphs (2)

1 Draw the graph of $y = 3x + 10$:

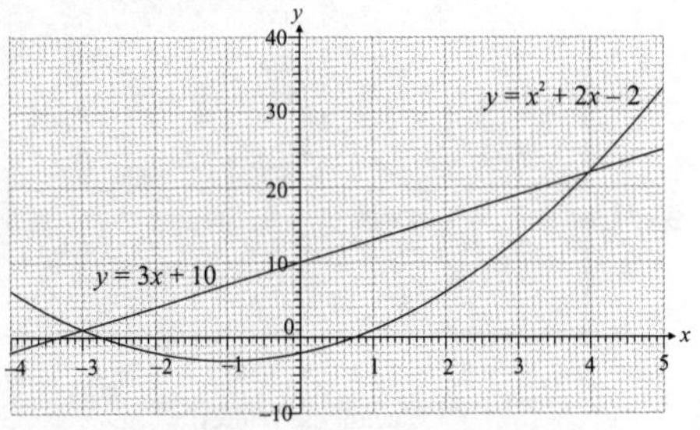

$x = -3$ (accept ±0.1), $y = 1$ (accept ±0.5) and $x = 4$ (accept ±0.1), $y = 22$ (accept ±0.5)
[4 marks available — 2 marks for correctly drawing the line y = 3x + 10, otherwise 1 mark for a straight line passing through one correct point, and 1 mark for each correct solution]

2 Find the equation of the line that should be drawn: $x^2 + x = 1$

$x^2 + x - 4 = -3$

$x^2 - x - 4 = -3 - 2x$ ***[1 mark]***

So the line $y = -2x - 3$ needs to be drawn to find the solutions ***[1 mark]***:

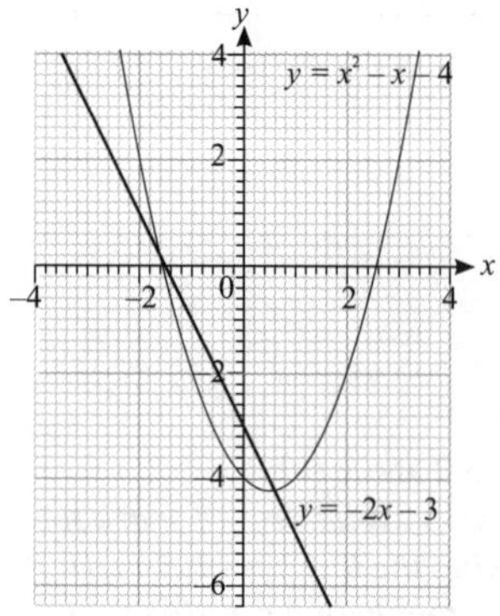

[2 marks for line drawn correctly, otherwise 1 mark for a straight line passing through one correct point]

The solutions to $x^2 + x = 1$ are:

$x \approx -1.6$ and $x \approx 0.6$ ***[1 mark]***

[5 marks available in total — as above]

Page 59: Real-Life Graphs (1)

1 a) i) £18 ***[1 mark]***

ii) $40 \div 100 = 0.4$, so it costs 40p per unit

[2 marks available — 1 mark for dividing the 'monthly cost' by 'units used' using values from the graph, and 1 mark for the correct answer]

b) Mr Barker should use Plan A because it is cheaper.

Using 85 units with Plan A would cost £26.50.

85 units with Plan B would cost £34.

[2 marks available — 1 mark for correctly stating which plan, 1 mark for giving a reason]

2 a)

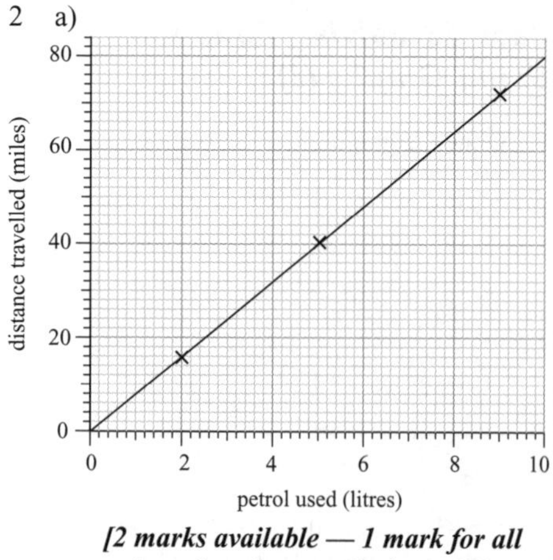

[2 marks available — 1 mark for all points plotted correctly, 1 mark for straight line joining points]

b) Gradient $= \frac{80 - 0}{10 - 0} = 8$ ***[1 mark]***

This means the car travels 8 miles for every litre of petrol used, so a 190 mile journey would use $190 \div 8 =$ 23.75 litres of petrol ***[1 mark]***.

[2 marks available in total — as above]

Page 60: Real-Life Graphs (2)

1 a) 5.5 gallons (allow 5.4 – 5.6 gallons) ***[1 mark]***

b) E.g. 20 litres = 4.5 gallons (allow 4.4 – 4.6 gallons)

$20 \times 4 = 80$, so 4.5 gallons $\times 4 =$ 18 gallons (allow 17.6 – 18.4 gallons)

[3 marks available — 1 mark for correct conversion factor, 1 mark for correct application of the conversion factor and 1 mark for answer within the range 17.6 – 18.4 gallons]

2 a)

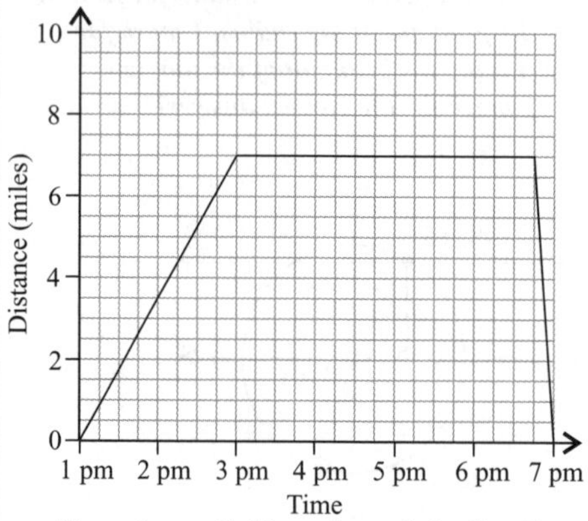

[3 marks available — 1 mark for line from (1, 0) to (3, 7), 1 mark for horizontal line for 3 hours and 45 minutes from (3, 7), 1 mark for line from (6.75, 7) to (7, 0)]

b) speed $= \frac{\text{distance}}{\text{time}} = \frac{7}{0.25} = 28$ mph

[2 marks available — 1 mark for a correct method, 1 mark for correct final answer]

Page 61: Gradients of Real-Life Graphs

1

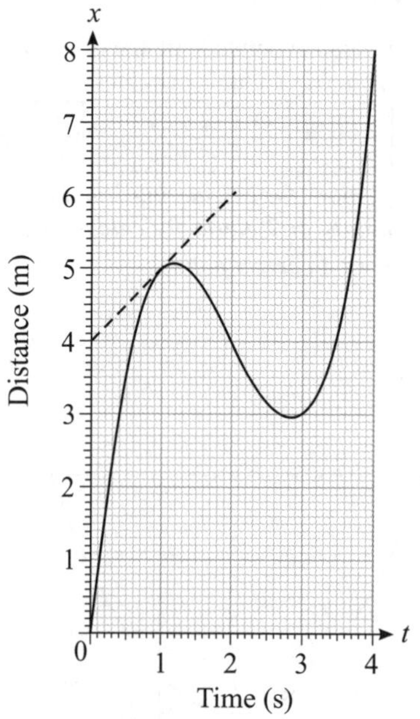

Speed = gradient of tangent $= \frac{6 - 4}{2 - 0} = \frac{2}{2}$ $= 1$ m/s

[2 marks available — 2 marks for answer between 0.5 and 1.5, otherwise 1 mark for correctly drawing the tangent]

2

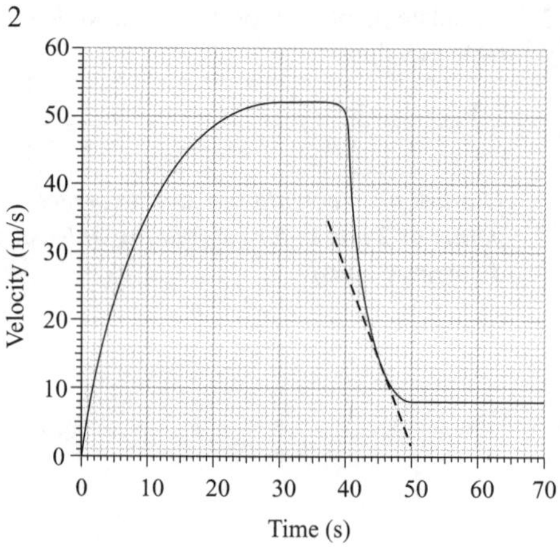

Gradient $= \frac{27 - 2}{40 - 50} = \frac{25}{-10} = -2.5$ m/s^2

[2 marks available — 2 marks for answer between –2 and –3, otherwise 1 mark for correctly drawing the tangent]

Section Five — Measures and Angles

Page 62: Metric Units

1 a) 1 litre = 1000 millilitres

$7.5 \times 1000 = 7500$

So 7.5 litres = 7500 ml ***[1 mark]***

b) 1 m = 100 cm

$8.7 \div 100 = 0.087$ m ***[1 mark]***

[2 marks available in total — as above]

2 1 m = 100 cm

$39\,200 \div 100 = 392$

$392 \div 100 = 3.92$ m^2

[2 marks available — 1 mark for correct method and 1 mark for correct final answer]

When the unit is squared, you have to use the conversion factor twice (so you use 100, and then 100 again). You could also divide 39 200 by 10 000 instead.

3 150 litres $\times$ 1000 ***[1 mark]*** = 150 000 cm^3

= 150 000 cm^3 $\div$ 1 000 000 ***[1 mark]***

= 0.15 m^3 ***[1 mark]***

[3 marks available in total — as above]

4 Start by converting the side lengths to the same measurement

1 m = 100 cm = 1000 mm

$3 \times 1000 = 3000$

So 3 m = 3000 mm ***[1 mark]***

Work out how many small cubes you could fit along each side of the large cube:

$3000 \div 60 = 50$ ***[1 mark]***

So in the large cube you could fit:

$50 \times 50 \times 50 = 125\,000$ small cubes ***[1 mark]***

[3 marks available in total — as above]

Page 63: Imperial Units

1 1 foot ≈ 30 cm
$9.5 \times 30 = 285$ cm ***[1 mark]***

2 64 pints = 64 ÷ 8 = 8 gallons ***[1 mark]***
8 gallons = 4 × 2 gallons ≈ 4 × 9 litres
[1 mark] = 36 litres ***[1 mark]***
[3 marks available in total — as above]

3 E.g. 1 kg ≈ 2.2 lb
2500 g ÷ 1000 = 2.5 kg
Convert kg into lbs: 2.5 × 2.2 = 5.5 lbs
5.5 ÷ 1.5 = 3.6666...
Maximum number of books = 3
[4 marks available — 1 mark for converting g to kg, 1 mark for converting kg into lb, 1 mark for dividing 5.5 by 1.5, 1 mark for correct answer]

4 4.5 litres ≈ 1 gallon
6.2 litres = 6.2 ÷ 4.5 = 1.377... gallons
8 km ≈ 5 miles
100 km = (100 ÷ 8) × 5 = 62.5 miles
Miles per gallon for car B: 62.5 ÷ 1.377...
= 45.362... mpg
Therefore car A is more efficient to hire.
[3 marks available — 1 mark for converting volumes to the same units, 1 mark for converting distances to the same units, 1 mark for finding the fuel efficiency in changed units]
You could also convert car A's miles per gallon into kilometres per litre to compare to car B. As long as you show all of your steps, you'll get the marks if your answer is correct.

Page 64: Speed

1 1 hour 15 minutes = 1.25 hours ***[1 mark]***
Distance = speed × time = 56 × 1.25
= 70 km ***[1 mark]***
[2 marks available in total — as above]

2 a) E.g. 2500 m = 2.5 km.
2.5 km = 2.5 ÷ 1.6 = 1.5625 miles.
102 s ÷ 60 = 1.7 minutes ÷ 60
= 0.02833... hours.
Speed = 1.5625 miles ÷ 0.02833... hours
= 55 mph (to nearest mph)
[3 marks available — 1 mark for converting 2500 metres to miles, 1 mark for converting 102 seconds into hours, 1 mark for the correct final answer]
It doesn't matter whether you do the conversion to miles per hour at the start or the end of the calculation — you could find the speed in m/s, km/s or km/h, and then change it to mph. Whichever way, you should get the same answer.

b) E.g. time = 1.5625 miles ÷ 50 mph
= 0.03125 hours
0.03125 hours × 60 × 60 = 113 s
(to nearest second)
[2 marks available — 1 mark for dividing the distance by the speed limit, 1 mark for the correct answer]

3 In 2020 he finished with a time of $t - 0.1t = 0.9t$ ***[1 mark]***
$s_1 = \frac{d}{t}$ and $s_2 = \frac{d}{0.9t}$ ***[1 mark]***
So, $s_1 t = 0.9 s_2 t$
$s_2 = \frac{s_1}{0.9} = 1.111... \times s_1$ ***[1 mark]***
So his percentage increase was 11.11% (2 d.p.) ***[1 mark]***
[4 marks available in total — as above]
There are other methods to get to the correct answer — as long as you show full working and get the answer right then you'll get full marks.

Page 65: Density

1 a) Volume = 360 ÷ 1800 ***[1 mark]***
= 0.2 m³ ***[1 mark]***
[2 marks available in total — as above]

b) Density = 220 ÷ 0.2 ***[1 mark]***
= 1100 kg/m³ ***[1 mark]***
[2 marks available in total — as above]

2 a) Volume = 4 cm × 4 cm × 4 cm
= 64 cm³ ***[1 mark]***
Mass = 7.9 × 64 ***[1 mark]***
= 505.6 g ***[1 mark]***
[3 marks available in total — as above]

b) 63.2 kg = 63 200 g ***[1 mark]***
Volume of large cube:
63 200 ÷ 7.9 = 8000 cm³ ***[1 mark]***
Side length of large cube:
$\sqrt[3]{8000} = 20$ cm ***[1 mark]***
Ratio of side lengths of the smaller and larger cubes:
4 cm : 20 cm = 1 : 5 ***[1 mark]***
[4 marks available in total — as above]

3 10 cm³ of brass contains 7 cm³ of copper and 3 cm³ of zinc.
7 cm³ of copper has a mass of
7 × 8.9 = 62.3 g
3 cm³ of zinc has a mass of
3 × 7.1 = 21.3 g
10 cm³ of brass has a mass of
62.3 + 21.3 = 83.6 g
Density of brass = 83.6 ÷ 10 = 8.36 g/cm³
[4 marks available — 1 mark for finding the mass of a stated volume of copper or zinc, 1 mark for finding the total mass of a stated volume of brass, 1 mark for attempting to find density using total mass ÷ total volume and 1 mark for correct final answer]

Page 66: Pressure

1 a) Area of A = 40 cm × 20 cm
= 800 cm²
= 800 ÷ 100 ÷ 100
= 0.08 m² ***[1 mark]***
Pressure = 40 N ÷ 0.08 m² ***[1 mark]***
= 500 N/m² ***[1 mark]***
[3 marks available in total — as above]

b) Three cuboids would have a weight of 3 × 40N = 120 N ***[1 mark]***
Area of B = 3 m × 0.4 m = 1.2 m²
[1 mark]
Pressure = 120 N ÷ 1.2 m²
= 100 N/m² ***[1 mark]***
[3 marks available in total — as above]

2 a) Area of circular base = $\pi \times (10)^2$
= 100π cm² ***[1 mark]***
100π cm² = $(100\pi \div 100 \div 100)$ m²
= 0.01π m² ***[1 mark]***
Weight = $650 \times 0.01\pi$ ***[1 mark]***
= 20.42035...
= 20.42 N (2 d.p.) ***[1 mark]***
[4 marks available in total — as above]

b) E.g. If the diameter is halved, the area of the circular base becomes:
$\pi \times (5)^2 = 25\pi$ cm² $= 0.0025\pi$ m²
Pressure = $6.5\pi \div 0.0025\pi$
= 2600 N/m²
2600 N/m² ÷ 650 N/m² = 4
If the diameter of the circle is halved the pressure increases and is 4 times greater.
[2 marks available — 1 mark for a correct method to find the pressure exerted by the cone with half the diameter, 1 mark for a correct comparison of the pressure exerted by the different cones]

Pages 67-68: Angle Rules and Parallel Lines

1 a) *B* and *H* <u>or</u> *E* and *C* ***[1 mark]***
b) *E* or *G* ***[1 mark]***
c) 60° because angle *A* and Angle *E* are corresponding angles. ***[1 mark]***

2 a) Angles on a straight line add up to 180°, so angle *FEC* = 180° – 14°
= 166° ***[1 mark]***
Angles in a quadrilateral add up to 360°, so *x* = 360° – 90 – 62° – 166°
= 42° ***[1 mark]***
[2 marks available in total — as above]

b) Angles in a triangle add up to 180° ***[1 mark]***, so *y* = 180° – 90° – 42°
= 48° ***[1 mark]***
[2 marks available in total — as above]

3 Let a be the third angle in the triangle.
$a = 180° - y - z$ (angles in a triangle add to 180°) ***[1 mark]***
$x = 180° - a$ (angles on a straight line add to 180°) ***[1 mark]***
So $x = 180° - (180° - y - z) = y + z$
[1 mark]
[3 marks available in total — as above]

4 Angles on a straight line add up to 180°, so angle $ABJ = 180° - 140° = 40°$ ***[1 mark]***
Allied angles add up to 180°, so angle $JAB = 180° - 150° = 30°$ ***[1 mark]***
Angles in a triangle add up to 180°, so angle $AJB = 180° - 40° - 30° = 110°$
[1 mark]
Angles on a straight line add up to 180°, so angle $x = 180° - 110° = 70°$ ***[1 mark]***
[4 marks available in total — as above]

5 Angle BDC = angle $BCD = x$
(triangle BCD is isosceles)
Angle $CBD = 180° - x - x = 180° - 2x$
[1 mark] (angles in a triangle add to 180°)
Angle BDE = angle $CBD = 180° - 2x$
[1 mark] (alternate angles)
Angle AED = angle $BDE = 180° - 2x$
[1 mark] ($ABDE$ is an isosceles trapezium so has a vertical line of symmetry)
$y = 360°$ – angle AED ***[1 mark]*** (angles round a point add to 360°)
So $y = 360° - (180° - 2x) = 180° + 2x$
[1 mark]
[5 marks available in total — as above]
There's more than one way to do these questions — as long as you show your working and explain each step you'll get the marks.

6 $5x + (4x - 9°) = 180°$ ***[1 mark]***
(Allied angles add up to 180°.)
Rearranging this: $9x = 189°$
Therefore $x = 21°$ ***[1 mark]***
$(4y - 12°) + 2y = 180°$ ***[1 mark]***
(Allied angles add up to 180°.)
Rearranging this: $6y = 192°$
Therefore $y = 32°$ ***[1 mark]***
[4 marks available in total — as above]

Pages 69-70: Angles in Shapes

1 Number of sides = 360° ÷ 24° ***[1 mark]***
= 15 ***[1 mark]***
[2 marks available in total — as above]

2 Exterior angle = 180° – 150° = 30°
[1 mark]
Number of sides = 360° ÷ 30° ***[1 mark]***
= 12 ***[1 mark]***
[3 marks available in total — as above]

3 Sum of interior angles = $180 \times (n - 2)$
$= 180 \times (6 - 2)$ ***[1 mark]***
$= 180 \times 4 = 720°$ ***[1 mark]***
$a = 720 - 87 - 145 - 154 - 158 - 68$
[1 mark] = 108° ***[1 mark]***
[4 marks available in total — as above]

4 Exterior angle of a pentagon = 360° ÷ 5 = 72°
Interior angle of a pentagon = 180° – 72° = 108°
Angle in an equilateral triangle = 180° ÷ 3 = 60°
$p = 360° - (108° + 60°)$ *(angles round a point add up to 360°)*
$= 360° - 168° = 192°$
[5 marks available — 1 mark for the correct final answer and 4 method marks, e.g.: 1 mark for calculating the exterior angle of the pentagon, 1 mark for calculating the interior angle of the pentagon, 1 mark for calculating the angle of the triangle and 1 mark for using the 'angles around a point rule'.]

5 E.g.:

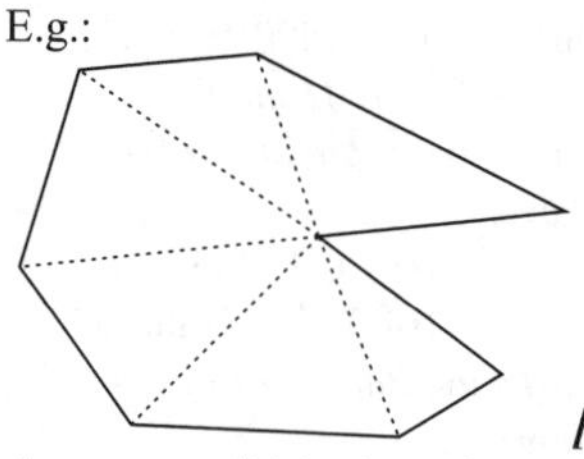

[1 mark]
Any correct division into 6 triangles is acceptable, as long as all of the angles of each triangle are part of the internal angles of the shape.
Angle sum of polygon = 6 × 180° ***[1 mark]***
= 1080° ***[1 mark]***
[3 marks available in total — as above]

6 a) x is the same as an exterior angle, so $x = 360° \div 8$ ***[1 mark]***
$x = 45°$ ***[1 mark]***
[2 marks available in total — as above]
You could also say that the triangle containing angle x could be drawn from each side of the octagon, so 8 lots of x would form angles round a point, so 8x = 360°.

b) The line OB bisects the internal angle, so $y = (180° - 45°) \div 2$ ***[1 mark]***
$y = 67.5°$ ***[1 mark]***
[2 marks available in total — as above]

7 Interior angle of regular n-sided polygon
= 180° – exterior angle
$= 180° - (360° \div n)$

Interior angle of regular octagon = 180° – (360° ÷ 8) = 135°
Interior angle of regular hexagon = 180° – (360° ÷ 6) = 120°
Angle CBK = angle ABC – angle IJK = 135° – 120° = 15°
[3 marks available in total — 1 mark for using correct method to find interior angle of octagon or hexagon, 1 mark for both interior angles correct, 1 mark for correct answer]

Page 71: Bearings

1 a)

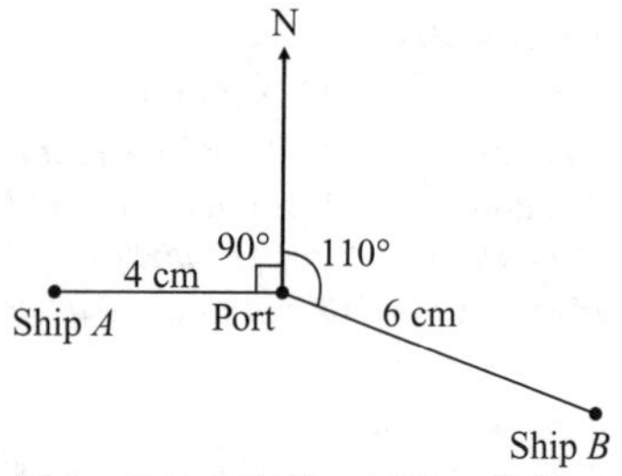

[4 marks available — 1 mark for Ship A 4 cm from the port, 1 mark for correct bearing for ship A, 1 mark for ship B 6 cm from the port, and 1 mark for correct bearing for Ship B]
This diagram has been drawn smaller to make it fit — your measurements should match the labels given on the diagram here.

b) 102° (accept answers between 100° and 104°) ***[1 mark]***

c) 180° – 102° = 78°
360° – 78° = 282° (accept answers between 280° and 284°)
[2 marks available — 1 mark for correctly using the answer from part b), 1 mark for correct answer]
You could also do this by adding 180° to 102°.

2 a)

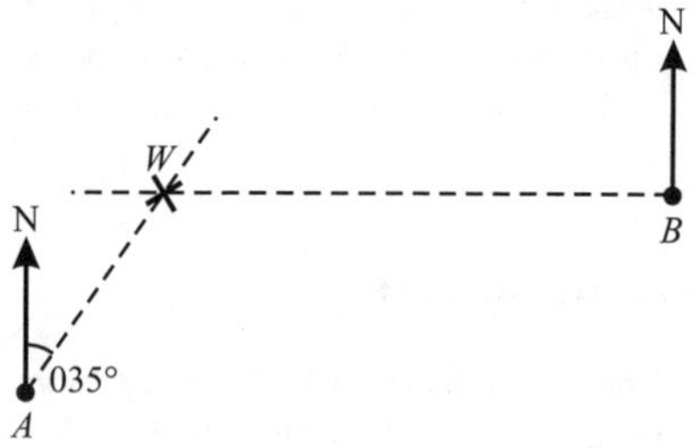

[2 marks available — 1 mark for correct bearing of 035° and 1 mark for marking W directly west of B]

b)

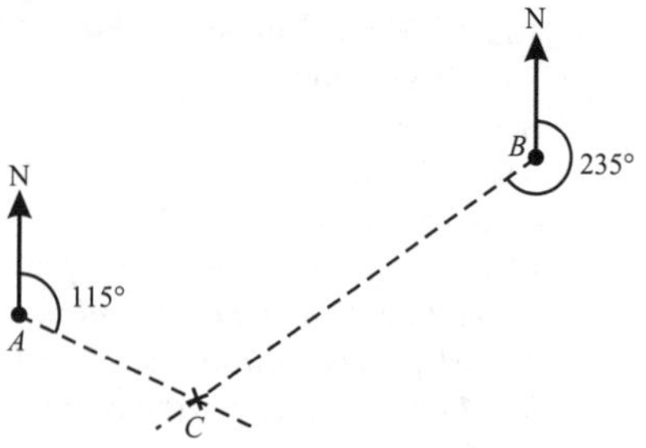

[3 marks available — 1 mark for correct bearing from A, 1 mark for correct bearing from B and 1 mark for correctly identifying intersection at point C]

c) 164° (accept answers between 162° and 166°) ***[1 mark]***

Pages 72-74: Circle Geometry

1 a) Angle $BCD = 150° \div 2 = 75°$ ***[1 mark]***
(Angle at the centre is 2 × angle at circumference.) ***[1 mark]***
[2 marks available in total — as above]
b) Opposite angles in a cyclic quadrilateral sum to 180°. ***[1 mark]***

2 Angle $DBC = 62°$ because angles in the same segment are equal. ***[1 mark]***
Angle $ABC = 90°$ because the angle in a semicircle is a right angle. ***[1 mark]***
Angle $x = 90° - 62° = 28°$ ***[1 mark]***
[3 marks available in total — as above]

3 a) $x = 28°$ ***[1 mark]*** $y = 24°$ ***[1 mark]***
[2 marks available in total — as above]
b) Angles in the same segment are equal. ***[1 mark]***

4 Angles ODE and OBE are both 90° because a tangent always meets a radius at 90°. ***[1 mark]***
Angle $DOB = 100°$ because angles in a quadrilateral add up to 360°. ***[1 mark]***
Angle $DCB = 50°$ because an angle at the centre is twice the angle at the circumference. ***[1 mark]***
Angle $DAB = 130°$ because opposite angles of a cyclic quadrilateral sum to 180°. ***[1 mark]***
[4 marks available in total — as above]

5 Angle $DCO = 90°$ because a tangent always meets a radius at 90°. ***[1 mark]***
Angle $DOC = 180° - 90° - 24° = 66°$ because angles in a triangle add up to 180°. ***[1 mark]***
Angle $AOC = 66° \times 2 = 132°$ because tangents from the same point are the same length, so create two identical triangles, meaning angle DOC = angle DOA. ***[1 mark]***
Angle $ABC = 66°$ because an angle at the centre is twice the angle at the circumference. ***[1 mark]***
Angle $CBE = 180° - 66° = 114°$ because angles on a straight line add up to 180°. ***[1 mark]***
[5 marks available in total — as above]

6 Angle FBD = angle $BCD = 102°$ from the alternate segment theorem. ***[1 mark]***
Angle $CDB = 180° - 147° = 33°$ because angles on a straight line add up to 180°. ***[1 mark]***
Angle $CBD = 180° - 102° - 33° = 45°$ because angles in a triangle add up to 180°. ***[1 mark]***
Angle CAD = angle $CBD = 45°$ because angles in the same segment are equal. ***[1 mark]***
[4 marks available in total — as above]

7 a) Angle DAB = Angle $BDE = 53°$ from the alternate segment theorem. ***[1 mark]***
Angle $DOB = 2 \times$ Angle $DAB = 106°$ because an angle at the centre is twice the angle at the circumference. ***[1 mark]***
[2 marks available in total — as above]
You could have done this one by splitting the triangle DOB into two identical right-angled triangles and working out the angles.
b) OB and OD are both radii, so OBD is an isosceles triangle.
The radius OC crosses chord BD at right-angles, so it bisects BD ***[1 mark]*** and divides the isosceles triangle OBD in half, which means angle COB = 0.5 × angle DOB ***[1 mark]***.
[2 marks available in total — as above]

Page 75: Pythagoras' Theorem

1 $AB^2 = 4^2 + 8^2$ ***[1 mark]***
$AB = \sqrt{16+64} = \sqrt{80}$ ***[1 mark]***
$AB = 8.94$ cm (2 d.p) ***[1 mark]***
[3 marks available in total — as above]

2 Difference in x-coordinates $= 8 - 2 = 6$
Difference in y-coordinates $= 7 - -1 = 8$
[1 mark for both]
So length of line segment $= \sqrt{6^2+8^2}$ ***[1 mark]***
$= \sqrt{36+64}$
$= \sqrt{100} = 10$ ***[1 mark]***
[3 marks available in total — as above]

3 Let h be the height of the triangle:
$13^2 = 5^2 + h^2$ ***[1 mark]***
$h = \sqrt{169-25} = \sqrt{144}$ ***[1 mark]***
$h = 12$ cm ***[1 mark]***
Area, $A = \frac{1}{2} \times 10 \times 12$
$A = 60\text{ cm}^2$ ***[1 mark]***
[4 marks available in total — as above]

4 Length of EA:
$28.3^2 = 20^2 + EA^2$ ***[1 mark]***
$EA = \sqrt{800.89 - 400}$
$EA = 20.02...$ ***[1 mark]***
Length of CE:
$54.3^2 = 20^2 + CE^2$ ***[1 mark]***
$CE = \sqrt{2948.49 - 400} = 50.48...$ ***[1 mark]***
Perimeter $= 28.3 + 54.3 + EA + CE$
$= 153.1$ cm (1 d.p) ***[1 mark]***
[5 marks available in total — as above]

Page 76: Trigonometry

1 $\sin x = \frac{14}{18}$ ***[1 mark]***
$x = \sin^{-1}\left(\frac{14}{18}\right)$ ***[1 mark]***
$x = 51.1°$ (1 d.p) ***[1 mark]***
[3 marks available in total — as above]

2 $\tan 60° = \frac{4}{y}$
$y = \frac{4}{\tan 60°} = 2.31$ m (2 d.p.)
[3 marks available — 1 mark for correct use of tan formula, 1 mark for correctly substituting 60° and 4, 1 mark for the correct answer]

3 The angle between the ground and the ramp should be 3.6°.
$\tan 3.6° = \frac{12}{x}$
$x = \frac{12}{\tan 3.6°}$
$x = 191$ cm (3 s.f)
[3 marks available — 1 mark for correct use of tan formula, 1 mark for correctly substituting 3.6° and 12, 1 mark for the correct answer]

4 Call the distance from the centre of the circle to the centre of an edge x.
The radius bisects the interior angle forming angle a.

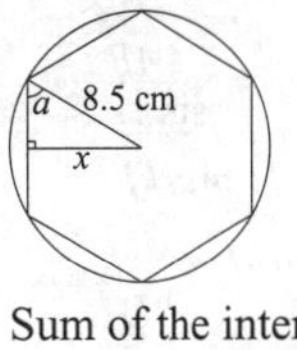

Sum of the interior angles of a hexagon = $4 \times 180° = 720°$
Each interior angle of a hexagon = $720° \div 6 = 120°$
$a = 120 \div 2 = 60°$
$\sin 60° = \frac{x}{8.5}$
$x = 8.5 \times \sin 60°$
$x = 7.36$ cm (2 d.p)
[6 marks available — 1 mark for correct method to find interior angle of a hexagon, 1 mark for correct interior angle of a hexagon, 1 mark for the correct size of angle a, 1 mark for correct use of sin formula, 1 mark for correctly substituting 60° and 8.5, 1 mark for correct answer]
You could also use the calculation cos 30° × 8.5 to find the value of x. As long as you make sure you show your working, you'll get full marks if your answer is correct.

Pages 77-78: The Sine and Cosine Rules

1 a) $AC^2 = 10^2 + 7^2 - (2 \times 10 \times 7 \times \cos 85°)$ ***[1 mark]***
$AC = \sqrt{149 - 140 \times \cos 85°}$
$= 11.7$ cm (3 s.f) ***[1 mark]***
[2 marks available in total — as above.]
b) Area $= \frac{1}{2} \times 10 \times 7 \times \sin 85°$ ***[1 mark]***
$= 34.9\text{ cm}^2$ (3 s.f) ***[1 mark]***
[2 marks available in total — as above]

2 a) $\frac{BD}{\sin 30°} = \frac{8}{\sin 70°}$ ***[1 mark]***
$BD = \frac{8}{\sin 70°} \times \sin 30°$ ***[1 mark]***
$BD = 4.26$ m (3 s.f) ***[1 mark]***
[3 marks available in total — as above]

b) $\frac{4}{\sin BDC} = \frac{4.26}{\sin 60°}$ ***[1 mark]***

$\sin BDC = \frac{\sin 60°}{4.26} \times 4$

Angle $BDC = \sin^{-1}(0.813...)$ ***[1 mark]***

Angle $BDC = 54.4°$ (3 s.f) ***[1 mark]***

[3 marks available in total — as above]

3 First find one angle using the cosine rule: E.g. use angle CAB

$\cos A = \frac{14^2 + 12^2 - 19^2}{2 \times 14 \times 12}$ ***[1 mark]***

$A = \cos^{-1}\left(\frac{-21}{336}\right)$

$A = 93.58...°$ ***[1 mark]***

Area $= \frac{1}{2} \times 14 \times 12 \times \sin 93.58...°$ ***[1 mark]***

Area $= 83.84$ cm^2 (2.d.p) ***[1 mark]***

[4 marks available in total — as above]

4 Angle $ABD = 180° - 90° - 31° - 12° = 47°$

Angle $ACB = 180° - 12° - 47° = 121°$

[1 mark for both]

Use the sine rule: $\frac{3.3}{\sin 12°} = \frac{AB}{\sin 121°}$

$AB = \frac{3.3}{\sin 12°} \times \sin 121°$ ***[1 mark]***

$AB = 13.6050...$ m ***[1 mark]***

Find length BD: $\cos 47° = \frac{BD}{13.6050...}$

$BD = \cos 47° \times 13.6050...$ ***[1 mark]***

$BD = 9.2786... = 9.28$ m (3 s.f.) ***[1 mark]***

[5 marks available in total— as above]

There's more than one way of doing this question. As long as you've used a correct method to get the right answer you'll still get the marks.

5 $\sin 30° = \frac{x}{AC}$

$AC = \frac{x}{\sin 30°} = 2x$ cm ***[1 mark]***

Angle $CAD = 90° - 30° = 60°$

$CD^2 = (2x)^2 + (3x)^2 - (2 \times 2x \times 3x \times \cos 60°)$ ***[1 mark]***

$CD^2 = 4x^2 + 9x^2 - 6x^2 = 7x^2$

$CD = \sqrt{7x^2} = x\sqrt{7}$ cm ***[1 mark]***

Perimeter of $ACD = 2x + 3x + x\sqrt{7}$

$= (5 + \sqrt{7})x$ cm (so $a = 5$ ***[1 mark]***, $b = 7$ ***[1 mark]***)

[5 marks available in total — as above]

Page 79: 3D Pythagoras and Trigonometry

1 $BH^2 = 6^2 + 3^2 + 4^2$ ***[1 mark]***

$BH = \sqrt{61}$ ***[1 mark]***

$BH = 7.81$ cm (3 s.f.) ***[1 mark]***

[3 marks available in total — as above]

2 $FG = 80 \div 2 \div 8 = 5$ cm

$DF^2 = 8^2 + 2^2 + 5^2$ ***[1 mark]***

$DF = \sqrt{93}$ ***[1 mark]***

The angle between the diagonal DF and the plane $CDHG$ is the angle it makes with the line DG, so

$\sin FDG = \frac{5}{\sqrt{93}}$ ***[1 mark]***

$FDG = \sin^{-1}\left(\frac{5}{\sqrt{93}}\right)$ ***[1 mark]***

$= 31°$ (2 s.f.) ***[1 mark]***

[5 marks available in total — as above]

3 Using Pythagoras' theorem on triangle AXV:

$AX^2 = 8.9^2 - 7.2^2 = 27.37$, so $AX = \sqrt{27.37}$ ***[1 mark]*** and $AC = 2\sqrt{27.37}$ ***[1 mark]***

Now using Pythagoras' theorem on triangle ABC:

$AB^2 = (2\sqrt{27.37})^2 - 4.2^2 = 91.84$ ***[1 mark]***,

so $AB = \sqrt{91.84} = 9.583...$

$= 9.58$ cm (3 s.f.) ***[1 mark]***

[4 marks available in total — as above]

Section Six — Shapes and Area

Page 80: Properties of 2D Shapes

1 a) rhombus ***[1 mark]***

b) isosceles triangle ***[1 mark]***

2 a)

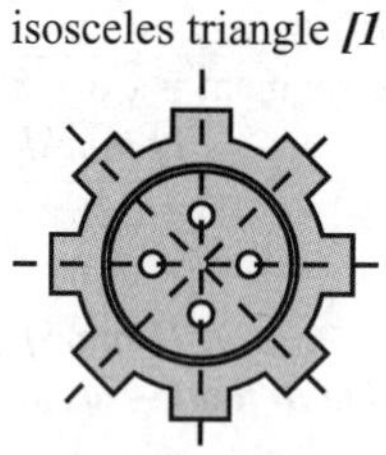

[2 marks available — 2 marks if all four lines of symmetry correctly drawn, otherwise 1 mark if two out of four lines of symmetry correctly drawn]

b) 4 ***[1 mark]***

3 a) E.g.

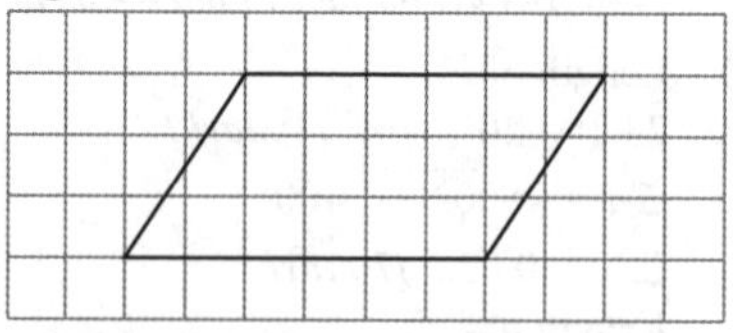

[2 marks available — 2 marks for drawing a parallelogram, otherwise 1 mark for drawing a shape which has two of the listed properties]

b) No, because e.g. all the sides and angles in a regular polygon are the same, and all regular polygons have at least one line of symmetry. ***[1 mark for 'no' and at least one correct reason]***

Page 81: Similar Shapes

1 Scale factor from $EFGH$ to $ABCD$ = $9 \div 6 = 1.5$ ***[1 mark]***

$EF = 6 \div 1.5 = 4$ cm ***[1 mark]***

$BC = 4 \times 1.5 = 6$ cm ***[1 mark]***

[3 marks available in total — as above]

2 63 m = 6300 cm

Scale factor = $6300 \div 60$ ***[1 mark]***

= 105 ***[1 mark]***

Height of flagpole = 8 cm × 105 = 840 cm = 8.4 m ***[1 mark]***

[3 marks available in total — as above]

The triangles created between Cian's eyes and his finger and his eyes and the flagpole are similar.

3 Lines AD and EF are parallel (they're both parallel to BCG)

Angles in a rectangle are 90° so angle ABC = angle CEF

Corresponding angles are equal so angle BAC = angle ECF

Corresponding angles are equal so angle ACB = angle CFE

Triangles ABC and CEF have all three angles the same so are similar.

[3 marks available — 1 mark for showing one angle is the same, 1 mark for showing that the rest are the same (the third angle can be implied from two angles the same), 1 mark for stating that the triangles are similar because their angles are the same]

Pages 82-83: Perimeter and Area

1 Area of rhombus = ½ × diagonal × diagonal ***[1 mark]***

= ½ × 4 × 5 = 10 mm^2 ***[1 mark]***

Area of kite = ½ × diagonal × diagonal ***[1 mark]***

= ½ × 4 × 12 = 24 mm^2 ***[1 mark]***

Total area = 10 + 24 = 34 mm^2 ***[1 mark]***

[5 marks available in total — as above]

2 Lawn area = (30 m × 10 m) – (π × (5 m)^2) = 221.460... m^2

Boxes of seed needed = 221.460... m^2 ÷ 10 m^2 = 22.15

So Lynn must buy 23 boxes.

Total cost = 23 × £7 = £161

[5 marks available — 1 mark for a correct method for finding the lawn area, 1 mark for correctly calculating the lawn area, 1 mark for dividing the area by 10 m² to find the number of boxes, 1 mark for the correct number of boxes, 1 mark for the correct answer]

3 Shorter parallel side of the trapezium = 52 cm – 16 cm – 16 cm = 20 cm
To see this, split the shape into two triangles and a rectangle. The two triangles are both isosceles, so the base of each triangle is 16 cm long.
Area of trapezium = 0.5 × (52 + 20) × 16 = 576 cm^2
[3 marks available — 1 mark for finding shorter parallel side of trapezium, 1 mark for correct method to calculate area of trapezium, 1 mark for correct answer]

4 Area of triangle = 0.5 × 2x × 2x ***[1 mark]***
= 2x^2 ***[1 mark]***
Area of square = x^2
$2x^2 - x^2 = 9$ cm^2 ***[1 mark]***
$x^2 = 9$ cm^2 so $x = 3$ cm ***[1 mark]***
Perimeter of square = 4 × 3 cm = 12 cm ***[1 mark]***
[5 marks available in total — as above]

5 Circumference of full circle = 2 × π × 6 = 12π cm
Length of arc = (30 ÷ 360) × circumference of circle
= (30 ÷ 360) × 12π = π cm
Perimeter of sector = π + 6 + 6 = 15.1 cm (3 s.f.)
Area of full circle = π × 6^2 = 36π cm^2
Area of sector = (30 ÷ 360) × area of circle
= (30 ÷ 360) × 36π = 3π cm^2
= 9.42 cm^2 (3 s.f.)
[5 marks available — 1 mark for a correct method for calculating the length of the arc, 1 mark for correct arc length, 1 mark for correct perimeter of sector, 1 mark for a correct method for finding the area of the sector, 1 mark for correct area of sector]

6 Each straight section = 2 × radius = 2 × 9 = 18 cm ***[1 mark]***
Each curved section = $\frac{1}{3}$ × circumference of circle
= $\frac{1}{3}$ × 2 × π × 9 ***[1 mark]***
= 6π cm ***[1 mark]***
Total length = 3 × 18 + 3 × 6π
= 110.5 cm (1 d.p.) ***[1 mark]***
[4 marks available in total — as above]

Page 84: Plans and Elevations

1

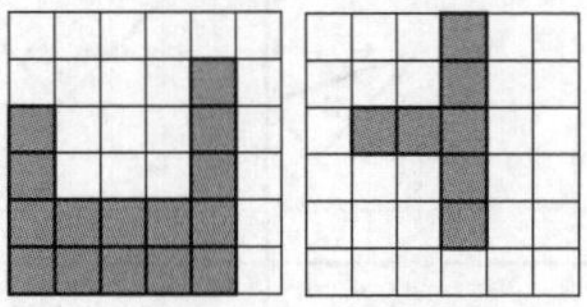

Front elevation Plan view

[3 marks available — 1 mark for a correct front elevation diagram, 1 mark for a correct plan view diagram in any orientation, 1 mark for demonstrating an understanding of elevations]
The third mark here is pretty vague — basically it means that even if your drawings aren't bang on, you can still pick up a mark if the examiner can see that you had the right idea.

2 Split the shape into two cuboids, looking at the front elevation. The bottom cuboid has 4 × 2 × 4 = 32 cubes in it. The cuboid at the top has 2 × 2 × 4 = 16 cubes in it.
So there are 32 + 16 = 48 cubes in the shape.
[2 marks available — 1 mark for a correct calculation, 1 mark for the correct answer]
You might have split your shape up differently — as long as your working is correct and you get the correct answer, you'll get all the marks.

3

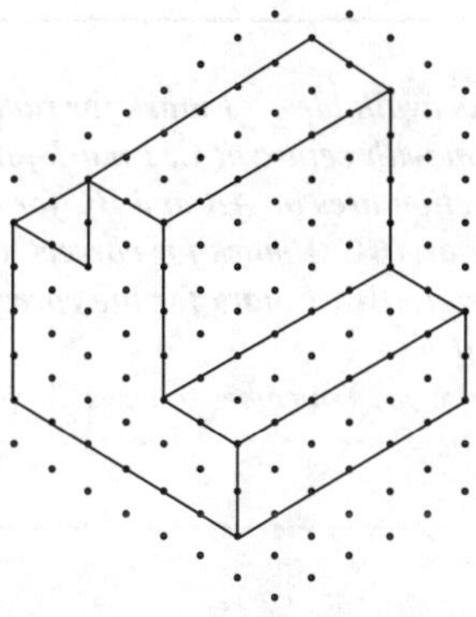

[2 marks available — 2 marks for a correct diagram, otherwise 1 mark for demonstrating an understanding of elevations — e.g. all the appropriate vertices of the cross-section have straight lines extending from them, but they're not all the same length]

Pages 85-86: 3D Shapes — Surface Area & Volume (1)

1 Area of pool base = π × (2 ÷ 2)^2 = π m^2 ***[1 mark]***
Volume of pool = π × 0.4 = 0.4π m^3 ***[1 mark]***
Volume of water Amy should use = 0.4π × $\frac{3}{4}$ ***[1 mark]*** = 0.94 m^3 (2 d.p.) ***[1 mark]***
[4 marks available in total — as above]

2 A regular hexagon is made up of 6 identical triangles.
Area of triangle = 0.5 × 8 × 7 = 28 cm^2 ***[1 mark]***
Area of whole hexagon cross-section = 28 × 6 = 168 cm^2 ***[1 mark]***
Volume of prism = cross-sectional area × length = 168 × 6 = 1008 cm^3 ***[1 mark]***
[3 marks available in total — as above]

3 113 = $\frac{1}{3}$ × πr^2 × 12 ***[1 mark]***
r^2 = 8.992...
r = 3.00 (3 s.f.) ***[1 mark]***
[2 marks available in total — as above]

4 Volume = $\frac{4}{3}\pi r^3$ = 478 cm^3 ***[1 mark]***
$r = \sqrt[3]{\frac{3 \times 478}{4\pi}}$ = 4.8504... cm ***[1 mark]***
Surface area = $4\pi r^2 = 4\pi \times (4.8504...)^2$ ***[1 mark]***
= 295.6 cm^2 (1 d.p.) ***[1 mark]***
[4 marks available in total — as above]

5 Volume of cone = $\frac{1}{3}(\pi \times 6^2 \times 18)$
= 216π cm^3 ***[1 mark]***
So $\frac{4}{3}\pi r^3$ = 216π cm^3 ***[1 mark]***
r^3 = 162 ***[1 mark]***
r = 5.4513... cm = 5.45 cm (3 s.f.) ***[1 mark]***
[4 marks available in total — as above]

6 The area of the net is a quarter of a circle, so
$\frac{1}{4}\pi r^2$ = 64 cm^2 ***[1 mark]***
$r = \sqrt{\frac{64 \times 4}{\pi}}$ ***[1 mark]***
= 9.027... cm ***[1 mark]***
So the slant height of the cone (l) = 9.027... cm.
The curved area of the cone = πRl
(where R is the radius of the circular base)
πRl = 64 cm^2
So R = 64 ÷ 9.027... π ***[1 mark]***
= 2.26 cm (2 d.p.) ***[1 mark]***
[5 marks available in total — as above]

Page 87: 3D Shapes — Surface Area & Volume (2)

1 Volume of cuboid = 1.5 × 0.4 × 0.5
= 0.3 m^3 ***[1 mark]***
Height of removed cone = 0.5 – 0.3
= 0.2 m ***[1 mark]***
Volume of frustum =
$(\frac{1}{3} \times \pi \times 0.3^2 \times 0.5) - (\frac{1}{3} \times \pi \times 0.12^2 \times 0.2)$ ***[1 mark]***
= 0.015π – 0.00096π
= 0.01404π = 0.0441... m^3 ***[1 mark]***
Volume of water = 0.3 – 0.0441...
= 0.256 m^3 (3 s.f.) ***[1 mark]***
0.256 × 100 × 100 × 100 = 256 000 cm^3
= 256 000 ÷ 1000 = 256 litres (3 s.f.) ***[1 mark]***
[6 marks available in total — as above]

2 a) The removed cone is one-third of the height of the original cone, so has height 12 cm ***[1 mark]***
Volume of frustum
= $(\frac{1}{3} \times \pi \times 15^2 \times 36) - (\frac{1}{3} \times \pi \times 5^2 \times 12)$ ***[1 mark]***
= 2700π – 100π = 2600π cm^3
= 8168.14 cm^3 (to 2 d.p.) ***[1 mark]***
[3 marks available in total — as above]

b) Slant height of removed cone = $39 - 26 = 13$ cm.
Curved area of frustum
$= (\pi \times 15 \times 39) - (\pi \times 5 \times 13)$
[1 mark]
$= 585\pi - 65\pi = 520\pi$ ***[1 mark]***
Area of top and base $= 5^2\pi + 15^2\pi$
$= (25 + 225)\pi$
$= 250\pi$ ***[1 mark]***
Surface area $= 520\pi + 250\pi$
$= 770\pi$ cm^2
$= 2419.03$ cm^2 (to 2 d.p.)
[1 mark]
[4 marks available in total — as above]

Pages 88-89: Loci and Construction

1 a)

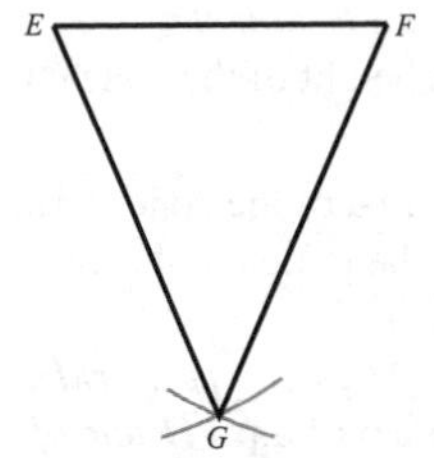

(diagram not actual size)
[2 marks available — 1 mark for arcs drawn with a radius of 4.5 cm, 1 mark for completed triangle]

b)

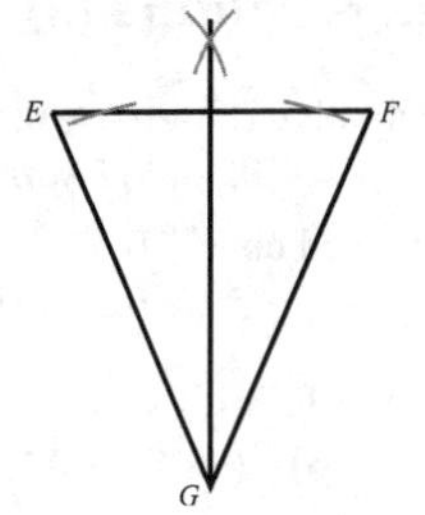

[2 marks available — 1 mark for correct construction arcs, 1 mark for correct perpendicular]

2

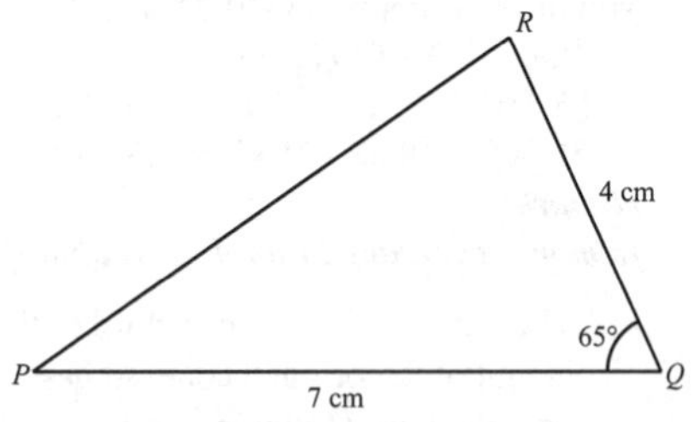

(This diagram isn't actual size — but your measurements should match those given.)
[3 marks available — 1 mark for a correct 65° angle (± 1°), 1 mark for two correct line lengths (± 1 mm), 1 mark for a fully correct diagram]

3

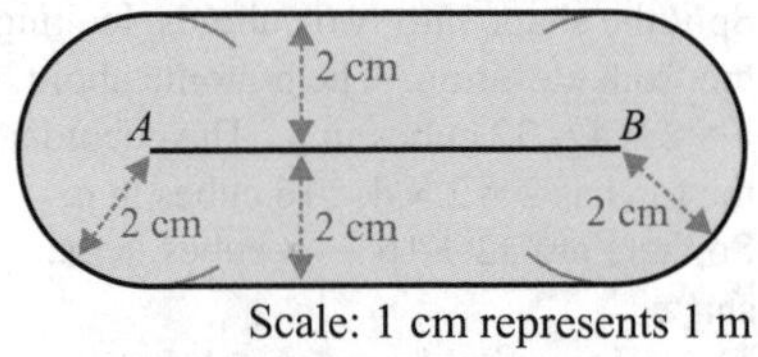

Scale: 1 cm represents 1 m
[2 marks available — 1 mark for correct semicircles, 1 mark for correct shaded area]

4

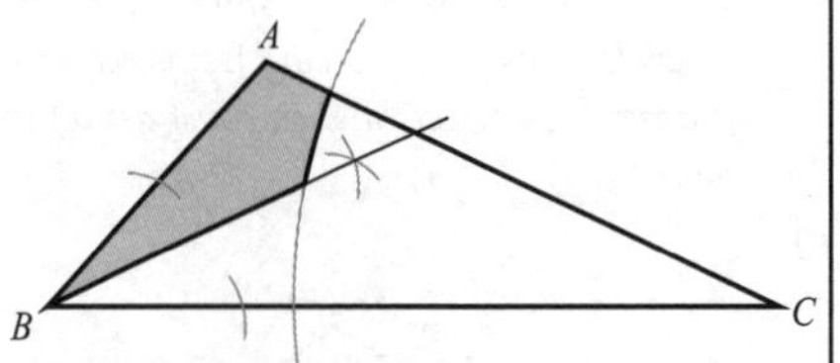

[4 marks available — 1 mark for radius of 6.5 cm with centre at C, 1 mark for construction arcs on AB and BC for angle bisector at ABC, 1 mark for correct angle bisector at ABC, 1 mark for the correct shading]
Make sure you remember to leave in your construction lines.

5

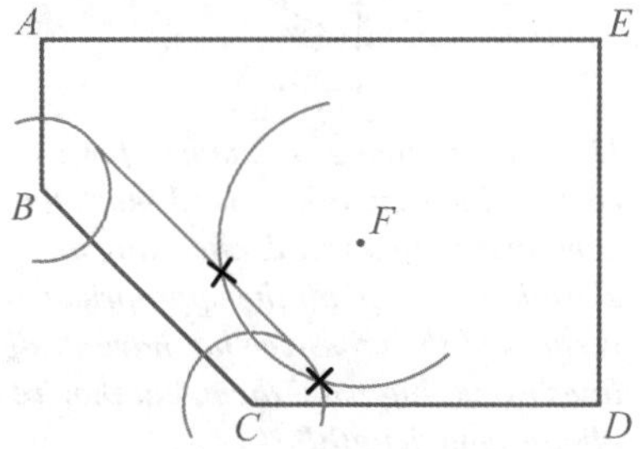

[4 marks available — 1 mark for arcs with radius of 1 cm centred at B and C, 1 mark for a line parallel to BC 1 cm from BC, 1 mark for an arc with radius of 2 cm centred at F, 1 mark for correct crosses at the intersections]

6 a)

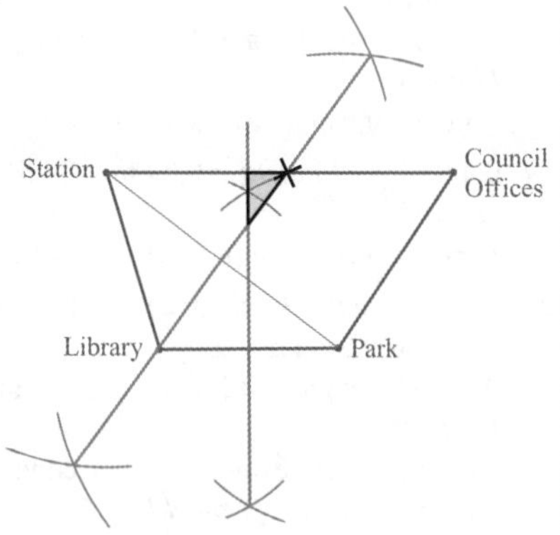

[5 marks available — 1 mark for each pair of correct arcs (centred at Library and Park and at Station and Park), 1 mark for each correct perpendicular bisector (of line between Library and Park and line between Station and Park), 1 mark for correct shaded area]

b) See diagram.
[1 mark for cross in the correct place]

Page 90: Translation, Rotation and Reflection

1 a) $\begin{pmatrix} 2 \\ -5 \end{pmatrix}$
[2 marks available — 1 mark for $\begin{pmatrix} \pm 2 \\ \pm 5 \end{pmatrix}$***, 1 mark for fully correct answer]***

b)

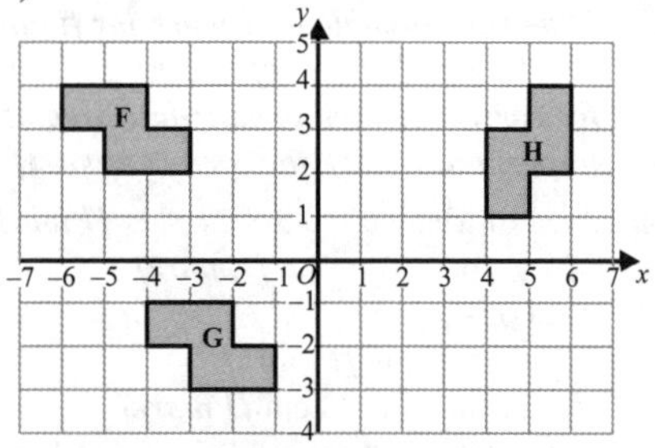

[2 marks available — 1 mark for a rotation of 90° clockwise around any point, 1 mark for correct centre of rotation]

2 a) Rotation 90° anti-clockwise around the point (0, 0)
[3 marks available — 1 mark for rotation, 1 mark for correct angle and direction of rotation, 1 mark for correct centre of rotation]

b)

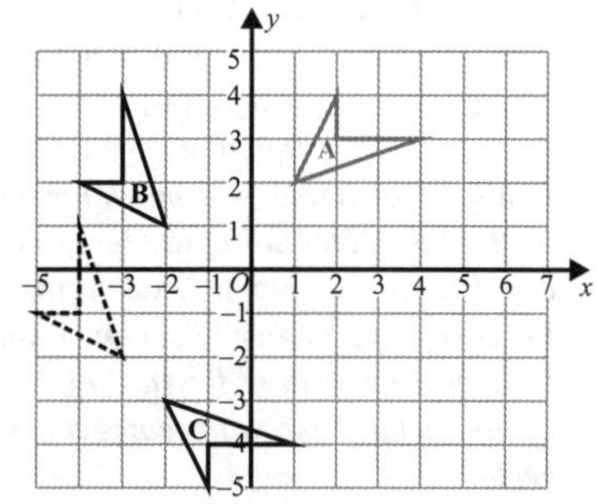

[4 marks available — 2 marks for a correct translation, otherwise 1 mark for a translation by the correct amount in only one direction, and 2 marks for a correct reflection, otherwise 1 mark for a reflected shape in the wrong position]

Page 91: Enlargement (1)

1

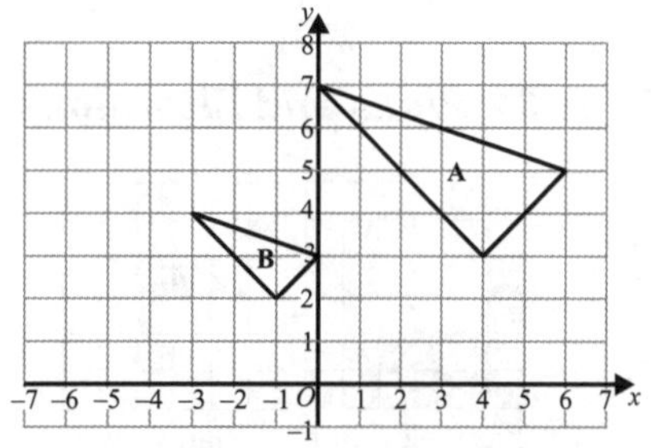

[3 marks available — 3 marks for correct shape in correct position, otherwise 1 mark for correctly enlarged shape but wrong centre of enlargement used, 1 mark for one coordinate correct]

2

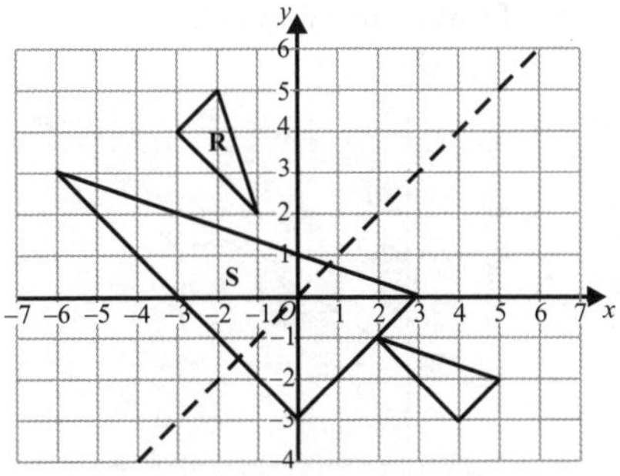

[4 marks available — 4 marks for correct shape S in correct position, otherwise 1 mark for correctly reflected shape, 1 mark for correctly enlarged shape but wrong centre of enlargement used, 1 mark for one coordinate of shape S correct]

3 $1^3 : 7^3 = 1 : 343$ ***[1 mark]***

4 Area of enlarged shape = 7×3^2 ***[1 mark]***
$= 63$ cm^2 ***[1 mark]***
[2 marks available in total — as above]

Page 92: Enlargement (2)

1

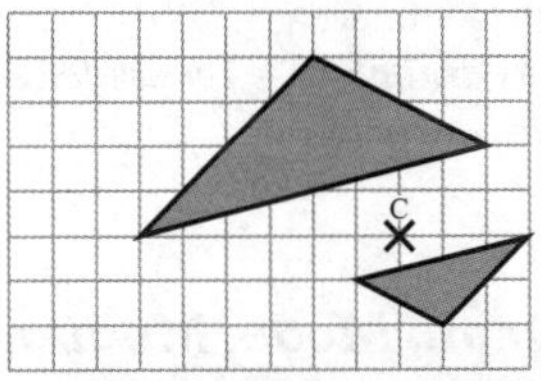

[3 marks available — 3 marks for correct shape in correct position, otherwise 1 mark for correctly enlarged shape but wrong centre of enlargement used, 1 mark for one coordinate correct]

2 Let x be the scale factor for length from cylinder A to cylinder B.
$x^3 = \frac{64}{27}$, so $x = \sqrt[3]{\frac{64}{27}} = \frac{4}{3}$ ***[1 mark]***
Then $x^2 = \frac{4^2}{3^2} = \frac{16}{9}$, ***[1 mark]***
so s.a. of cylinder B $= 81\pi \times \frac{16}{9}$ ***[1 mark]***
$= 144\pi$ cm^2 ***[1 mark]***
[4 marks available in total — as above]

3 a) If n is the scale factor from **A** to **C**:
$n^2 = 108\pi \div 12\pi = 9$ so $n = 3$
Volume of **A** $= 135\pi$ cm$^3 \div 3^3 = 5\pi$ cm^3
[4 marks available — 1 mark for finding n^2, 1 mark for finding n, 1 mark for dividing volume of A by n^3, 1 mark for correct answer]

b) If m is the scale factor from **A** to **B**:
$m^2 = 48\pi \div 12\pi = 4$ ***[1 mark]***
$m = 2$ ***[1 mark]***
Perpendicular height of **B** = 4 cm × 2 = 8 cm ***[1 mark]***
[3 marks available in total — as above]

Section Seven — Statistics and Probability

Page 93: Sampling and Data Collection (1)

1 a) E.g. How many different after-school activities do you attend each week?

0	1 – 2	3 – 4	5 or more
☐	☐	☐	☐

[2 marks available — 1 mark for an appropriate question, 1 mark for at least 3 boxes which don't overlap and which cover all possible answers]

b) E.g. The results of her survey are likely to be biased as she is only asking people who attend an after-school activity. ***[1 mark]***
The key idea here is "bias" — the results of her survey are likely to be an unfair representation of what all pupils at the school do.

2 a) Proportion of people in sample who travelled by car = 22 ÷ 50 = 0.44 ***[1 mark]***
Estimate of number of people at match who travelled by car
= 0.44 × 5000 ***[1 mark]***
= 2200 ***[1 mark]***
[3 marks available in total — as above]
You could have followed a different method here — e.g. divide 5000 by 50 and then multiply 22 by the result to scale it up to the full population.

b) E.g. He could ask a larger sample of people at the game. ***[1 mark]***

c) E.g. Daisy has made the assumption that Mario's sample is a fair representation of the people at her match. ***[1 mark]***
Or you could say she has assumed that the proportions who travelled by car to the two matches are roughly the same.
E.g. her estimate is unreliable because she hasn't sampled people from the correct population. ***[1 mark]***
[2 marks available in total — as above]

Page 94: Sampling and Data Collection (2)

1 a) E.g. she needs to find the fraction of the total number of teenagers in each age group, then multiply each of these by the sample size (100) to get the number of teenagers from each group to be included in the sample. She should then choose these teenagers at random.
[2 marks available — 1 mark for a description of the calculation, 1 mark for saying to select the sample at random]

b) Teenagers aged 14
= (total aged 14 ÷ total teenagers) × size of sample
= (192 ÷ 800) × 100 ***[1 mark]***
= 24 ***[1 mark]***
[2 marks available in total — as above]

2 (487 ÷ 2033) × 150 ***[1 mark]***
= 35.932... = 36 ***[1 mark]***
[2 marks available in total — as above]

3 Total number of students =
167 + 162 + 150 + 125 + 116
= 720 ***[1 mark]***
(116 ÷ 720) × 75 ***[1 mark]***
= 12.083... = 12 ***[1 mark]***
[3 marks available in total — as above]

Page 95: Venn Diagrams

1 Percentage not in F or S = 20% ***[1 mark]***
$20\% = \frac{20}{100} = \frac{1}{5}$ ***[1 mark]***
[2 marks available in total — as above]

2 a)

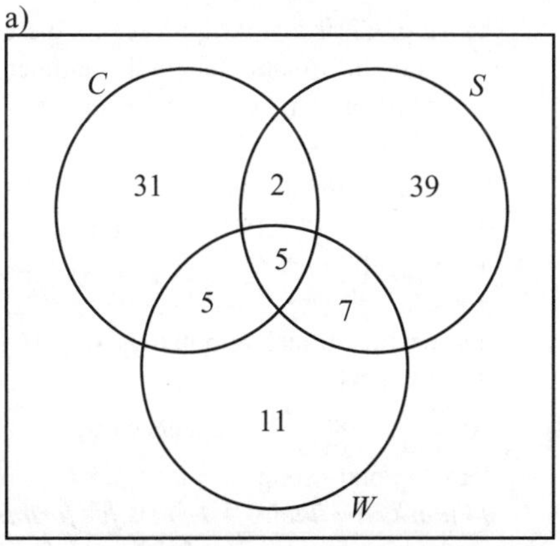

[3 marks available — 3 marks for a completely correct diagram, otherwise 1 mark for at least 2 correct entries or 2 marks for at least 4 correct entries]

b) 31 + 5 + 5 + 2 + 7 + 39 = 89 ***[1 mark]***
You could also do 100 – 11 to get this answer.

c) $\frac{2}{39 + 2 + 5 + 7}$ ***[1 mark]***
$= \frac{2}{53}$ ***[1 mark]***
[2 marks available in total — as above]

Page 96: Pie Charts

1 a) Total number of people =
12 + 18 + 9 + 21 = 60
Multiplier = 360 ÷ 60 = 6
Plain: 12 × 6 = 72°
Salted: 18 × 6 = 108°
Sugared: 9 × 6 = 54°
Toffee: 21 × 6 = 126°

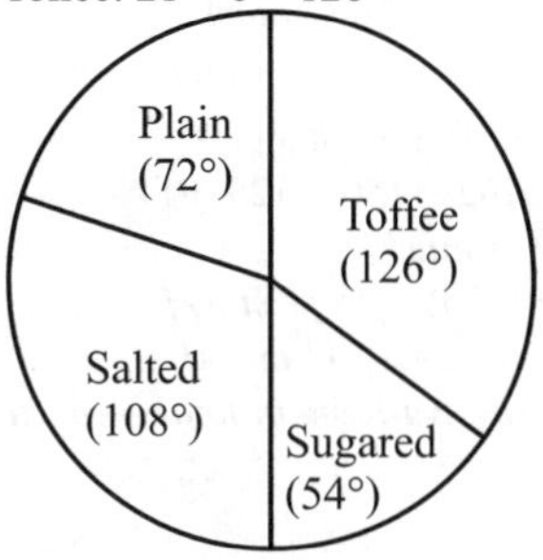

[4 marks available — 1 mark for one sector correctly drawn, 1 mark for a second sector correctly drawn, 1 mark for a complete pie chart with all angles correct, 1 mark for correct labels]

b) E.g. Chris is not right because there is no information about the number of people in the ice-cream survey.
[1 mark]

2 There are 360° in a circle, so
$2x° + 3x° + 4x° + x° + 90° = 360°$
$10x° = 270°$
$x = 27$
The sector for leek & potato is $3x° = 3 \times 27° = 81°$,
so $\frac{81°}{360°} \times 80 = 18$ students chose leek & potato soup.
[4 marks available — 1 mark for forming an equation in terms of x, 1 mark for solving to find the value of x, 1 mark for a correct method to find the number of students, 1 mark for the correct answer]

Page 97: Other Charts and Graphs

1 The data shows a slight downward trend in the numbers of swallows seen. ***[1 mark]***

2 Number of left-handed females
= 23 – 9 = 14
Total number of females = 14 + 126 = 140
Fraction of females who are left-handed
$= \frac{14}{140} = \frac{1}{10}$
[4 marks available in total — 1 mark for a correct calculation to find the number of left-handed females, 1 mark for a correct calculation to find the total number of females, 1 mark for a correct fraction with left-handed females over total females, 1 mark for correctly simplifying the fraction.]

3 a) A Start/Begin box and Stop/End box are both missing ***[1 mark]***.

b)

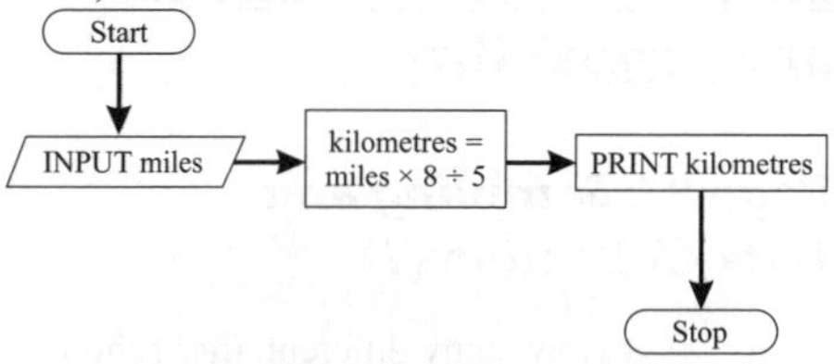

[2 marks available — 1 mark for adding the start box before input and the stop box after print, 1 mark for the correct shape of box]

Page 98: Scatter Graphs

1 a)

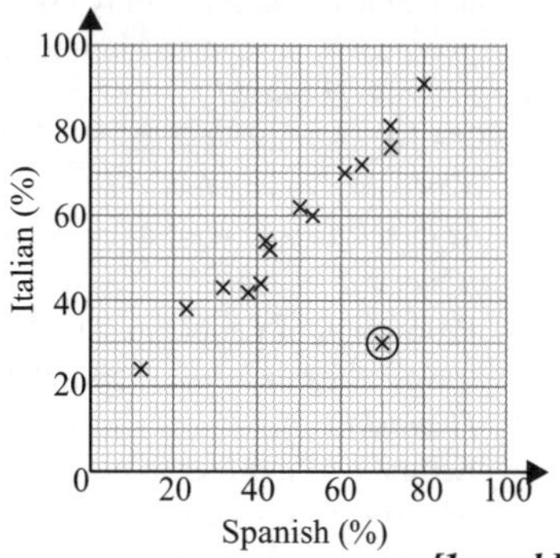

[1 mark]

b) Strong positive correlation ***[1 mark]***

c)

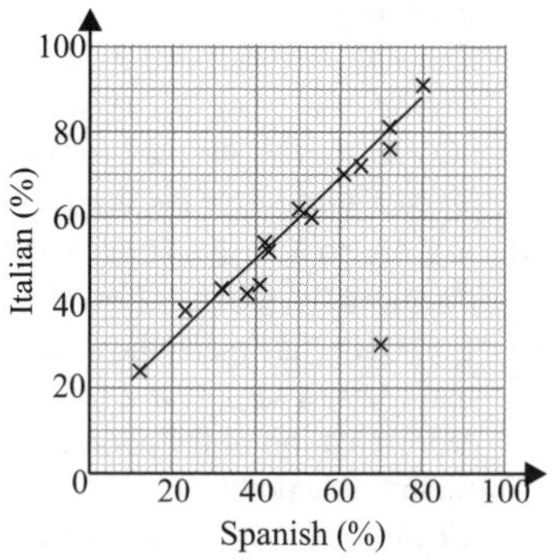

[1 mark for line of best fit passing between (10, 16) & (10, 28) and (80, 82) & (80, 96)]

2 a)

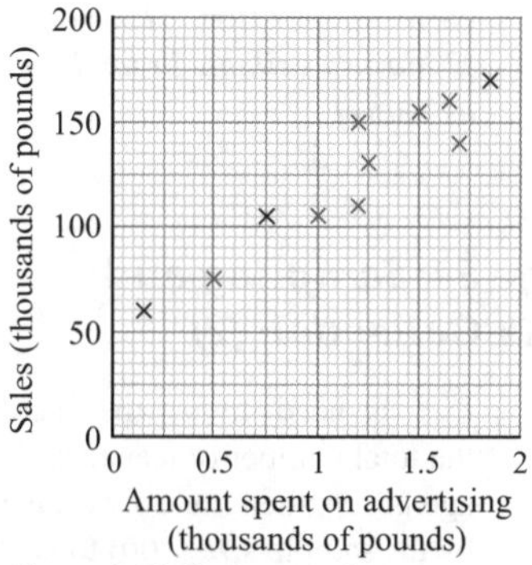

[1 mark if all three points are plotted correctly]

b) Draw a line of best fit:

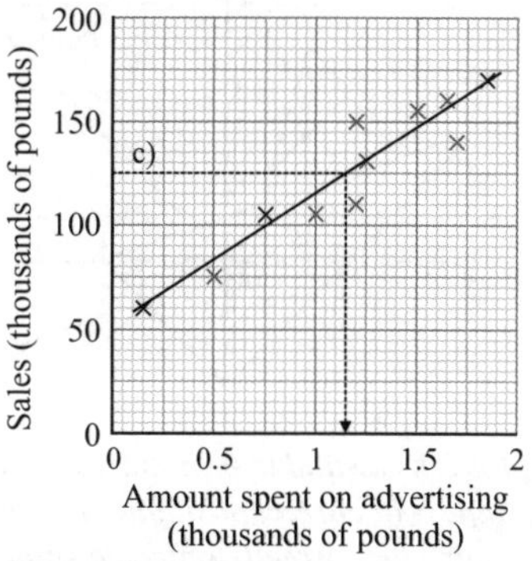

See graph — £1150
[2 marks available — 1 mark for drawing a line of best fit, 1 mark for reading off the correct answer, allow answers ± £100]

c) E.g. using the trend to predict sales for a value of £3000 might be unreliable because the value is outside their range of data and they don't know whether the same pattern would continue. However, the data shows strong positive correlation, so the trend will probably continue.
[2 marks available — 1 mark for each sensible comment]

Page 99: Mean, Mode, Median and Range

1 a) Yes, the mean number is higher than 17 because the 11th data value is higher than the mean of the original 10 values. ***[1 mark]***

b) You can't tell if the median number is higher than 15, because you don't know the other data values. ***[1 mark]***

2 a) 23, 26, 36 (in any order)
range = 13, median = 26
[2 marks available — 1 mark for all three weights correct, 1 mark for both range and median correct]

b) Original total weight of herd =
32 + 23 + 31 + 28 + 36 + 26 = 176
New total weight of herd =
4 × 27.25 = 109 ***[1 mark]***
Change in total weight =
176 – 109 = 67 ***[1 mark]***
so, goats weighing 31 kg and 36 kg
[1 mark]
[3 marks available in total — as above]

3 Call the five consecutive numbers n, $n + 1$, $n + 2$, $n + 3$ and $n + 4$
Median = middle value = $n + 2$
Mean =
$$\frac{n+(n+1)+(n+2)+(n+3)+(n+4)}{5}$$
$$= \frac{5n+10}{5}$$
$$= n + 2$$
Difference between mean and median = $(n + 2) - (n + 2) = 0$
[3 marks available — 1 mark for writing correct expressions for five consecutive numbers, 1 mark for a correct expression for the mean, 1 mark for showing that the difference between the expression for the mean and the expression for the median is zero]

Page 100: Frequency Tables — Finding Averages

1 a) $8 + 3 + 5 + 8 + 4 + 1 = 29$
[2 marks available — 1 mark for the correct calculation, 1 mark for the correct answer]

b) $(0 \times 8) + (1 \times 3) + (2 \times 5) + (3 \times 8) + (4 \times 4) + (5 \times 1) = 58$
[2 marks available — 1 mark for the correct calculation, 1 mark for the correct answer]

c) $58 \div 29 = 2$
[2 marks available — 1 mark for the correct calculation, 1 mark for the correct answer]

2 a) $(0 \times 2) + (2 \times 4) + (3 \times 7) + (5 \times 11) + (7 \times 6) + (8 \times 3) + (10 \times 3)$ ***[1 mark]***
$= 180$ ***[1 mark]***
[2 marks available in total — as above]

b) i) $180 \div (2 + 4 + 7 + 11 + 6 + 3 + 3) = 5$
[2 marks available — 1 mark for the correct calculation, 1 mark for the correct answer]

ii) 5 ***[1 mark]***

iii) Value in position $(36 + 1) \div 2 = 18.5$
18th value = 5 and 19th value = 5, so median = 5
[2 marks available — 1 mark for the correct position, 1 mark for correct value]

Page 101: Grouped Frequency Tables

1 a) The modal class is the one with the highest frequency, so that's $3 \leq x \leq 5$ ***[1 mark]***

b) $(10 + 1) \div 2 = 5.5$, so the median is halfway between the 5th and 6th values, so it lies in the group containing the 5th and 6th values, which is $3 \leq x \leq 5$ ***[1 mark]***

c) $((1 \times 2) + (4 \times 4) + (7 \times 3) + (10 \times 1)) \div 10$
$= 49 \div 10 = 4.9$ cm
[4 marks available — 1 mark for all mid-interval values, 1 mark for calculation of frequency × mid-interval value, 1 mark for dividing sum of frequency × mid-interval values by sum of frequencies, 1 mark for the correct answer]

2 a) $((24 \times 4) + (28 \times 8) + (32 \times 13) + (36 \times 6) + (40 \times 1)) \div 32$
$= 992 \div 32 = 31$ seconds
[4 marks available — 1 mark for all mid-interval values, 1 mark for calculation of frequency × mid-interval value, 1 mark for dividing sum of frequency × mid-interval values by sum of frequencies, 1 mark for the correct answer]

b) There were 32 pupils and $13 + 6 + 1 = 20$ got a time of more than 30 seconds ***[1 mark]***, $(20 \div 32) \times 100 = 62.5\%$ ***[1 mark]***
[2 marks available in total — as above]

c) E.g. You couldn't use these results because you don't know the ages of the pupils in the sample, or whether any of the times were run by boys, so you can't tell if the results would fairly represent 16-year-old boys.
[1 mark for a sensible comment]

Pages 102-103: Averages and Spread

1 a)

0	3 4 4 5 5 5 7 8 8 9
1	0 1 2 5
2	0

Key: 0 | 3 = £3

[3 marks available — 1 mark for correct entries, 1 mark for correct order, 1 mark for key]

b) E.g. the interquartile range will remain the same, as all the values have decreased by 50p. This 50p will cancel out when you subtract the lower quartile from the upper quartile. ***[1 mark]***

2 a) IQR = 72 – 52 ***[1 mark]***
= 20 km ***[1 mark]***
[2 marks available in total — as above]

b) E.g. the interquartile range doesn't include outliers, which Rachel's longest distance is likely to be, so it should be a more reliable measure of the spread. ***[1 mark]***

c) 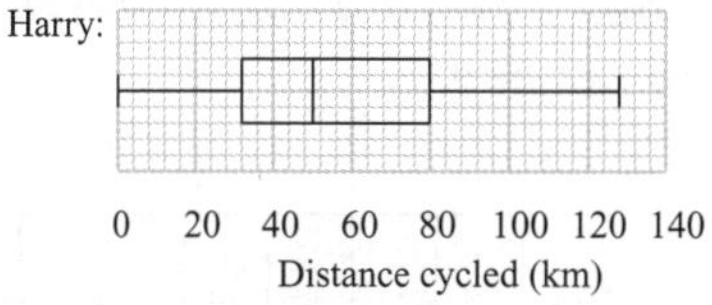

[2 marks available — 2 marks for a fully correct box plot, otherwise 1 mark for correctly showing at least 3 of lower endpoint, upper endpoint, median, lower quartile and upper quartile]

d) E.g. comparing the box plots, the IQR of Rachel's distances is much smaller than the IQR of Harry's distances and Rachel's range is also smaller, so I agree that her distances were more consistent.
[2 marks available — 1 mark for correctly comparing the values of the range or IQR, 1 mark for a correct conclusion (supported by a correct comparison)]

3 Put the data in order: 29, 31, 31, 31, 33, 38, 40, 42, 42, 45, 46 ***[1 mark]***
11 values in the list so median = $(11 + 1) \div 2$ = 6th value = 38 ***[1 mark]***
$Q_1 = (11 + 1) \div 4$ = 3rd value = 31 ***[1 mark]***
$Q_3 = 3 \times (11 + 1) \div 4$ = 9th value = 42 ***[1 mark]***
IQR = 42 – 31 = 11 ***[1 mark]***
[5 marks available in total — as above]

4 E.g. the median time taken by the boys is the same as the median time taken by the girls, so on average the boys and girls took the same time. The interquartile range for the boys is smaller than the interquartile range for the girls, so the times taken by the boys were more consistent than the times taken by the girls.
[2 marks available — 1 mark for a correct comparison of the median, 1 mark for a correct comparison of the interquartile range OR range (for both marks, at least one comparison must be given in the context of the data)]
'In the context of the data' means you need to explain what your comparison shows about the times taken by the boys and girls.

5 Median (June) = 29
Median (Nov) = 15
Interquartile range (June) = 37 – 15 = 22
Interquartile range (Nov) = 22 – 7 = 15
E.g. the median rainfall was higher in June than in November, suggesting that rainfall is higher on average in June. The interquartile range was also greater in June than in November, suggesting that the amount of rainfall is more varied in June.
[6 marks available — 1 mark for the June median, 1 mark for the November median, 1 mark for the June interquartile range, 1 mark for the November interquartile range, 1 mark for a suitable comment on the median, 1 mark for a suitable comment on the interquartile range]

Pages 104-105: Cumulative Frequency

1 a)

Exam mark (%)	≤ 20	≤ 30	≤ 40	≤ 50	≤ 60	≤ 70	≤ 80	≤ 100
Cumulative Frequency	3	13	25	49	91	107	116	120

[1 mark]

b)

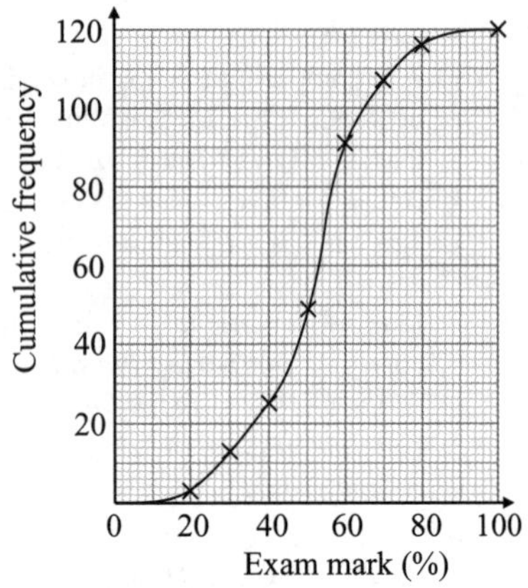

[3 marks available — 1 mark for all points plotted at correct class boundaries, 1 mark for all points from part a) plotted at correct heights, 1 mark for joining them with a smooth curve or straight lines]

A common mistake in exams is not plotting the points at the top end of the interval.

c) Median plotted at 60 gives a value of 53%
[1 mark, accept answers ± 1%]

d) Lower quartile at 30 gives a value of 43%
Upper quartile at 90 gives a value of 60%
Interquartile range = 60 – 43 = 17%
[2 marks available — 1 mark for correct method, 1 mark for correct answer, accept answers ± 2%]

e) $\frac{1}{5}$ of pupils got lower than grade C,
$\frac{1}{5}$ of 120 = 24 pupils
So the lowest to get a grade C was the 25th pupil.
Reading from the graph at a cumulative frequency of 25 gives 40%, so the mark needed to get a grade C was about 40%.
[3 marks available — 1 mark for finding the number of pupils who got lower than grade C, 1 mark for drawing a line across from 25 on the cumulative frequency axis, 1 mark for an answer in the range 38-42%]

2 a) i) Number of journeys between 27 and 47 mins = 49 – 28 = 21
[2 marks available — 1 mark for reading the cumulative frequencies off at 27 and 47 minutes, 1 mark for correct answer]

ii) 48 journeys took 40 minutes or less, so 2 journeys took longer.
Percentage of total number = (2 ÷ 50) × 100 = 4%
[2 marks available — 1 mark for correct method, 1 mark for correct answer]

b) The answers are estimates because they're based on grouped data, rather than the actual data values. ***[1 mark]***

c)

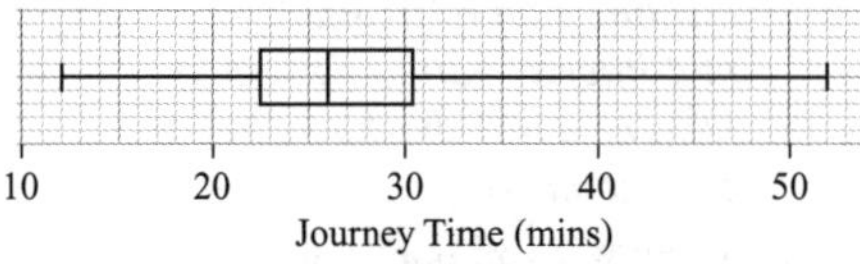

[3 marks available — 1 mark for plotting end points correctly, 1 mark for plotting median correctly (± 0.5) and 1 mark for plotting lower and upper quartiles correctly (± 0.5)]

Pages 106-107: Histograms and Frequency Density

1 To find the scale, find the frequency density of one bar.
Frequency density = frequency ÷ class width = 15 ÷ 20 = 0.75.
So the height of the first bar is 0.75.
The height of the third bar is 30 ÷ 10 = 3.

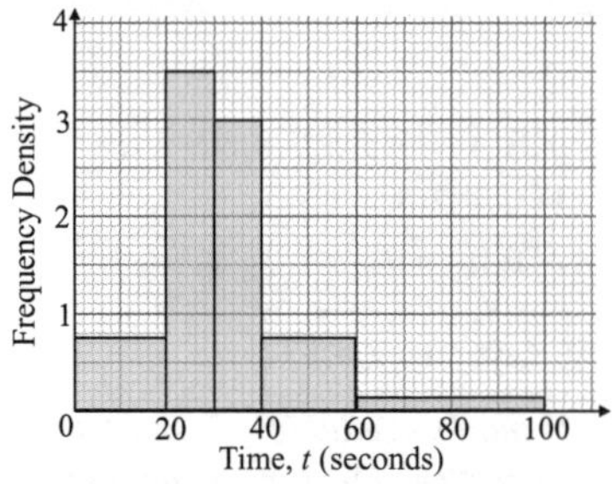

The frequency of the second row is 3.5 × 10 = 35.

Time, t (s)	Frequency
$0 < t \le 20$	15
$20 < t \le 30$	35
$30 < t \le 40$	30
$40 < t \le 60$	15
$60 < t \le 100$	5

[3 marks available — 1 mark for the correct scale on the frequency density axis, 1 mark for the correct entry in the table, 1 mark for the correct bar on the histogram]

2

Time, m (minutes)	Frequency (f)	Mid-interval Value (x)	fx
$40 \le m < 60$	20 × 1 = 20	50	1000
$60 \le m < 70$	10 × 7 = 70	65	4550
$70 \le m < 80$	10 × 4 = 40	75	3000
$80 \le m < 120$	40 × 2 = 80	100	8000
$120 \le m < 140$	20 × 3 = 60	130	7800
Total	270		24 350

Mean for children = 24 350 ÷ 270 = 90.185... = 90.2 minutes (to 1 d.p.)

E.g. the data supports the hypothesis since the mean time for the adults is longer than the mean time for the children, and the large samples mean the results should represent the populations.
[4 marks available — 1 mark for a correct method to find the frequencies, 1 mark for multiplying the frequencies by the mid-interval values, 1 mark for the correct mean, 1 mark for a correct conclusion based on a comparison of the means]

3 a) Estimate of number of lambs between 3.5 and 4 kg = 0.5 × 22 ***[1 mark]*** = 11
11 + (1 × 26) + (1 × 16) + (2 × 3) ***[1 mark]***
= 59 out of 100 = 59% ***[1 mark]***
[3 marks available in total — as above]

b)

Weight, w kg	$0 < w \le 2$	$2 < w \le 4$	$4 < w \le 5$	$5 < w \le 6$	$6 < w \le 8$
Frequency	4	28	30	28	10
Frequency Density	2	14	30	28	5

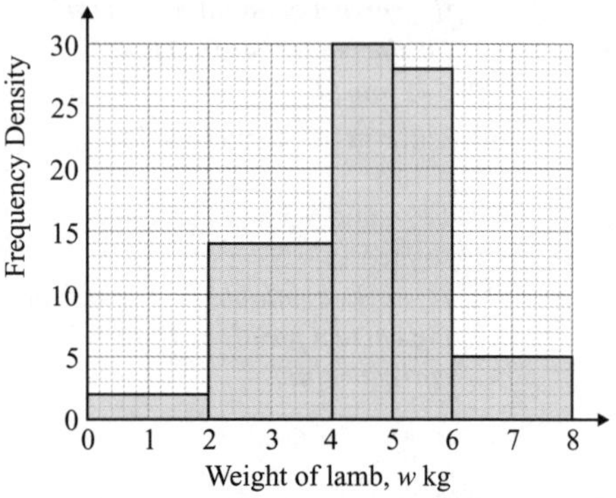

[3 marks available — 1 mark for the correct frequency densities, 1 mark for correctly labelling the axes and drawing 5 bars with no gaps, 1 mark for the correct histogram]

c) E.g. the second histogram shows more lambs with heavier weights and fewer with lighter weights than the first, which suggests that, in general, the lambs are larger on the second farm.
[1 mark for a correct comment based on a comparison of the histograms]

Page 108: Probability Basics

1 a) P(strawberry) = $\frac{2}{2+5} = \frac{2}{7}$ ***[1 mark]***

b) P(banana) = $\frac{5}{7}$

$2 \times$ P(strawberry) = $2 \times \frac{2}{7} = \frac{4}{7}$

so Ailbhe is wrong, she is more than twice as likely to pick a banana sweet.
[2 marks available — 1 mark for finding the probability of choosing a banana sweet, 1 mark for saying Ailbhe is wrong with a valid explanation]

2 Number of red counters = $p - n$ ***[1 mark]***
Probability of getting a red counter = $\frac{p-n}{p}$ ***[1 mark]***
[2 marks available in total — as above]

3 P(stripy sock) = $2y$ ***[1 mark]***
$0.4 + y + 2y = 1$ ***[1 mark]***
$3y = 0.6$
$y = 0.2$ ***[1 mark]***
[3 marks available in total — as above]

Page 109: Counting Outcomes

1

		Dice					
	+	1	2	3	4	5	6
Cards	2	3	4	5	6	7	8
	4	5	6	7	8	9	10
	6	7	8	9	10	11	12
	8	9	10	11	12	13	14
	10	11	12	13	14	15	16

P(scoring more than 4)
$= \frac{\text{number of ways to score more than 4}}{\text{total number of possible outcomes}}$
$= \frac{28}{30} = \frac{14}{15}$
[3 marks available — 1 mark for finding the total number of possible outcomes, 1 mark for finding the number of ways to score more than 4, 1 mark for the correct answer]

2 Combinations of sandwich and drink = $5 \times 8 = 40$
Combinations of sandwich and snack = $5 \times 4 = 20$
Combinations of sandwich, snack and drink = $5 \times 4 \times 8 = 160$
Total number of possible combinations = $40 + 20 + 160 = 220$
[3 marks available — 1 mark for the correct number of combinations for one meal deal, 1 mark for the correct number of combinations for the other two meal deals, 1 mark for the correct answer]

3 a) Total number of different ways for the spinners to land
$= 4 \times 4 \times 4 \times 4 \times 4 = 4^5 = 1024$
[1 mark]

b) Number of ways of not spinning any 1's $= 3 \times 3 \times 3 \times 3 \times 3$
$= 3^5 = 243$ ***[1 mark]***

So P(not spinning any 1's) = $\frac{243}{1024}$
[1 mark]

[2 marks available in total — as above]

4 $4 \times 4 \times 4 \times 4 \times 4 \times 4 = 4096$ ***[1 mark]***
Number of ways for all lights not to be green or yellow $= 2 \times 2 \times 2 \times 2 \times 2 \times 2 = 64$ ***[1 mark]***
P(no lights green or yellow) = $\frac{64}{4096} = \frac{1}{64}$
[1 mark]
[3 marks available in total — as above]
You could also solve this using the AND/OR rules — find the probability that one light is red OR blue, and use the AND rule to extend that to all six lights.

Pages 110-111: Probability Experiments

1 a) $50 \times 0.12 = 6$
[2 marks available — 1 mark for correct method, 1 mark for the correct answer]

b) E.g. On a fair dice, the theoretical frequency of each number is 0.166..., so as 1 has a much higher relative frequency and 5 has a much lower relative frequency, the dice is probably not fair.
[2 marks available — 1 mark for 'not fair' or similar, 1 mark for an explanation including numbers or relative frequency]

c) E.g. No, each dice roll is random, so in a small number of trials like 50 she is likely to get different results. ***[1 mark]***

2 a)

Number on counter	1	2	3	4	5
Frequency	23	25	22	21	9
Relative Frequency	**0.23**	**0.25**	**0.22**	**0.21**	**0.09**

[1 mark]

b) Elvin is likely to be wrong. The bag seems to contain fewer counters numbered 5. ***[1 mark]***

c) P(odd number) = 0.23 + 0.22 + 0.09 ***[1 mark]***
= 0.54 ***[1 mark]***
[2 marks available in total — as above]

3 a) i) $\frac{1}{2} \times 8 = 4$ ***[1 mark]***

ii) E.g. Danielle predicted correctly five times, which is close to the number you'd expect her to get correct if she was just guessing, so there is no evidence that she can predict the flip of a coin. ***[1 mark]***

b) i)

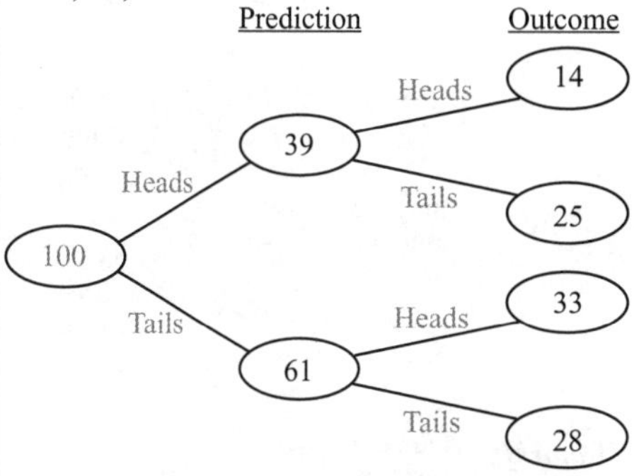

[3 marks available — 1 mark for the numbers 39 and 61 in the correct places, 1 mark for the numbers 14 and 25 in the correct places, 1 mark for the numbers 33 and 28 in the correct places]

ii) Relative frequency of predicting the outcome correctly
= relative frequency of 'heads, heads' or 'tails, tails'
$= \frac{14 + 28}{100}$
$= \frac{42}{100}$ or $\frac{21}{50}$ or 0.42 or 42%
[2 marks available — 1 mark for 14 + 28, 1 mark for the correct answer]

c) E.g. The experiment in part b) has more trials so the results are more reliable. ***[1 mark]***

Page 112: The AND/OR Rules

1 a) P(multiple of 3) = 0.2
P(square number) = 0.3 + 0.25 = 0.55
The two categories don't overlap, so use the OR rule:
P(multiple of 3 or square number) = 0.2 + 0.55 = 0.75
[2 marks available — 1 mark for a correct method, 1 mark for the correct answer]

b) P(2 on second spin only)
= P(not 2) × P(2)
= (1 – 0.15) × 0.15 ***[1 mark]***
= 0.85 × 0.15 = 0.1275 ***[1 mark]***
[2 marks available — as above]

2 a) P(loses) = 1 – 0.3 = 0.7
P(loses 3 games) = 0.7 × 0.7 × 0.7
= 0.343 ***[1 mark]***

b) P(wins a prize) =
1 – P(doesn't win a prize)
= 1 – (0.7 × 0.7) ***[1 mark]***
= 1 – 0.49 = 0.51
0.51 > 0.5, so he is correct ***[1 mark]***
[2 marks available in total — as above]

Page 113: Tree Diagrams (1)

1 a)

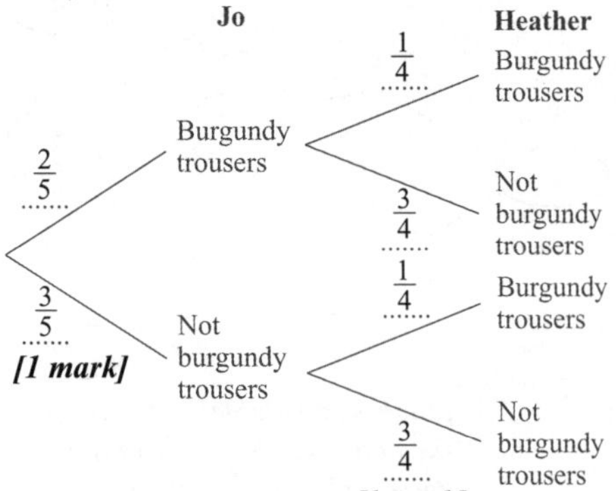

[2 marks available in total — as above]

b) P(neither wear burgundy trousers) =

$\frac{3}{5} \times \frac{3}{4}$ ***[1 mark]*** $= \frac{9}{20}$ ***[1 mark]***

[2 marks available in total — as above]

2 a) P(Paul's point) = P(1, 2, 3 or 6) = $\frac{2}{3}$

P(Jen's point) = $1 - \frac{2}{3} = \frac{1}{3}$

[1 mark for both probabilities]

You can draw a tree diagram to help you:

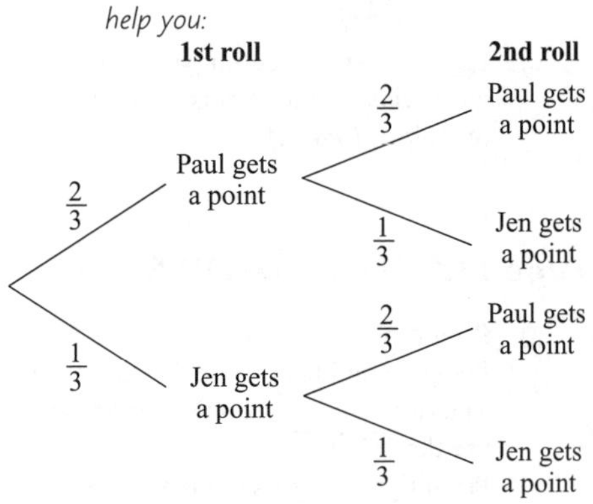

P(they draw after two rolls)

= P(they both get 1 point)

$= \left(\frac{2}{3} \times \frac{1}{3}\right) + \left(\frac{1}{3} \times \frac{2}{3}\right)$ ***[1 mark]***

$= \frac{2}{9} + \frac{2}{9} = \frac{4}{9}$ ***[1 mark]***

[3 marks available in total — as above]

b) P(Paul wins) =

P(Paul wins 3-0) + P(Paul wins 2-1) =

$\left(\frac{2}{3} \times \frac{2}{3} \times \frac{2}{3}\right) + \left(\frac{2}{3} \times \frac{2}{3} \times \frac{1}{3}\right) +$

$\left(\frac{2}{3} \times \frac{1}{3} \times \frac{2}{3}\right) + \left(\frac{1}{3} \times \frac{2}{3} \times \frac{2}{3}\right)$

$= \frac{8}{27} + \frac{4}{27} + \frac{4}{27} + \frac{4}{27} = \frac{20}{27}$

[3 marks available — 1 mark for finding the probability of Paul winning 3-0, 1 mark for finding the probabilities of Paul winning 2-1, 1 mark for the correct final answer]

You could draw another tree diagram showing 3 rolls if you're struggling to find the right probabilities.

Page 114: Tree Diagrams (2)

1 a)

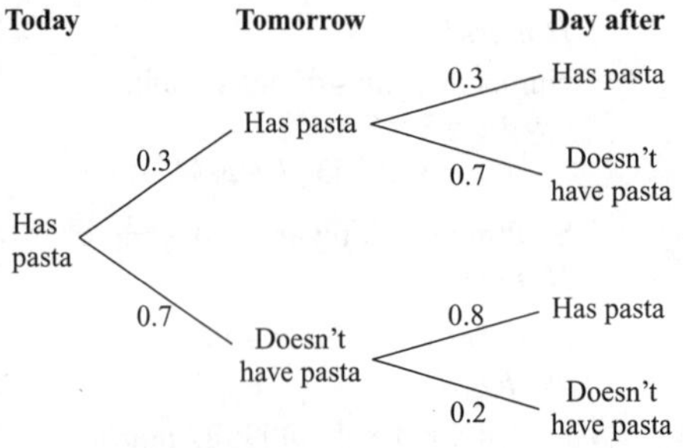

[2 marks available — 1 mark for the correct probabilities for tomorrow, 1 mark for the correct probabilities for the day after]

b) P(pasta on 1 of the next 2 days) =

P(pasta then no pasta) +

P(no pasta then pasta)

= (0.3 × 0.7) + (0.7 × 0.8) ***[1 mark]***

= 0.21 + 0.56 = 0.77 ***[1 mark]***

[2 marks available in total — as above]

2 a) P(2nd is also milk) = $\frac{6}{11}$ ***[1 mark]***

1 milk chocolate has been taken, so there are 6 milk chocolates left out of 11 remaining chocolates.

b) P(at least one milk) = 1 – P(no milk)

= 1 – P(white then white)

$= 1 - \left(\frac{5}{12} \times \frac{4}{11}\right)$ ***[1 mark]***

$= 1 - \frac{20}{132} = \frac{112}{132} = \frac{28}{33}$ ***[1 mark]***

[2 marks available in total — as above]

c) P(milk and white) =

P(milk then white) +

P(white then milk)

$= \left(\frac{7}{12} \times \frac{5}{11}\right) + \left(\frac{5}{12} \times \frac{7}{11}\right) = \frac{35}{66}$

[2 marks available — 1 mark for a correct method, 1 mark for the correct answer]

You might find it helpful to draw a tree diagram for parts b) and c).